THE QUANTUM BLUEPRINT

THE QUANTUM BLUEPRINT

Unravelling the Divine Code

Salah-Eddin Gherbi

Copyright © 2025 by Salah-Eddin Gherbi

All rights reserved. No part of this book may be reproduced in any form either by electronic or mechanical means, including information storage and retrieval systems, without written permission from the publisher, except by a reviewer who may quote brief passages in a review.

First Edition

ISBN 978-1-83709-116-4
Imprint: Vektor Publishing

https://salaheddin.substack.com

INTRODUCTION

INTRODUCTION

In a time when the paths of science and spirituality often seem to diverge, "The Quantum Blueprint: Unravelling the Divine Code" presents a unique bridge. Authored by Salah-Eddin Gherbi, a visionary in soul alchemy, healing, and intuitive numerology, this book stands out by seamlessly blending modern scientific intrigue with ancient mystical wisdom. Gherbi's extensive research and experience in these fields make him a credible source of knowledge. It offers readers an enlightening journey through the intricate tapestry of consciousness, revealing the profound interconnectedness of all things. This unique blend of science and spirituality intrigues and opens readers' minds.

Drawing from a rich background that includes extensive research into Gematria, scripture, and sacred geometry, Gherbi explores the deep-seated connections between numbers, letters, and the very fabric of the Universe. His previous work, "The Fifth Element: The Rainbow Bridge Between the Dimensions," laid the groundwork for this exploration, delving into the mysteries encoded within the Holy Bible.

"The Quantum Blueprint" is not just a book; it is a map that guides the reader through intricate layers of consciousness, from the physical to the spiritual. The book is organized into sections corresponding to different aspects of the divine code, providing the reader with a clear and structured path. Gherbi's insights into Hebrew and Greek Gematria, coupled with his understanding of Kabbalah, offer a unique lens through which to view the microcosm and macrocosm. His work deciphers some of the hidden codes that underpin the construct of reality, offering a new light on concepts such as the origins of the Royal Cubit about the dimensions of the Sun and the Jesus Code embedded in the first verse of Genesis and the reconstitution of the lost geometric pattern on the floorplan of the St. Mary's Chapel of Glastonbury Abbey. This book of revelation introduces the concept of the divine code—a

INTRODUCTION

universal language composed of letters, numbers, geometry, colors, and sounds (frequencies). This code is the blueprint of Genesis, from the origins of creation to what is unfolding in the present moment, a testament to the order and harmony that govern the Universe. From the first word of Genesis *Bereisheit* (בראשית) "In the beginning," "In Principle," "In Wisdom," to the intricate design of the New Jerusalem Diagram, Stonehenge and Rosslyn Chapel, Gherbi elucidates how these ancient symbols and structures reflect the divine order. Gherbi unveils an excellent link between early Christianity and ancient Celtic cultures, converging on the location of the first Christian church of England built by Joseph of Arimathea and his followers. Drawing in the reader to explore the mysteries with greater depth, he combines Gematria and geometry to reveal the connection of the Rose Pattern with the zodiacal blueprint and a possible location of Joseph's grave at Glastonbury Abbey.

The narrative seamlessly intertwines scientific principles with esoteric knowledge, encouraging readers to expand their understanding of consciousness. Concepts such as the Quantum Word, the Primary Being, the Great Image, and Hyperdimensional Light are explored in depth, revealing the profound wisdom embedded in our Universe and the nature of our divine blueprint. The book also touches upon practical applications of this knowledge, such as how understanding the divine code can help in personal and spiritual transformation and how we can apply the concept of the Quantum Word to daily life. This depth of wisdom will stimulate the readers' intellect and enlighten their journey.

More than a research work, "The Quantum Blueprint: Unravelling the Divine Code" catalyzes transformation. It invites the reader to embark on a journey of personal growth, to look beyond the surface, to perceive the underlying patterns that connect us all, and to embrace the divine wisdom that

INTRODUCTION

flows through every aspect of existence. This invitation sets the tone for the book's content, inspiring and engaging readers. The book's potential to encourage personal growth and transformation will resonate with those interested in the intersection of science and spirituality, particularly those exploring consciousness and personal development.

SYNOPSIS

SYNOPSIS

1. Humankind's Blueprint

- This chapter paves the way by exploring the nature of consciousness. It uncovers the profound wisdom embedded in numbers and geometric patterns, laying the groundwork for understanding the complex interplay between the material and spiritual worlds.

2. Quantum Word

- Explore the mystical aspects of language and its power to shape reality. Examining the Hebrew word *Chel'kiyk* (חלקיק) and its connection to elemental particles uncover the profound relationship between time, matter, and the Torah, demonstrating how ancient texts encode quantum principles.

3. The First Word

- This chapter investigates the significance of the first word in Genesis, revealing its numerical and geometric importance and how it encapsulates the universe's divine order. It provides an in-depth look at the origins of creation as described in the Hebrew Bible.

4. Introduction to Kabbalah

- Delve into Kabbalistic teachings, focusing on the Tree of Life, the spheres (sephiroth), and levels of consciousness (undifferentiated, differentiated, and emanating) that shape our reality. This chapter provides essential insights into the spiritual dimensions of existence and their connection to physical reality.

SYNOPSIS

5. The First Verse of Genesis

- This chapter reveals how ancient scriptures contain hidden mathematical and cosmic patterns. Decode the numerical and geometric significance of the Bible's opening verse, offering a blueprint for understanding the divine order. Explore the significance of the value PI π and its decimals in the decoding and how it relates to the first verse of Genesis.

6. The Sign of the Covenant

- Investigate the deep symbolism and significance of the Covenant, understanding its representation in sacred texts and its enduring implications for humanity. It highlights the connection between divine promises and the natural phenomenon of the rainbow, as viewed on Earth by us all and from the heavens in Elohim's-eye-view.

7. The Primary Being

- Examine the concept of the Primary Being, exploring its essence in consciousness and its role in the universe's structure. This chapter delves into spiritual fire (ether) symbolism as a unifying element. Explore the three aspects of the candlelight mirroring the nature of spiritual flame, vivifying and nurturing every man's and woman's soul coming into existence.

8. The Great Image

- Dive into the unification of the feminine and masculine principles through the Tree of Life in Kabbalah, revealing the divine blueprint of creation as "Androgynous," "Christ" nature, and the balance of forces in the universe. Discover the archetype of the Great Image and its reflections across various cultural contexts.

9. The Rings of *Yod*

- Investigate the mystical significance of the Rings of *Yod* (') embedded within the first verse of Genesis, uncovering their meanings and intricate connections to the divine code and universal harmony. This chapter develops further the hidden facets of the Bible's opening verse and its ties with the Primary Being.

10. The Jesus Code

- Decode the hidden numerical, symbolic, and geometrical messages associated with Jesus, unveiling their spiritual significance and role in the divine blueprint. This chapter encodes the different names of Jesus at the very core of the first verse of Genesis.

11. Hyperdimensional Light

- Explore the concept of hyperdimensional light, which challenges our traditional understanding of light and reality. Discover its potential to reveal higher dimensions by introducing hyper dodecahedron and its link with the Jesus Code in the first verse of Genesis, a bridge between the physical and the metaphysical.

12. The Root of the Royal Cubit

- Trace the origins and importance of the royal cubit in sacred geometry. Delve into the ancient Egyptian Royal Cubit and its profound connections with the dimensions of the Sun. This chapter challenges the readers to uncover the link between the Royal Cubit and the cosmos. The exploration highlights the harmonious relationship between these measurements and universal principles, bridging ancient wisdom with astronomical phenomena.

13. Key 117

- This chapter explores the use of the number 117 in sacred architecture, its relationship with the Great Pyramid's proportions, and its role in revealing universal patterns and cosmic harmony through the science of gematria. Uncover the mystical significance of 117, its connections to biblical texts, and their geometric and esoteric meanings.

14. The New Jerusalem Diagram

- This chapter examines the New Jerusalem Diagram, a geometric representation of the heavenly city described in the Book of Revelation by John Michell. Various ancient structures, including Stonehenge and Glastonbury Abbey, reflect the diagram's proportions. Discover how the Hebrew letters of the first verse of Genesis form the building blocks of the New Jerusalem Diagram, a universal harmony and cosmic design through sacred geometry and Gematria bridging the heavens and the earth.

15. St. Mary's Chapel of Glastonbury Abbey

- This chapter delves into St. Mary's Chapel's rich history and geometric precision. The chapter also touches on the importance of the Vesicae Piscium, the geometric layout setting every masonic part of the original building into a harmonious place. It invites the readers to reflect on the Rose Pattern embedded within the square foundation of the Wattle Church circle, which Joseph of Arimathea and his followers built. This chapter compares different geometric schemes of the chapel: Bligh Bond's hexagonal scheme and John Michell's octagonal scheme within the New Jerusalem Blueprint. Discover how the chapel's design encodes the proportions of Solomon's Temple using the Sumerian Cubit.

SYNOPSIS

16. Stonehenge, a Prototype of the New Jerusalem

- This chapter explores the geometric and numeric correlations between Stonehenge and the New Jerusalem Diagram from the Book of Revelation. It delves into how Stonehenge is a cosmic temple, embodying universal harmony through its layout. The chapter also highlights the connection between Stonehenge and St. Mary's Chapel, emphasizing their shared foundation in a universal blueprint and their significance in sacred geometry and gematria.

17. The Reconstitution of the Lost Pattern

- This chapter investigates the efforts to rediscover and restore the lost pattern on the floor plan of St. Mary's Chapel. Once reconstituted, it explores how this lost pattern can reveal profound insights into the divine blueprint and universal principles. The chapter emphasizes the connection between the Rose Pattern and the zodiacal blueprint, highlighting their potential to bridge ancient wisdom with modern understanding.

18. The Power of Speech

- This chapter delves into the power of speech encoded in the structure of the first letter of the Torah, *Beit* (ב). It highlights that everything comes into existence through the power of the divine word (frequency); The Creator endowed Adam and his descendants with the same power. This chapter invites the readers to explore the deeper layers of gematria encoded in the Hebrew Bible, which emphasizes the divine blueprint and links the concepts explored in the previous chapters.

SYNOPSIS

19. The Prophecy of Melkin

- This chapter explores the enigmatic Prophecy of Melkin, revealing its historical context and potential meanings. It examines how the prophecy relates to the divine code in St. Mary's Chapel with the Fibonacci spiral and its implications for humanity's spiritual journey. By decoding Melkin's prophecy, readers gain insights into hidden knowledge and future revelations in ancient texts. The chapter also touches on the potential precise location of Joseph of Arimathea's grave, revealing insights through the lens of sacred geometry and gematria.

20. The Celtic Cross Connection

- This chapter delves into the ancient wisdom, symbolism, and significance of the Celtic Cross, tracing its origins and connection to the divine blueprint. It explores how the cross's design encodes sacred geometry and cosmic principles, offering profound spiritual insights. The chapter bridges the Celtic Cross and links it with early Christianity. It highlights a unified design between the Celtic Cross, the Rose Pattern, and the Zodiacal Blueprint of St. Mary's Chapel, expanding the New Jerusalem Diagram.

21. Rosslyn Chapel

- This chapter uncovers some of the mysteries of Rosslyn Chapel, exploring its intricate carvings and symbolic architecture. It reveals how the chapel is a repository of sacred geometry and esoteric knowledge connected to the divine code. By examining Rosslyn Chapel and its link to Solomon's Temple, the unified design of the New Jerusalem Diagram, and the first verse of Genesis, readers discover its significance in the quest for spiritual understanding.

CONTENT

Introduction & Synopsis .... 6 & 10
Humankind's Blueprint 18
Quantum Word 38
The First Word 46
Introduction to Kabbalah 56
The First Verse of Genesis 62
The Sign of the Covenant 82
The Primary Being 92
The Great Image 110
The Rings of Yod 116
The Jesus Code 133
Hyperdimensional Light 146
The Root of the Royal Cubit 154
Key 117 161
The New Jerusalem Diagram 166
St. Mary's Chapel of Glastonbury Abbey 174
Stonehenge, a Prototype of the New Jerusalem 204
The Reconstitution of the Lost Pattern 209
The Power of Speech 217
The Prophecy of Melkin 222
The Celtic Cross Connection 230
Rosslyn Chapel 244
Appendix 254
List of Figures 265
Acknowledgement 271
Autobiography 272

HUMANKIND'S BLUEPRINT

According to Pythagoras: "All is number." Numbers and their qualities layer consciousness. Teaching numbers can bring them to life with esoteric insights and wisdom with the eye of wisdom. Divine Wisdom manifests everything from the unknowable and non-existent planes. Numbers are wisdom, but their language is very particular and covers many dimensions and layers only the intuitive eye can perceive. The voice speaks from the Heart of All and knows the language of symbols, colors, and anything presented as a form that can express Divine Wisdom. Have you ever felt that the universe aligns everything perfectly for us to experience? A perfect order connects everything from microcosm to macrocosm. From the beginning to the end, from the *Alpha* (α) to the *Omega* (Ω), from the *Aleph* (א) to the *Tav* (ת), everything is witnessed by the Divine Eye. From the bigger picture perspective, everyone is not just a person but contains the whole universe experiencing itself and becoming conscious and aware of itself. The journey invites us to enter the depths of the waters, where our feet can finally touch the ground. Once reached, the individual journeys from the deep to the higher waters, where the unconscious is processed. Like a snake shedding its skin, we release the layers of our unconscious parts, often unseen but felt and experienced. It is the heart which navigates the immensity of the waters. We as individuals have the power to seek more deeply, alone at the dashboard of our consciousness, where all the answers lie. The individual perceives through the lens of their mind without necessarily having a conscious, concrete, and spontaneous experience of their divine blueprint.

The expression of consciousness is a multifaceted marvel, encompassing numbers, gematria, geometry, colors, sound, and symbols. The beauty lies in understanding how these diverse elements are intricately interconnected, unveiling the profound truths of our reality. The mystical and wise awareness of Divine Revelation perceives this reality, not the rational mind. It's not a straight line from A to B, but a

HUMANKIND'S BLUEPRINT

harmoniously spiraling line, expanding and contracting, ultimately returning to the zero-energy point. This singularity point is where everything transitions from non-existence to existence, a pure silence devoid of sound or thought. It's the Divine Womb, the receptacle of all forms and manifestations.

The interconnectedness of these different expressions of consciousness is a symphony that resonates with the heart, dispelling any doubts about the nature of our consciousness. It's a consciousness that is not just ours but purely divine and intricately connected with everything in existence. We are not isolated entities, but integral parts of a grand design expressed in the Heavens and the Earth.

As human beings experiencing life on Earth, are we not a mirror of the grand design expressed in the Heavens and the Earth? The simplest geometric figure, the triangle, and two words in Hebrew, *Adam* (אדם) and *Yahweh* (יהוה) can illustrate this fact. It is a concept involving numbers, Hebrew letters, and geometry that goes beyond mere ideas to reveal how everything in the universe is interconnected.

Let's delve into the depth of the Hebrew language through the first word, *Adam* (אדם). Originally, Adam comes from the Hebrew word *Adamah* (אדמה) meaning "ground," "earth," and "soil."

The gematria value of Adam in Hebrew is **45**.

The book of Genesis reveals the man's first name, which means red earth or man.

מ ד א
40 4 1
Adam

HUMANKIND'S BLUEPRINT

A profound meaning within the Hebrew name of Adam:

א is *Aleph*, "The strong leader,"

ד is *Dalet*, "that opens the doorway and enters the path,"

מ is *Mem*, "that leads to life or death."

In ancient times, *Aleph* (א) symbolized a strong leader who guided and protected (Ox). A door represented *Dalet* (ד) and *Mem* (מ) was the waters of life or death or destruction (chaos). Adam was born free to lead itself to its own life or death. Despite being a great leader or guide, Adam chose the doorway to death and forgot his true divine nature. His choice led to the fall of humanity (all his descendants).

This fall retains all individuals with the same design: "a strong leader that opens the doorway that leads to life or death." In our free will, we can raise our consciousness above the waters of chaos or destruction to remember our true essence, divine and perfect, emphasizing our power to shape our spiritual journey.

HUMANKIND'S BLUEPRINT

Yahweh (יהוה) means "Lord."

The gematria value of Yahweh in Hebrew is 26. The Hebrew consonants *Yod* (י), *Heh* (ה), *Vav* (ו) and *Heh* (ה) spell *YHVH* (יהוה). This word, used in the Old Testament manuscripts, is known as the Tetragrammaton.

י ה ו ה
10 5 6 5

Yod (י) of numerical value 10 is the first manifestation of existence, the first primordial intelligence, "light." Everything comes into existence from that light before taking any form, shape, sound, or other expressions of the One Quintessence.

The light comes through Adam's crown (the man) and acts as the spirit, bridging God, Goddess, and man and woman. It is the spirit floating above the waters of consciousness to originate life. Yahweh reveals the eternal and timeless nature of God's and Goddess' existence. The Hebrew letters of the word *Yahweh* (יהוה) express the three tenses of the Hebrew verb "to be." Time allows movement in space in the world of "matter," a condensed manifestation of spirit in the densest dimensions. The spirit element, the light, is the first primordial intelligence that manifests whilst transcending time and space. Like an Artist, it can paint anything and anywhere on the canvas through God's and Goddess' Will, although the phenomenon occurs through the universe's natural laws.

HUMANKIND'S BLUEPRINT

Present Tense

ה ו ה י

5 6 6 5

"He/She is" = 22

Past Tense

ה י ה

5 10 5

"He/She was" = 20

Future Tense

י ה י ה

5 10 5 10

"He/She was" = 30

The gematria value of the timeless nature of God's and Goddess's existence ("He/She was, He/She is, He/She will be," יהיה היה הווה) is 72. This number is well-known as being the 72-fold name of God and Goddess. The 72 names of God and Goddess is a formula of 72 combinations that Moses used to part the Red Sea. The three consecutive verses from Exodus 14:19-21 contain 72 letters, a rare phenomenon. We can organize the letters from these three verses into 72 distinct triplets. In *Kabbalah* (קבלה), they teach us that if we reverse the order of the letters in the middle set, the 72 triplets become 72 "names" of God and Goddess.

They are the carriers of powerful frequencies or energies that individuals could need. Each three-letter combination is considered an angelic force. Departing the Red Sea symbolizes overcoming matter with the fire of spirit.

Fig 1. Table of the 72 names of God and Goddess.

כהת	אכא	ללה	מהש	עלם	סיט	ילי	והו
הקם	הרי	מבה	יזל	ההע	לאו	אלד	הזי
חהו	מלה	ייי	נלך	פהל	לוו	כלי	לאו
ושר	לכב	אום	ריי	שאה	ירת	האא	נתה
ייז	רהע	חעם	אני	מנד	כוק	להח	יחו
מיה	עשל	ערי	סאל	ילה	ויל	מיך	ההה
פוי	מבה	נית	ננא	עמם	החש	דני	והו
מחי	ענו	יהה	ומב	מצר	הרח	ייל	נמם
מום	היי	יבם	ראה	חבו	איע	מנק	דמב

HUMANKIND'S BLUEPRINT

Scripture states that God and Goddess made *Eve* (חוה) from a rib They took (subtracted from Adam) (Genesis 2:21-23). If we subtract the value of Eve's name (19) from Adam's (45), the result is remarkably 26.

$$\underset{40\ 4\ 1}{\text{מ ד א}} - \underset{5\ 6\ 8}{\text{ה ו ח}} = \underset{5\ 6\ 5\ 10}{\text{ה ו ה י}}$$

$$\underset{45}{\text{Adam}} - \underset{19}{\text{Eve}} = \underset{26}{\text{Yahweh}}$$

Equivalently:

$$\underset{19}{\text{Eve}} + \underset{26}{\text{Yahweh}} = \underset{45}{\text{Adam}}$$

A profound meaning in the Hebrew name of Eve:

ח is *Chet*, "The inner room or chamber,"

ו is *Vav*, "that joins or connects together,"

ה is *Heh*, "that reveals or shows."

In ancient times, people called *Chet* (ח) the inner room or chamber. They represented *Vav* (ו) with a hook or peg that connects, serving as the connecting "hook" of the Holy Tent (Tabernacle). *Heh* (ה) signifies the divine breath, revelation, and light. *Eve* (חוה) is the Inner Room or Holy Graal (the cup) that receives understanding, the spirit, the light, and the divine breath to reveal.

Eve revealed the light of the perfect man in God's and Goddess' image as she is the Inner Chamber or Holy Grail that receives understanding.

Hence the mathematical equation:

Eve (19) + Yahweh (26) = Adam (45)

הגביע הקדוש

Ha-Gavia Ha-Kadosh

Holy Grail

Fig 2. The Holy Grail.

Eve (19) is the combination of the first and last positive digits (1 and 9).

Adam (45) is the sum of all the single positive digits (1 through 9).

$$1 + 2 + 3 + 4 + 5 + 6 + 7 + 8 + 9 = 45$$

The ancient ones universally understood that there are 360 degrees in an ideal circle. The perfect man mirrors the ideal circle, considering that:

$$3^2 + 6^2 + 0^2 = 45 = \text{Adam}$$

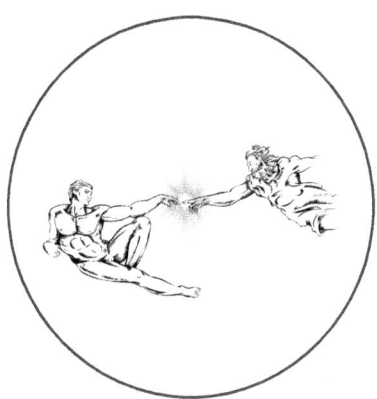

Fig 3. The Ideal Circle.

PI (π) is the ratio between the circumference and diameter of a circle. The numerical position where the first instance of the sequence 360 occurs in the decimal expansion of PI (π) is 285, the sum of all the single positive digits (1 through 9) squared.

$$1^2 + 2^2 + 3^2 + 4^2 + 5^2 + 6^2 + 7^2 + 8^2 + 9^2 = 285$$

The alchemical combination of Adam and Eve completes creation, mirroring through the geometric expression of the ideal circle (360 degrees) with PI (π) value.

HUMANKIND'S BLUEPRINT

Yahweh reveals the human design in God's and Goddess' image, incorporating the four Worlds of the *Kabbalah* ("Receiving," קבלה) *Atziluth* (אצליות), *Briah* (בריאה), *Yetzirah* (יצירה) and *Assiah* (עשיה) each respectively representing an element and an attribute:

- Fire, the World of Emanation, the Spiritual World.
- Air, the World of Creation, the Mental World.
- Water, the World of Formation, the Emotional World.
- Earth, the World of Action, the Physical World.

The first emanation of light descends into the four worlds to manifest out of the non-existence and the unknowable, like a lightning flash to create, form, and act upon.

The fifth world is the simultaneous presence of the four worlds, working and connecting in the form of man or woman, though not yet manifest. *Adam Kadmon* (אדם קדמון) means "the primordial man." The entire universe identifies the primordial man with the soul or essence of all things. *Kadmon* (קדמון) means "primary of all primaries," the first pristine emanation, emerging from *Ein Sof* ("infiniteness or limitlessness," אין סוף), the transcendental par excellence.

Analogous to the simultaneous presence and works of the four elements (fire, air, water, and earth), the primordial man can refer to the fifth element, the ether, the perfect man, the completion of the Great Alchemical Work, and the capstone of the Pyramid, which is God's and Goddess' manifestation in the form of a man or woman. The pure, lucid state of God's and Goddess' Consciousness is concealed and hidden in all of us. The "lucid and luminous light" has yet to be accessed and manifested to reveal the primordial man and woman as a mirror (or image) of God and Goddess.

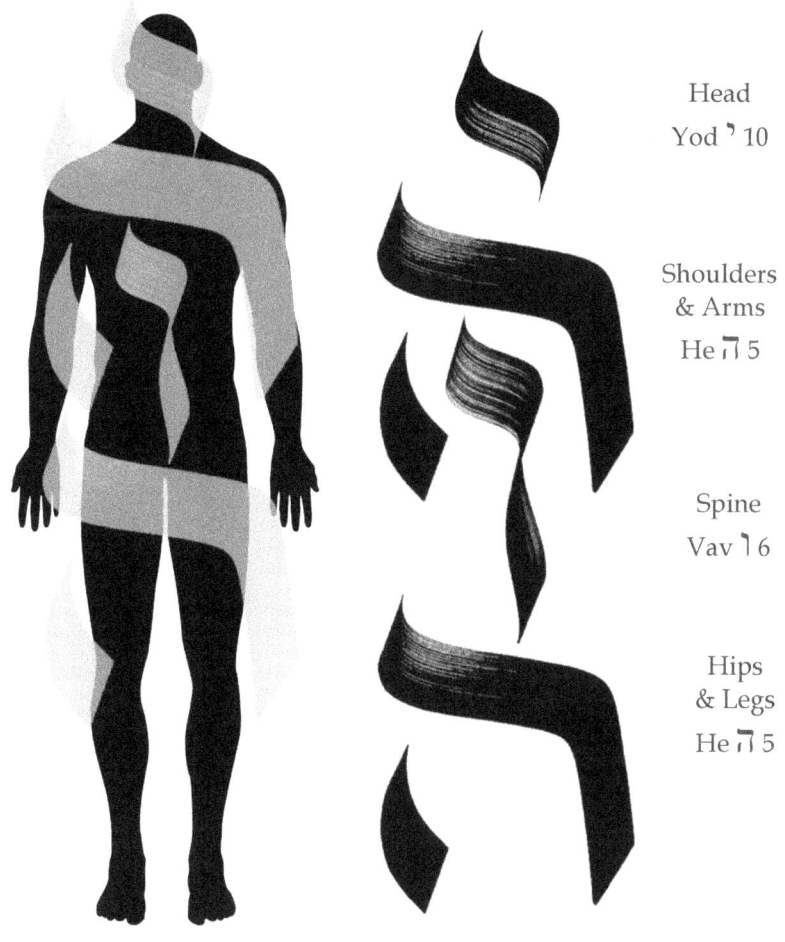

Fig 4. The Tetragrammaton — Man in Yahweh's Image.

26 is the mean between 13 (the number of lunar months in a year) and 52 (the number of solar weeks in a year):

$$13 \times 2 = 26$$
$$26 \times 2 = 52$$

HUMANKIND'S BLUEPRINT

Adam is considered the first human in Judaism, Christianity, and Islam. In the Sufi tradition, Adam symbolizes the "perfect man." Adam, written in the equivalent Ancient Egyptian alphabetical characters, becomes Atam or Atum. In Ancient Egypt, Atam or Atum is like *Yod* (י), the first realization of existence or primordial intelligence, "light." As such, he is depicted in complete human form, in the image of the Hebrew consonants of Yahweh in descending order: *Yod* (י), *Heh* (ה), *Vav* (ו) and *Heh* (ה).

Atam or Atum means "he who completes or perfects." Adam is the man who initially is perfect before falling with all his descendants. The soul of the man or woman must undergo a long alchemical evolutive process to be complete or perfect again, purified from all of its impurities, emerging out of the depth of the unconscious into the light of consciousness. Similarly, alchemists pursued the transformation of lead metal into gold, and this mutation can only occur at the core of the metal, not just at its surface.

The high mound where Adam, Atam, or Atum stands is the Ancient Egyptian Benben Stone, the Philosopher's Stone. People believe this agent transmutes base metals into gold and indefinitely prolongs life.

The word Neb mirrors Ben:

Ben means:	Neb means:
Primordial Stone	Gold
Mound of creation	Pure
First stage of creation	Master

In Ancient Egypt, the Benben stone symbolized the Phoenix, which could revive itself and be reborn. It also describes the name given to the top of an obelisk or the capstone placed on top of a pyramid.

Fig 5.
The Phoenix and Pyramidion.

HUMANKIND'S BLUEPRINT

In the perfect and complete design of man and woman, as Adam and Eve, the union reflects the harmonious balance of creation. Geometrically, it represents an ideal circle in Yahweh's work.

The Hebrew word for "Hand" is *Yawd* (יד).

יד

4 10

Hand

14

The first Hebrew consonant of *Yahweh* (יהוה), *Yod* (י), depicts the "Hand" that worked to complete Adam and Eve. A man's or woman's fingers have 14 joints.

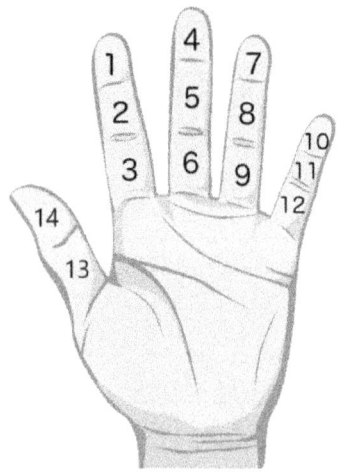

Fig 6. Joints of the Hand.

The Hand (14) occurs at position 1 in the value of PI π counting from the first digit after the decimal point.

3.14

Adam and Eve were made by Yahweh's Hand in God's and Goddess' image, embodying God's and Goddess' existence's timeless nature.

Adding up the standard gematria values of *Adam* (אדמ), *Eve* (חוה), *Yahweh* (יהוה) and their timeless nature ("He/She was, He/She is, He/She will be," יהיה היה הווה) altogether, it results in a well-known number that every man and woman witness in nature as a reminder of their divine essence they indeed are. The expression of this number underlies a geometric shape, the spiral, which is the medium pervading all spaces and dimensions, and the veil between *Ein Sof* ("infiniteness," or "limitlessness," אין סוף) the eternal nature of God's and Goddess' existence and the finite or limited nature of all things coming into existence.

$$\begin{array}{ccccccc} \text{Eve} & + & \text{Yahweh} & + & \text{Adam} & + & \text{Timeless} \\ 19 & + & 26 & + & 45 & + & 72 & = \\ & & 90 & & & + & 72 & = \\ & & & 162 & & & & \end{array}$$

The golden ratio, represented as 1:1.62, approximates the exact value of 1.61803399+.

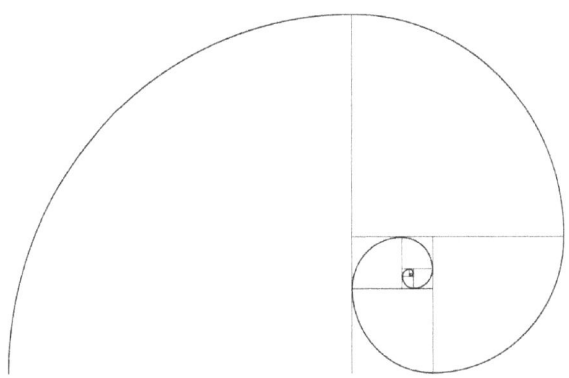

Fig 7. The Fibonacci Spiral / Golden Ratio.

HUMANKIND'S BLUEPRINT

Interestingly, the total sum value of *Adam* (אדמ), *Eve* (חוה), and *Yahweh* (יהוה) is 90, which is a quarter of an ideal circle. Yahweh took one of Adam's ribs to create Eve, as described in Genesis 2:21. The Hebrew word *Tsela* (צלע) means "rib" or "side." It can also mean figuratively the quarter of a circle, which is 90 degrees.

ע   ל   צ

70   30   90

190

צ is *Tsade*, "The fishing hook,"

ל is *Lamed*, "That incites,"

ע is *Ayin*, "the will of good or bad."

Tsela (צלע) is the quarter of an ideal circle, which sets Adam as a leader or guide with the free will to choose between good and evil. The first letter begins with *Tsade* (צ) which has a numerical value of 90 and involves the combination of *Adam* (אדמ), *Eve* (חוה), and *Yahweh* (יהוה). The total value of *Tsela* (צלע) is 190 of numerical value 19 when reduced (added without the zero; 7 + 3 + 9 = 19), the same numerical gematria value as the word *Hawwah* ("Eve," חוה).

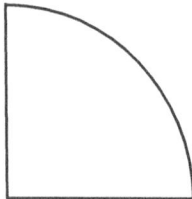

90 degrees
Tsela (צלע)

**Fig 8.
A quarter of a circle.**

So, a great question remains: did Adam have the free will before that Yahweh took one of his rib to make Eve?

HUMANKIND'S BLUEPRINT

God and Goddess made Adam and Eve in their image and likeness, each having the attributes of God (Male) and Goddess (Female).

Genesis 1:26 "Let us make humankind in our image, after our likeness (...)". Notice that the number of the verse is 26, which is the gematria value of *Yahweh* (יהוה).

Genesis 1:27: "creating them in the image of Elohim—creating them male and female."

The word *Elohim* (אלהים) is often associated with "God." However, Elohim's likeness comes from both genders, male and female, a divine image that Yahweh represents through the four Hebrew consonants *Yod* (י), *Heh* (ה), *Vav* (ו) and *Heh* (ה) (Fig 9).

B'tzelem ("In the Image," בצלם) has a gematria value of 162 in the Hebrew standard gematria (Fig 126), the golden ratio in nature on a scale of 100. It combines *Adam* (אדמ), *Eve* (חוה), *Yahweh* (יהוה) and the timeless nature of God's and Goddess' existence ("He/She was, He/She is, He/She will be," יהיה היה הווה). So, *Elohim* (אלהים) represents all the attributes of the timeless nature of God's and Goddess' existence (72 names). God and Goddess then made humankind with the characteristics of their divine qualities, each principle, masculine and feminine, and their union.

In the Hebrew Scripture, *B'tzelem Elohim* means "in the image of Elohim" (בצלם אלקים). Added to 86 for *Elohim* ("The Mighty Ones") is 248.

```
    א ל ה י ם         ב צ ל ם
    40 10 5 30 1     40 30 90 2
         86               162
```

HUMANKIND'S BLUEPRINT

Fig 9. The Tetragrammaton - Humankind in the Image of Elohim.

In Kabbalistic Gematria, scholars assume or misrepresent YHVH as exclusively masculine, revealing Him as either between the genders or as of both genders. YHVH's male-female polarity reveals itself because each consonant represents each member of the Divine Family: Faher *Yod* (י), Mother *Heh* (ה), Son *Vav* (ו) and Daugher *Heh* (ה). *Yahweh* ("Lord," YHVH, יהוה) embodies both male and female.

Elohim (אלהים) does not refer to a particular gender. It is the plural form of *Eloah* ("The Mighty One," אלוה). The term *Elohim* (אלהים) derives from *Eloah,* the singular form of Elohim, which comes from *El* ("The Strong One," אל).

The phrase *Btzelem Elohim* ("In the Image of Elohim," בצלם אלהים) in Genesis 1:27 describes how humankind (both men and women) reflects the perfect image of *El* ("The Strong One, אל) and expresses the divine attributes of *Elohim* ("The Mighty Ones," אלהים).

We can observe this image in the construction of the universe's microcosm and macrocosm, as well as in the anatomy of a human being. Numbers carry information, highlighting the essence of the interconnectedness of all things on every scale.

The number 248 is one of the critical numbers that the Hebrew language reveals in this matter. The gematria value of *Khmer* ("Matter" or "Substance," חמר) is 248.

ר   מ   ח

200   40   8

In physics, particles can be matter particles or force particles, but more abstractly, everything is a form of some substance. All things, not "things," are some forms of abstract matter. Because there is also not "nothing," all particles are a form of substance.

Btzelem Elohim ("In the Image of Elohim," בצלם אלהים) would refer to the Substance One from *El* ("The Strong One, אל) which is everything made of, including the universe's building blocks (the elementary particles). In modern Hebrew, the word for an elementary particle is *chel'kiyk* (חלקיק) whose numerical value is also 248. This Hebrew term will be the focus of the next chapter, *Quantum Word.*

QUANTUM WORD

The number 248 and some of its multiples are very special in Mathematics and Physics. Some exceptional Lie groups, E8 in particular, play a foundational role.

Wilhelm Killing discovered the exceptional Lie algebra E8 in the 1880s, and Elie Cartan proved the existence of the corresponding Lie group E8, both of which hold rich historical significance. In 1900, Thorold Gosset discovered the E8 root system, which consisted of 240 root vectors across R8, while working as an English amateur mathematician. The root system is a vital structure in Lie group theory to study the exceptional group E8. The exceptional Lie group E8 thus has a dimension of 240 + 8 = 248, a unique property that sets it apart from other simple Lie groups, emphasizing its exclusivity and importance in mathematics.

Fig 10. A 2D projection of the E8 root system.
Picture credit: American Institute of Mathematics

QUANTUM WORD

The modern Hebrew word *chel'kiyk* ("elemental particle," חלקיק) is not just a linguistic term but a bridge that connects Hebrew to the concept of an elemental particle. Derived from *chelek* ("part," חלק) whose the addition of the two-letter Hebrew suffix (יק) indicates extreme smallness, conveys the meaning of "a tiny part."

The term *chel'kiyk* (חלקיק) denotes any tiny entity or unit. One of its most common uses is in the phrase *chel'kiyk sh'niyah* ("an infinitesimal part of a second," חלקיק שניה). In the Torah, the term "part" refers to the second smallest unit of time, derived from the original base word *chel'kiyk* (חלקיק). A minute contains 18 of these parts, so each "part" equals three and a third seconds (3.333333+ secs). In any event, "an infinitesimal part of a second"(חלקיק שניה) expresses the smallest unit of time.

The second word, "second" (שניה) is equal to 365, which is the number of days in a solar year. It also refers to the number of prohibitive commandments in the Torah, the complement of 248, and the number of positive commandments. So, the value of the idiom חלקיק שניה, "an infinitesimal part of a second," is 613. One particle of a second (the smallest unit of time) captures and encapsulates the entire Torah. Like energy, we can quantify time into basic discrete units. Therefore, the best way to describe the smallest quanta of time would be the idiom *chel'kiyk sh'niyah* ("an infinitesimal part of a second," חלקיק שניה) which has a numerical value of 613.

The smallest quanta of time, the seed of reality quantized in an instant of time, captured and encapsulated not only the entire Torah (The Word) but also matter, the possible entire map of the elementary particles of the universe of numerical value 248, which is the Substance One.

QUANTUM WORD

What would be the value of the smallest quanta of time? Considering that a "part," the second smallest unit of time is 3.333333+ secs. The smallest quanta of time is the division of this part into 613 most minor units.

$$1 \text{ smallest quanta of time} = 10 \div 1839 = 0.0054377379+$$

Interestingly, the number 1839 is an essential factor within the atomic structure. All matter is composed of atoms, the smallest individual units of elements. Each atom comprises three subatomic particles: protons, neutrons, and electrons. Together, these three particles account for an atom's mass and charge. The mass of electrons is tiny compared to protons and neutrons. The atomic nucleus holds protons and neutrons, resulting in most atomic mass occurring within the nucleus. Neutrons are the heaviest subatomic particles and weigh 1839 times more than an electron. This mathematical relationship, where the smallest quanta of time are 10 times the neutron-to-electron mass ratio ($m_e \div m_n = 1 \div 1839$), a dimensionless quantity in Physics, demonstrates that the fabric of subatomic particles in the universe intrinsically links to time, further reinforcing the significance of the number 248 in the context of physics and mathematics.

$$1 \text{ smallest quanta of time} = 10 \times (m_{e^-} \div m_n)$$

The mass of a proton is slightly less than that of a neutron. The protons weigh 1836 times more than an electron.

$$613 \times 3 = 1839 \text{ (Neutron)}$$
$$612 \times 3 = 1836 \text{ (Protons)}$$

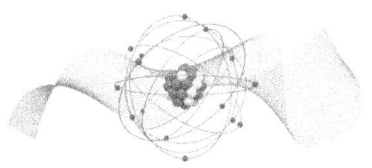

QUANTUM WORD

The numbers 612 and 613 are remarkably the numerical values of many words in Hebrew, like *BaTorah* ("In the Torah," בתורה). The universe's infinitesimal and smallest building blocks to form matter, whilst expressing the smallest quanta of time in space, were captured and encapsulated in Yahweh's Word.

BaTorah ("In the Torah," בתורה) is a mathematical identity fully satisfying to the most discerning of intellects:

בתורה

613

The following words also have the same numerical value as 613. *B'rit Aleph* ("The First Covenant," ברית א); *Barati* ("I created," בראתי); *Et HaAur* ("The Light," את האור).

B'rit ("Covenant," ברית) is of numerical value 612. It is the only word which has the same root meaning as 613. *Kol Mitsvot YHVH* ("All the Commandments of the Lord," כל מצות יהוה) is of numerical value 612.
Sheva Pawmim ("Seven Times," שבע פעמים) is also of numerical value 612.

כל מצות יהוה

612

Torah (תורה) is of numerical value 611. Same as *Ashish* ("Foundation," אשיש).

אשיש

611

QUANTUM WORD

The Greek Word *Stoma* ("Mouth" or "Opening," στόμα) is of numerical value 611.

$$\text{στόμα}$$
$$611$$

Graphe ("Scripture," στόμα) is of numerical value 612.

$$\text{γραφη}$$
$$612$$

The numbers 611, 612, and 613 have an excellent mathematical relationship, indicating that the Spoken Word of Yahweh manifested all matter (atoms).

$$611 + 612 + 613 = 1836 = 612 \times 3$$

"Opening the Covenant I created"
"Opening all the Commandments of the Lord in the Torah"
"Torah Scripture the Light"
"Opening Seven Times the First Covenant"
"Opening Seven Times in the Torah"

The above idioms are captured and encapsulated in the mass of a proton 1836 if the mass of an electron is 1. The presence of a proton, electron, and neutron is the active embodiment of the Spoken Word of Yahweh. It naturally manifests all things with the smallest units of matter and the smallest quanta of time ($10 \div 1839 = 0.0054377379+$).

QUANTUM WORD

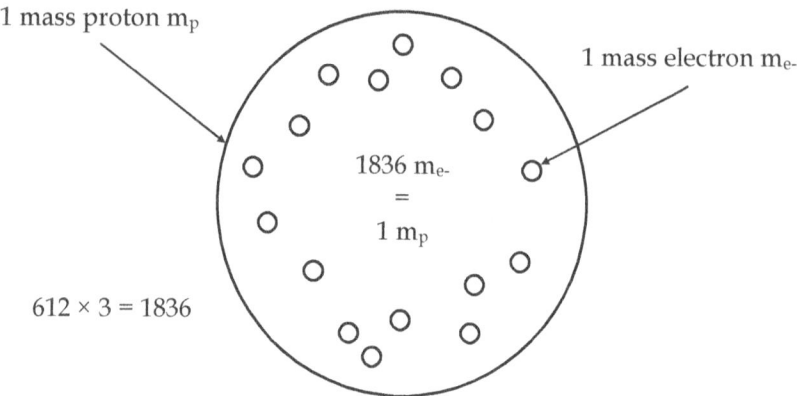

612 Gematria value of:
- "Scripture" (στόμα).
- "Covenant" (ברית).

613 Gematria value of:
- "The Light" (את האור).
- "In the Torah" (בתורה).

In terms of mass, the neutron and proton have only a gap of three electrons. The triangle reminds us of the trinity of God's and Goddess' expression.

10 is the gematria value of the Hebrew letter *Yod* (י), the single point from which all creation emerges, the foundation of all foundations. In Kabbalah, it is the first and highest level of creation.

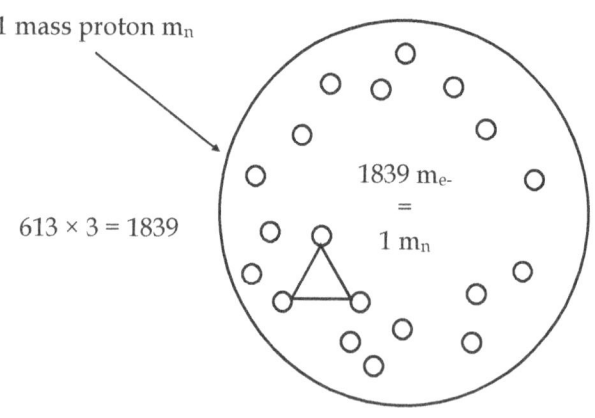

1 smallest quanta of time
$= 10 \times (m_{e^-} \div m_n)$
= 10 Sephiroth weighted by the quotient of the electron mass and the neutron mass.

Fig 11.
Matter and Time encapsulate the Spoken Word.

We already know that the numerical value of the idiom *Btzelem Elohim* ("In the Image of Elohim," בצלם אלהים) is 248. The image of *Elohim* ("The Mighty Ones," אלהים) manifests the smallest quanta of time, which derives from *Eloah* ("The Mighty One," אלוה).

חלקיק שניה

365   248

613

Btzelem Elohim ("In the Image of Elohim," בצלם אלהים) is the combination of *Adam* (אדמ), *Eve* (חוה), *Yahweh* (יהוה) and God's and Goddess' timeless nature ("He/She was, He/She is, He/She will be," יהיה היה הווה). The smallest quanta of time, although measured in basic discrete units of 613, the essence of its manifestation with *Khmer* ("Matter" or "Substance," חמר) of numerical value 248 is beyond time itself. Throughout anatomical history, sources have varied significantly regarding the total bone count in the adult skeleton. Galen, who lived from 129 CE to 216 CE, attributed 248 bones to his work, and later, Ibn Abbas confirmed this count in 1437. The Mishnah in Oholos 1:8 lists 248 bones in the human body.

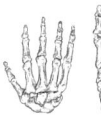

- 30 in the feet
- 6 in each toe
- 10 in the ankle
- 2 in the shin
- 5 in the knee
- 1 in the thigh
- 3 in the hip
- 11 ribs
- 30 in the palms
- 6 in the fingers
- 2 in the forearms
- 2 in the elbows
- 1 in the upper arms
- 4 in the shoulder

This totals 101 on each side, or a total of 202. In addition, there are 18 vertebrae: the 12 thoracic vertebrae, the 5 lumbar vertebrae, and the sacrum/coccyx.

- 9 in the head
- 8 in the neck
- 6 by the "openings of the heart"
- 5 around its cavities

THE FIRST WORD

THE FIRST WORD

The first letter of the Hebrew Alphabet, *Aleph* (א), holds a profound significance. It is not merely a letter but a symbol of the number 1, representing the Great Spirit, the One, the origin of all things. The structure of the first letter of the alphabet, the first word, and the first verse of the Bible profoundly embeds the concept of the One Source.

So, when we look at the inner structure of the *Aleph* (א), we construct it out of two other letters of the alphabet, *Yod* (י) and *Vav* (ו) into a group of three of these letters: two *Yods* (יי) and a *Vav* (ו). As mentioned, *Vav* (ו) is the connector, hook, or nail, usually translated as "and." Here, it connects the two *Yods* (יי) which interpreters can view as all things connected. As above, so below. The sum of these letters is 10 + 6 + 10 = 26, the number value of the name *Yahweh* (יהוה). In full gematria (Fig 127), the sum of these letters is 20 + 12 + 20 = 52, which is the gematria of *Elohim* (אלהים) in the position of the letters in the Hebrew Alphabet, respectively the sum is 24 + 10 + 5 + 12 + 1 = 52.

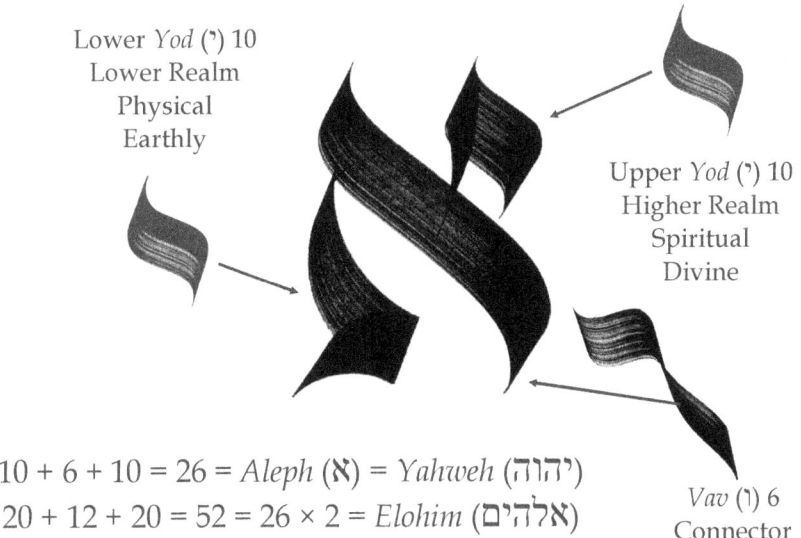

Fig 12.
The inner structure of the Hebrew letter *Aleph* (א).

THE FIRST WORD

As mentioned, 26 is the mean between 13 (lunar months in a year) and 52 (solar weeks in a year). Therefore, the masculine principle (solar cycle) and the feminine principle (lunar cycle) combined in the name of *Yahweh* (יהוה) and *Elohim* (אלהים) remind us of our divine nature beyond the genders as the unity of all aspects (father, mother, daughter, and son). Moreover, there are some essential Hebrew correspondences for the number 13, *Ekhad* ("One," אחד) and *Ahavah* ("Love," אהבה).

א ח ד
4 8 1

א ה ב ה
5 2 5 1

The number 13, a mirror number of 31, *El* ("The Strong One," אל) holds profound spiritual significance. It is the seventh Fibonacci number, following the sequence of numbers 1, 1, 2, 3, 5, 8, and 13. This spiritual significance is not just a mathematical curiosity, but a profound truth encoded in the very fabric of the Hebrew language and its letters.
From the first letter, *Aleph* (א) of numerical value 1, comes naturally the element that pervades all spaces and dimensions and embodies the threefold nature of all things in the universe, with the right and left sides and the center. It is the foundation of structure expressed in an orderly and precise way.
The letter *Shin* (ש) representing the threefold nature, is a key element in understanding the Hebrew alphabet. The letter *Vav* (ו) constructs the inner structure of the 21st letter of the Hebrew alphabet, which in turn is part of the inner structure of the letter *Aleph* (א).

El 31 | 13 אחד One / אהבה Love

THE FIRST WORD

Three *Vavs* (ווו) construct the letter *Shin* (ש). Thus, *Aleph* (א) conceived and bore the following letter, *Shin* (ש), with a numerical value of 300. The number 3, accompanied by the number 1, is the origin of all things, "the One," which can be read as 13, "One," or "Love," mirroring the number 31, *El* ("The Strong One, אל).

With three *Vavs* (ווו), the total sum is 18. The Hebrew word *Chai* (חי) meaning life, consists of two Hebrew letters, *Chet* (ח) equivalent to the number eight, and *Yod* (י), associated with the number ten, which together add up to 18. The letter *Shin* (ש) corresponds to life itself, the breath of life, the spirit or fifth element, the ether.

Many layers allow us to interpret the letter *Shin* (ש). It alludes to be present in the threefold nature of all things in unison. Accompanied by the letter *Aleph* (א), the word *Eish* ("Fire," אש) appears naturally in Hebrew. From the origin of all things, *Aleph* (א), the ether comes forth as the letter *Shin* (ש) and then the fire element is conceived through the union of the letters *Shin* (ש) and *Aleph* (א).

The numbers 1836 (18 x 2 = 36) and 1839 (18 x 2 + 3 = 39) encode life. They represent the mass of a proton and neutron

3 × *Vavs* (ווו) (6) = 18

The Holy Spirit expresses life through its three-fold nature as "the Spirit of the Primal Fire." Its fiery nature is evident in the meaning of *Eish* ("Fire," אש)

Fig 13. The Hebrew letter *Shin* (ש).

THE FIRST WORD

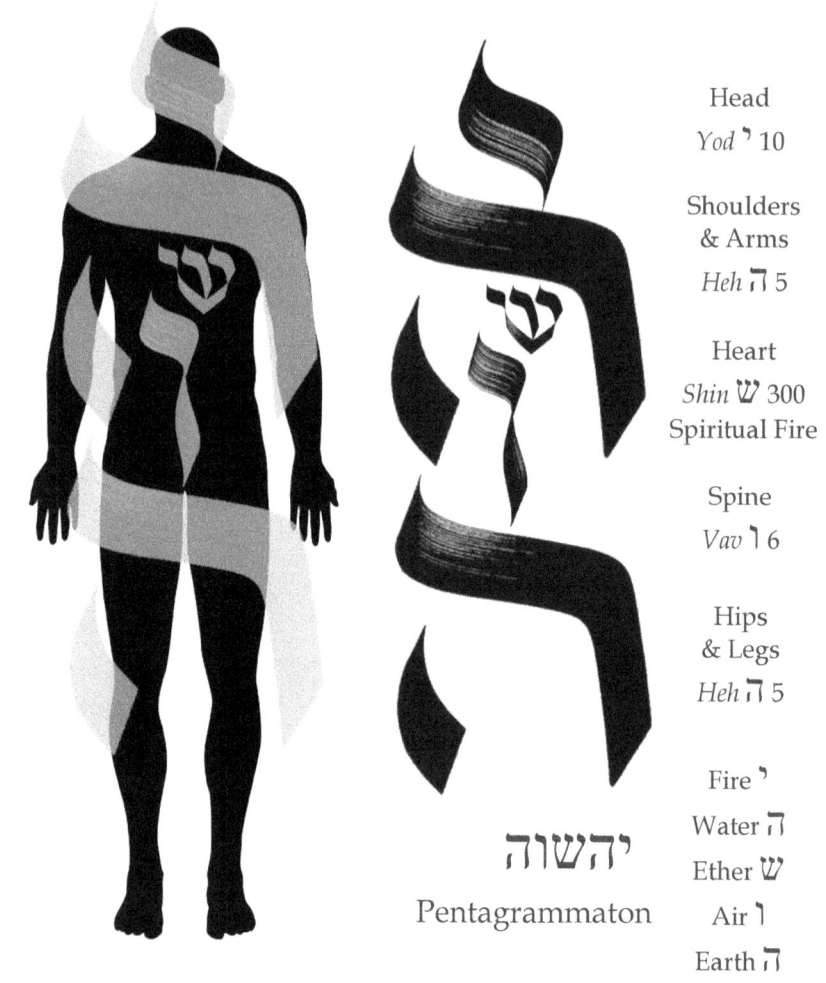

Fig 14.
The Pentagrammaton - The Integration of *Shin* (ש).

When we place the Hebrew letter *Shin* (ש) amid the first design Tetragrammaton (YHVH), we reconcile the opposing masculine (fire and air) and feminine (water and earth) energies within the Self. It represents the path of the "Spirit of the Primal Fire" in the Tree of Life, Kabbalah, alluding to the awakening of the Holy Spirit and its integration within the Self. It encodes the Hebrew name of *Yahshuah*, *Yeshua* ("Jesus," ישוע), spelled *YHShinVH* (יהשוה), the Pentagrammaton.

THE FIRST WORD

Hebrew letters are the instruments and building blocks of the creation. They are cosmic strands of DNA. Their shapes, sounds, and sequences radiate a wide range of forces.

Genesis in the Bible is a genetic map encoding not only Adam but also the origins of the construct on every scale, microcosm, and macrocosm. It begins with the first word of the first verse of Genesis *Bereisheit* ("In the beginning," בראשית):

$$ת\ י\ ש\ א\ ר\ ב$$
$$400\ \ 10\ \ 300\ \ 1\ \ 200\ \ 2$$
$$913$$

Bereisheit ("In the beginning," בראשית) is the signature of the number 13, representing the unified vibration of "Love" and "One" in the number 913. The total sum of 9, 1, and 3 is also 13, insisting on the universal vibration that the divine essence embodies, and it began with Love in the unity of all things. As mentioned before, the middle letters of *Bereisheit* (בראשית) form the word *Eish* ("Fire," אש). The Spirit of the Primal Fire, source of the ether, pervades all spaces and dimensions. It also encodes 13, as the letter *Aleph* (א) is 1, and the reduced number of *Shin* (ש) is 3. It has an affinity with the word "Pyramid." In the Greek language, the word *Pyramis* ("Pyramid," πυραμίς) means "Fire in the Middle." *Pyra* ("Fire," πυρά) was often synonymous with the word "light," and *Mis* ("Mid," μις) also describes a measurement (midpoint).

Eit Eish Ber

בר אש ית

Fig 15. Fire in the Middle.

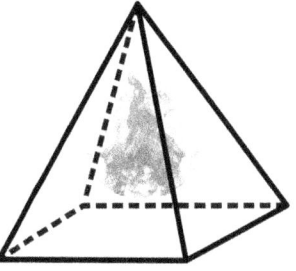

The two middle letters form *Eish* ("Fire," אש). The first word concealed the essence of the Spirit of the Primal Fire "in the beginning."

THE FIRST WORD

The number 13 is the seventh prime number, and the number of words in the first verse of Genesis is 7. Here, we already see that the sevenfold nature follows the threefold nature, and the sequence of this unfolding leads to a fundamental number in Physics: 137. The inverse ratio is the fine structure constant *Alpha* (α) governing the interaction between matter and light.

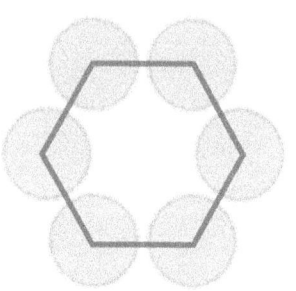

According to Genesis 1 and the verse in Exodus 20.11, the Lord created the heavens and the earth in six days and rested on the seventh day. A hexagonal ring of units symbolized the six days of creation.

**Fig 16.
Hexagonal Ring 6.**

When we arrange six units into a ring, we create a "free" space within it, providing an arena for further creation. We can then fill or seed the "free" space with another unit to form the centered hexagon 7, representing the completed seven-day period.

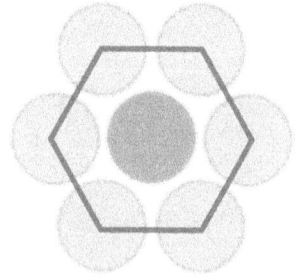

**Fig 17.
Hexagon 7.**

To further develop the creative process of creation, similar to atoms forming molecules and more significant structures, we can use the hexagon we created as the "day" unit for a second illustration of the six-day creation period.

Returning to the original ring of six units, we can create a ring of hexagons by replacing each unit with "Hexagon 7".

**Fig 18.
Hexagonal Ring 42.**

The space in the center takes on the shape of a hexagram, the star number of 13 units, which can be called "The Seal of Unity."

**Fig 19.
Snowflake 55.**

Elohim blessed the seventh day and made it holy. The "Seal of Unity," an ancient symbol of the Christ blueprint, amazingly symbolizes it. Thirteen is the standard gematria of the Hebrew words for *Ekhad* ("One," אחד) and *Ahavah* ("Love," אהבה). The gematria value of *Yahweh* ("Lord," יהוה) and the ordinal value of the English word "God" is 26 (13 x 2) (Appendix H).

The story of the creation in Genesis naturally builds the first fractal snowflake. As a symbol of growth and order, the center embodies God's and Goddess' Love and the essence of connectedness as One in all things. The "Seal of Unity" represents the Primal Fire of the Holy Spirit, which is ever-present ("In the beginning," בר אש ית).

THE FIRST WORD

The Torah reveals deeper meanings beyond the surface, and its crafting prevents simple understanding through mere reading. It requires the reader to look more deeply to question and challenge both the text and the reader as they seek its more profound wisdom and meaning. Every letter of every word has a purpose, and even the tiniest detail can change the reader's understanding of the Divine message. For example, the root structure of the first word of the first verse of Genesis, *Bereisheit* (בראשית) presents a complex challenge. Without knowing the root, it isn't easy to understand the word. This first word in the Torah is a grammatical oddity, which is to say that from the beginning, the text challenges language structure. This first challenge shows the reader the Torah's depth, revealing that there is no further to look if the first word is poorly understood and deeply deciphered in its meaning. In Hebrew, speakers build every word upon a basic two or three-root structure, and words that share a root convey connected meanings. The scholars consider the root of *Bereisheit* (בראשית) to be *Reish Aleph Shin* (ראש) which means "head," "mind," or "beginning." The letter *Beit* (ב) before the root would mean "in," hence "In the beginning." The last two letters don't make sense with this structure, yet every letter in the Torah has a purpose.

In the first word, *Bereisheit* (בראשית) there may be more than one root. The uniqueness of the word, rich in meaning, could transcend the human language itself. For example, the first three letters, *Beit Reish Aleph* (ברא) is the exact spelling as the second word, *Bara* (ברא) which means "created," a word only used for Elohim's creation. So, the word *Bereisheit* (בראשית) means both "beginning" and "divine creation." But there is more, as previously seen in the two middle letters of *Bereisheit* (בראשית) a third word buried within it, *Eish* ("Fire," אש). It seems to speak of the Primal Fire of the Holy Spirit involved with creation. It is generally associated with the ether, the fifth element, a superfluid pervading all dimensions.

THE FIRST WORD

We can delve deeper into the first word's meaning by interpreting the root *Reish Aleph Shin* (ראש) as "mind." The first four letters of the word *Bereisheit*, *Beit Reish Aleph Shin* (בראש) translate to "In the mind," while the last two letters, *Yod Tav* (ית) translate to "Creator." So, in another facet, the Hebrew word *Bereisheit* (בראשית) could mean "In the Creator's Mind," whose "the divine creation" emanated "In the beginning" from "the Primal Fire of the Holy Spirit," whichever lasted beyond the notion of space and time.

- Looking numerically at the inner structure of *Aleph* (א) (Fig 12), the Primal Fire is the connector *Vav* (ו) of gematria value 6, as the word *Bereisheit* (בראשית) has six Hebrew letters and connects the earthly and spiritual realms. As above, so below. The Primal Fire used for the divine creation has always been present on every scale, microcosm, and macrocosm. It is the Substance One, the ether, the primal force of all things created, manifested in Elohim's hands, and it seems to be coming from "Their Mind."
- Looking geometrically at the first fractal snowflake (Fig 19), built from the story of creation in Genesis, the core of the geometric pattern displays a six-fold symmetry observed in nature. Here, it is presented as "The Seal of Unity" or "the Star of David," representing the unification and balance between the feminine and masculine forces. The geometric pattern bears the number 6, a signature of the first word, *Bereisheit* ("In the beginning," בראשית).

Six pointed-star   Six Hebrew letters   *Vav* (ו) 6 Connector

Fig 20. Signature of 6.

INTRODUCTION TO KABBALAH

INTRODUCTION TO KABBALAH

The number 137, the 33rd prime number, beginning with 13, is the gematria value for *Ekhad* ("One," אחד) and *Ahavah* ("Love," אהבה). This number holds significant importance in Kabbalistic numerology as it corresponds to the standard value of the word *Kabbalah* ("Receiving," קבלה) which means "to receive, to accept." It symbolizes the unity and love that underpin the Kabbalistic teachings.

$$\begin{array}{cccc} ק & ב & ל & ה \\ 100 & 2 & 30 & 5 \end{array}$$
$$137$$

The Kabbalah derives from the Hebrew root *Kuf Beit Lamed* (קבל) which translates to "capacitor, condenser." Every subparticle of matter, human beings, planets, galaxies, and anything else would act as a capacitor or condenser, storing energy from the infinite and limitless source of light, *Ein Soph Aur* (אין סוף אור). The Divine Map, known as the Kabbalah, conducts the flow of creative energy through the Tree of Life. It has ten Sephiroth, each representing a jewel of wisdom, and three other mysterious and unknown Sephiroth above *Kether* (כתר) which means "crown," at the top, on the head of the Tree of Life. The description of these three is as follows:

- The first one is called *Ein* (אין) which in Hebrew means "nothingness" — **Undifferentiated Consciousness** in its purest original state, "I-less" or "ego-less."
- The second one, below *Ein* (אין) is called *Ein Soph* (סוף אין) "the limitless" — **Differentiated Consciousness** with "I," Self-Realization, the Monad (Point) before Emanation.
- The third aspect of the Absolute actively manifests as *Ein Soph Aur* (אין סוף אור) "the unfathomable light" — **Arising Consciousness**. The fabric of consciousness unfolds perpetually and eternally during the Physical Manifestation, the first emanation of the unknown, called *Christos* ("Christ," Χρίστος)

INTRODUCTION TO KABBALAH

On the usual diagram of the Kabbalah, there are ten Sephiroth, but we don't see the three above *Kether* (כתר), as they are unknown. However, they are just as important as the others, completing the Kabbalah through the "Seal of Unity" (13 Sephiroth).

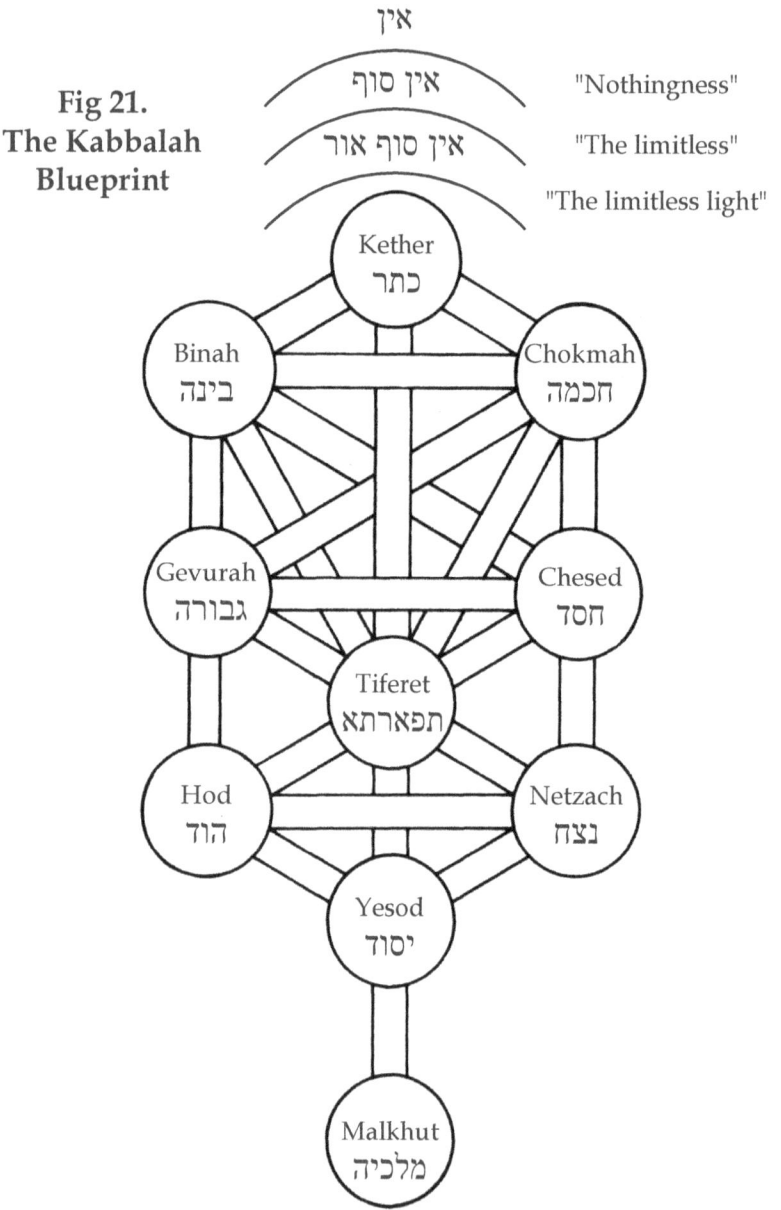

Fig 21. The Kabbalah Blueprint

INTRODUCTION TO KABBALAH

According to the Kabbalah, the world began as a "Middle" or "Central Point," *Nekudah Emtzait* (נקודה אמצעית) which expanded into an ideal circle. The Hebrew letter representing a dot or point is *Yod* (י), a dot that contains all 10 Sephiroth.

נקודה אמצעית

611   165

The numerical value of *Nekudah* ("Point," נקודה) is 165, the product of 15 and 11, the unification between the masculine and feminine principles encoded in the name of Yahweh YHVH (YH 15 x WH 11 = 165). The numerical value of 611, as previously mentioned, is the gematria value of *Torah* (תורה) *Ashish* ("Foundation," אשיש), and the Greek Word *Stoma* ("Mouth" or "Opening," στόμα)

So, the Middle Point contained everything spoken by the "Mouth" before coming into existence. It is the Greatest Foundation from which everything manifested from Yahweh's Word. The "Opening of the Mouth" begins with the first word of Genesis 1:1, *Bereisheit* (בראשית) which consists of six letters, aka the six days of creation. The first letter of *Bereisheit* (בראשית) is the Hebrew letter *Beit* (ב), the point of creation in the beginning, which is symbolized by the "Mouth" with a dot in the center (בּ), a sound/frequency out of the "Mouth."

Interestingly, *Nekudah Emtzait* ("Middle Point," נקודה אמצעית) has a standard gematria value of 776, and the 776th prime number is 5897, appearing strictly at location 10 in the digits of PI (π) after the decimal.

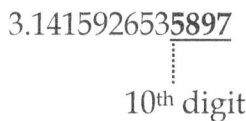

10th digit

INTRODUCTION TO KABBALAH

Beit (ב) / Mouth, the breathe of God and Goddess.

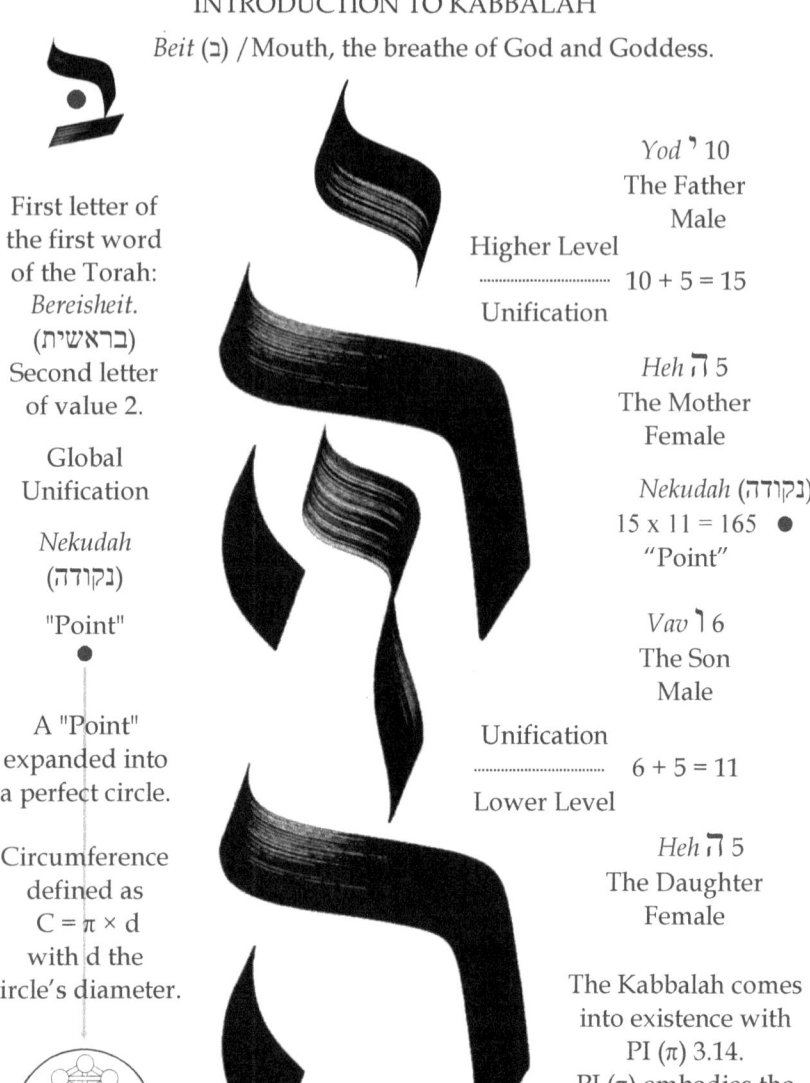

First letter of the first word of the Torah: *Bereisheit.* (בראשית)
Second letter of value 2.

Global Unification

Nekudah (נקודה)

"Point"
●

A "Point" expanded into a perfect circle.

Circumference defined as $C = \pi \times d$ with d the circle's diameter.

Yod י 10
The Father
Male

Higher Level
$10 + 5 = 15$
Unification

Heh ה 5
The Mother
Female

Nekudah (נקודה)
$15 \times 11 = 165$ ●
"Point"

Vav ו 6
The Son
Male

Unification
$6 + 5 = 11$
Lower Level

Heh ה 5
The Daughter
Female

The Kabbalah comes into existence with PI (π) 3.14.
PI (π) embodies the Spoken Word of God and Goddess; it is perfection.

Fig 22. The Emergence of Life.

Looking at the structure of the first verse of Genesis. There is a total of 28 Hebrew letters, the 7th triangular number. The position number 13, which represents the centroid of this triangular number, symbolizes the "Seal of Unity," associated with *Ekhad* ("One," אחד) and *Ahavah* ("Love," אהבה).

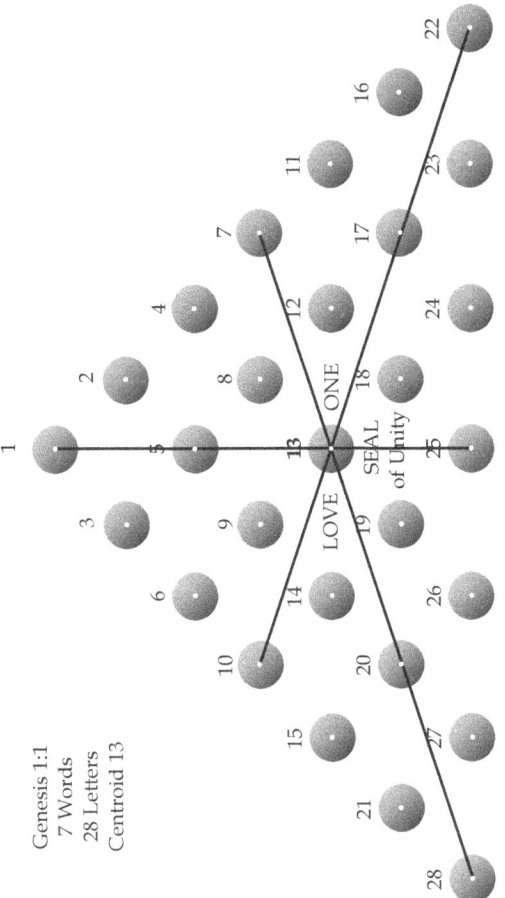

Fig 23. Triangular Number 7.

The centroid 13, known as the "Seal of Unity," holds the geometric and numerical structure of Genesis 1:1. Note that the gematria values of the first letter of each of these seven words sum to 22: *Beit* (ב) 2, *Beit* (ב) 2, *Aleph* (א) 1, *Aleph* (א) 1, *Heh* (ה) 5, *Vav* (ו) 6 and *Heh* (ה) 5. Their sum is 22, the number of letters in the Hebrew alphabet. A good approximation of PI (π) is 22 divided by 7; 3.142857+.

The opening word, *Bereisheit* ("In the beginning," בראשית) created Space and Time. Using PI (π), the initial "dot" was wholly and perfectly expanded into a circle.

THE FIRST VERSE OF GENESIS

THE FIRST VERSE OF GENESIS
GENESIS 1.1 has a total gematria value of 2701

In the beginning Elohim created the heavens and the earth.
Bereisheit bara Elohim et hashamayim v'et ha'aretz.

In the Beginning	בראשית	913
Created	ברא	203
Elohim	אלהים	86
Aleph Tav	את	401
the heavens	השמים	395
and	ואת	407
the earth	הארץ	296

THE FIRST VERSE OF GENESIS

It's intriguing that the first 611 digits of PI (π), when summed, equal 2701, is the gematria value of the first verse of Genesis. This connection underscores the profound truths encoded in the Bible and PI (π).

3.1415926535897932384626433832795028841971693993751058209749445923078164062862089986280348253421170679821480865132823066470938446095505822317253594081284811174502841027019385211055596446229489549303819644288109756659334461284756482337867831652712019091456485669234603486104543266482133936072602491412737245870066063155881748815209209628292540917153643678925903600113305305488204665213841469519415116094330572703657595919530921861173819326117931051185480744623799627495673518857527248912279381830119491298336733624406566430860213949463952247371907021798609437027705392171762931767523846748184676694051320005681271 4

As we decode the Bible, we realize that the value of PI (π) could be the Word of God and Goddess Itself, holding profound truths about the root of creation and its foundations. It is the code of creation. It is a complete record of what was said "In the Beginning" from the "Opening Mouth of God and Goddess," *Yahweh* ("Lord," יהוה).

The central word *Aleph Tav* (את) of the first verse of Genesis, though untranslated, is said to be the signature of *Elohim* ("The Mighty/Strong Ones," אלהים). *Aleph* (א) is the beginning, and *Tav* (ת) is the end of the Hebrew Alphabet. The New Testament also mentions this signature in Revelation 22:13, stating, "I am Alpha and Omega, the beginning and the end." It defines the comprehensiveness of Yahweh, implying that Yahweh includes all that can be. Yahweh contains everything as God and Goddess, which is also everything that has come into existence from the *Nekudah* (נקודה), a "Point Singularity." Yahweh transcends the space-time continuum and goes beyond the limitations set for Their creation.

THE FIRST VERSE OF GENESIS

The first verse of Genesis with the gematria value of 2701 can be visualized geometrically by the Triangular Number 73 (T_{73}), considering that 2701 = 666 x 3 + 703. 703 and 666 are Triangular numbers (the 37th and 36th respectively). According to the Kabbalah, an inner spiritual core surrounds every part of creation and the entire creation with an outer physical shell. The 703 Triangle fits in the exact center and represents the inner spiritual core. The surrounding 666 Triangles represent the external physical shell enclosing the spiritual core. 666 is the 36th Triangular Number and 6×6 = 36. Observe also that 6 surrounds both Genesis triangles through their perimeters.

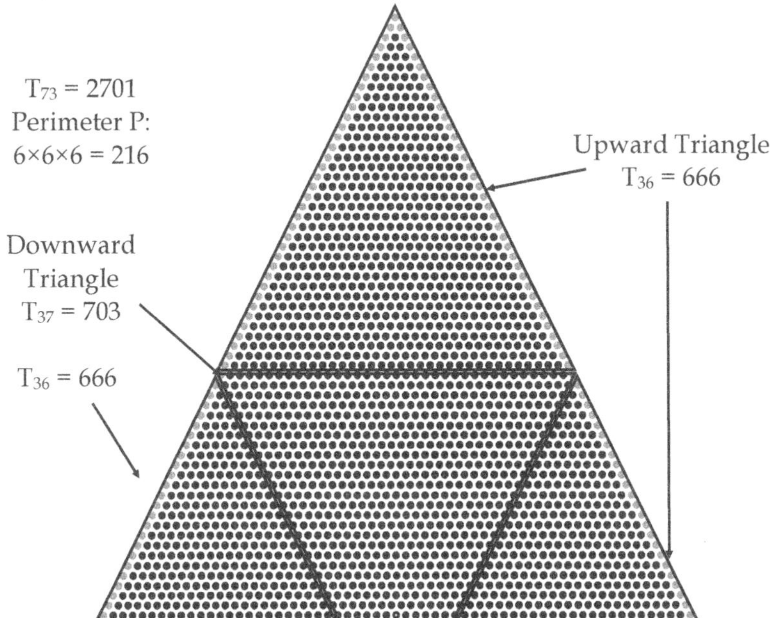

T_{73} = 2701
Perimeter P:
6×6×6 = 216

Upward Triangle
T_{36} = 666

Downward Triangle
T_{37} = 703

T_{36} = 666

**Fig 24.
Genesis Triangles.**

T_7 = 28
Perimeter P:
6+6+6 = 18

THE FIRST VERSE OF GENESIS
$$2701 = 3 \times 666 + 703 = 73 \times 37$$

The standard gematria value of *Chokmah* ("Wisdom," חכמה) is 73, while the ordinal gematria value is 37. These numbers carry profound spiritual implications, inviting us to delve deeper into their meanings.

	ח כ מ ה
Standard	5 40 20 8
	73
Ordinal	5 13 11 8
	37

The third- and fourth-star numbers are 37 and 73, and 37 is hexagonal. We can appreciate the relationship between these numbers when "Star Number 37" and "Hexagon 37" fit neatly inside "Star Number 73."

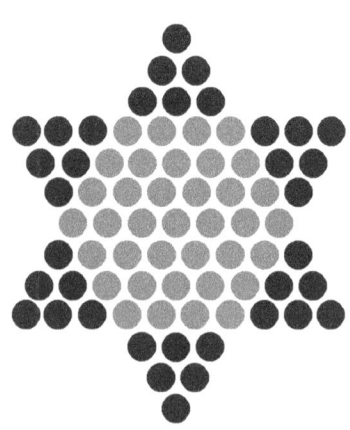

**Fig 25.
Star Number 73 and Hexagon 37.**

THE FIRST VERSE OF GENESIS

An interesting fact is that the sequence 2701 first appears in PI (π) at the 165th, 166th, 167th, and 168th decimal places:

3.1415926535897932384626433832795028841971693993751058209749445923078164062862089986280348253421170679821480865132823066470938446095505822317253594081284811174502841० **2701**

By adding the 165th, 166th, 167th, and 168th PI positions, we obtain 666, the 36th Triangular Number.

Let's recall that 165 is the gematria value of *Nekudah* ("Point," נקודה). Creation began as a "point," expanding into a perfect circle, ultimately forming the physical realm. The Great Architect used PI (π) to bring this circle into an ideal and whole way. In other words, Oneness, as the circle, is the Monad, a geometric symbol of Unity.
The sum of the first 165 digits of PI (π) is 737. 73 and 37 are reflective numbers. 737 is another version of 73 x 37, with three becoming one.

PI (π) is associated with the Holy Name *Sha-dai* (ש-די) standing for *Mi she'Amar Dai L'olamo* ("Whoever said 'enough is enough' for their Universe," מי שאמר די לעולמו). The infinite was constricted into the finite to make it possible for creation to exist. *Sha-dai* (ש-די) has a gematria value of 314, just like PI (π) starts at 3.14.

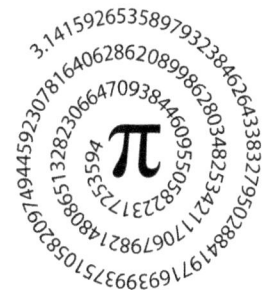

ש - ד י
10 4 300
314

Pi = 3.14+

THE FIRST VERSE OF GENESIS

PI (π) has so much depth and wisdom that a book would not be enough to cover it all. But here are a few questions rising to begin with.

- What would the Great Architect and its entire design represent for PI (π)?
- Did it set out to create space and time, *Bereisheit* ("in the beginning," בראשית), the first saying of creation, from the "initial dot" into a circle wholly and perfectly?

The Great Architect will place the structure at the center of the circle, allowing us to see and witness everything around all parts of the circle equidistantly.

- Is PI (π) the Living Word from the Opening Mouth of the Great Architect, a "Primary Being," *Metzuy Roshon* (מצוי ראשון) who brought into being all existence?

Note that PI (π) is the circumference of a circle divided by its diameter. Without PI (π), there is no circle, space, or time to contain anything. Everything would collapse back into a singularity point. Yahweh is timeless ("He/She was, He/She is, He/She will be," יהיה היה הווה), God's and Godess' nature. We can tell that PI (π) is the mathematical coding of Their Living Word at the starting point of creation, from the "singularity point" to a "perfect circle." They shaped it in Their image, reflecting Adam and Eve.

                    מצוי ראשון

Standard	703
Ordinal	109
Reduced	37

THE FIRST VERSE OF GENESIS

Interestingly, in a beautiful manner, *She'Amar Dai L'olamo* ("Who said 'enough is enough' for their Universe," שאמר די לעולמו) has a gematria of 737.

$$\begin{array}{cccc} \text{ש א מ ר} & \text{ל ע ו ל מ ו} & \text{ד י} \\ 200\ 40\ 1\ 300 & 6\ 40\ 30\ 6\ 70\ 30 & 10\ 4 \\ & 737 & \end{array}$$

The divine attribute used to "constrict" God's and Goddess' infinite light to make room for the physical is called the Sephira of *Gevurah* ("Might," "Restraint," גבורה).

	ג ב ו ר ה
Standard	5 200 6 2 3
	216 = 6 x 6 x 6
Ordinal	5 20 6 2 3
	36 = 6 x 6
Reduced	5 2 6 2 3
	18 = 6 + 6 + 6

There are 6 weekdays (time) and six directions of space from a center point: up, down, north, east, south, west. Thus, 6 represents the physical world. The surrounding 666 triangles and perimeters represent the creation of matter and time.

- 216 is the perimeter of the Triangular Number 73, totalling 2701, gematria value of Gen 1.1.
- 18 is the perimeter of the Triangular Number 7, totalling 28, the number of letters of Gen 1.1.

THE FIRST VERSE OF GENESIS

The creation involved "6 days of creation" (physical) followed by a 7th day Sabbath (spiritual). The 666 Triangles (and total perimeters) are folded as a "shell" around 703, representing the inner spiritual realm *Sabbath* (שבת) God's and Goddess' Temple, the divine spark that sustains everything.

Sabbath (שבת) has a gematria value of 702. With the center point, "the center of gravity," the location of the centroid of 2701, positioned at 1201, *Sabbath* (שבת) gives a complete structure of 703 (spiritual realm), including the 666 triangles (physical realm). The "Balance Point" is the innermost spiritual core, God's and Goddess' breath of divine essence, which vivifies man and woman's souls and grants wisdom. They are the intermediary between God and Goddess and the entire creation in the universe.

ש ב ת

400 2 300

702

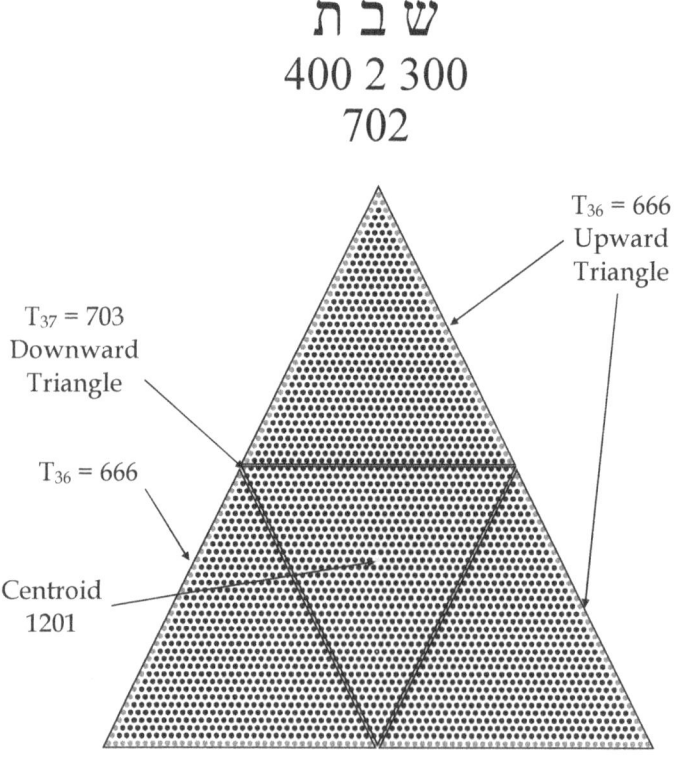

Fig 26. Centroid of Triangular Number 73.

THE FIRST VERSE OF GENESIS

1201 is the 197th prime number, and 197 ranks the 45th prime number. *Adam* (אדמ) of numerical value 45 hints Adam and Eve are the inner core of Their creation; They balance everything around them. Even the unimaginably vast universe and the different dimensions (inner as outer) are to teach them about the infinite essence of their divine nature, *Elohim B'tzelem* ("Elohim's image," בצלם האלהים).

Also note that $2701 = 26^2 + 45^2$. The gematria values of *Yahweh* (יהוה) and *Adam* (אדמ) are 26 and 45, respectively. The gematria value of *Chavah* ("Eve," חוה) is 19, and 45 - 26 = 19.

The number 37 is at the core of the mathematical structure of Genesis 1.1:

• $666 \div (6 + 6 + 6) = 37$, with 6 representing the physical world; 666 is the 36th Triangular Number and the perimeter of the Triangular Number 73.
• 6+ 6 + 6 =18 is the perimeter of the Triangular Number 7.
• 703 represents the core of the Triangular Number 73 (spiritual aspect).

37 is the reduced gematria of *Metzuy Roshon* ("Primary Being," מצוי ראשון) and ordinal gematria of *Chokmah* ("Wisdom," חכמה). The "Primary Being" brought all into existence with "Wisdom," establishing the foundation of the mathematical structure of Genesis 1.1. All that exists of the heavens, the earth, and what is between them came only from the truth of Their Being. The standard gematria of "Primary Being" in Hebrew is 703. The centroid located at 1201 refers to Adam and Eve (197th Prime Number and 197 is the 45th Prime Number) at the center of gravity of a "Primary Being" who spoke with "Wisdom." The "Primary Being" created Adam in Their image to serve as the intermediary between Them and all creation. The first Hebrew letter of Adam is *Aleph* (א) which represents "the strong leader" who can choose either life or death through his journey.

THE FIRST VERSE OF GENESIS

Interestingly, the 37th position of PI (π) contains the number 197.

3.1 4 1 5 9 2 6 5 3 5 8 9 7 9 3 2 3 8 4 6 2 6 4 3 3 8 3 2 7 9 5 0 2 8 8 4 **1 9 7**

---→ 37th digit

The sequence 2, 3, 5, 7, 11, 13, 17, 19, 23, 29, 31, 37 consists of the prime numbers up to 37. Their sum is 197.

The Hebrew word *Igul* ("Circle," עגול) has a standard gematria of 109 and an ordinal gematria value of 37:

	ע ג ו ל
Standard	30 6 3 70
	109
Ordinal	12 6 3 16
	37
Reduced	3 6 3 7
	19

The ordinal and standard gematria values of *Igul* ("Circle," עגול), 37 and 109, show a fascinating mathematical correlation with the reduced and ordinal gematria values of *Metzuy Roshon* ("Primary Being," מצוי ראשון). The reduced value 19 of *Igul* ("Circle," עגול) refers back to *Eve* (חוה).

In the star number 37, 19 is the centered hexagonal number. In the star number 13, the "Seal of Unity" as One Love, 7 is the centered hexagonal number. 197 is the concatenation of the two prime numbers, 19 and 7.

THE FIRST VERSE OF GENESIS

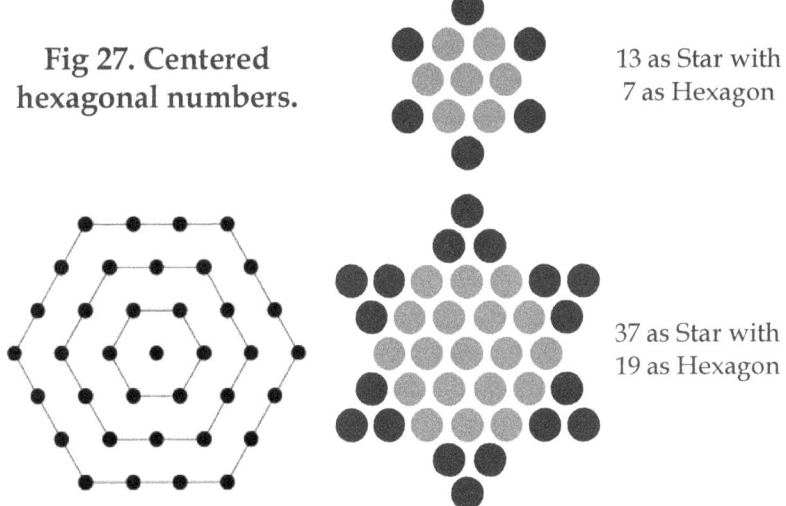

Fig 27. Centered hexagonal numbers.

13 as Star with 7 as Hexagon

37 as Star with 19 as Hexagon

The Triangular Number 73, with 2701 dots in total, holds everything into place in the creation. Its perimeter is 216, with a gematria value of *Gevurah* ("Might," "Restraint," גבורה), a sephirah of the Kabbalah, whose function is to hold the inner part, a total count of 2485, considering that 2701 - 216 = 2485.

2485 is the gematria of the five books of the Torah:

1. Genesis, *Bereisheit* ("Creation," בראשית).
2. Exodus, *Shemot* ("Names," שמות).
3. Leviticus, *Vayikrah* ("And he called," ויקרא).
4. Numbers *Bamidbar* ("In the Wilderness," במדבר).
5. Deuteronomy, *Hadevarim* ("The Second Word," הדברים).

בראשית
913

שמות
746

THE FIRST VERSE OF GENESIS

ויקרא
317

במדבר
248

הדברים
261

Interestingly, the ordinal gematria of the five books is 289, the standard gematria of *Bara Elohim* ("Elohim created," ברא אלהים) and the reduced gematria is 73, the standard gematria of *Chokmah* ("Wisdom," חכמה). Note that the total sum of the digits 289 and 2485 is 19, which is the reduced gematria of *Igul* ("Circle," עגול) and *Chokmah* ("Wisdom," חכמה).

$$2 + 8 + 9 = 19$$
$$2 + 4 + 8 + 5 = 19$$

Bara Elohim ("Elohim created," ברא אלהים) is the 2nd and 3rd word of the first book of Torah, *Bereisheit* ("Creation," בראשית) in the first verse of Genesis 1.1. 289 is 17 squared, and 17 is the gematria of *tov* ("Good," טוב) for creation is good, even though at the expense of *Tzimtzum* (צמצום) which means "contraction" or "withdrawal." 17 is also the reduced gematria of *Hikum* ("The universe," היקום). *Yahweh* (יהוה), as the Infinite *Ein Sof* (אין סוף) withdrew into itself to make room for the creation, which occurs by the first emanation of light from the Infinite into the newly provided space. This process began with *Nekudah* ("Point," נקודה) which expanded into a perfect circle. Later, the divine light is constricted and enclosed in finite "vessels," breaking under the strain of the light, whereby disharmony and evil enter the world.

THE FIRST VERSE OF GENESIS

The recall aims to clear the world of evil, reconstruct the divine realm, return the divine sparks to their source, and rebuild *Adam Kadmon* ("The primordial man," אדם קדמון), who represents the highest configuration of the holy light. The primordial man embodies the entire universe and the soul or essence of all existence. *Kadmon* (קדמון) means "primary of all primaries," the first pristine emanation, emerging from *Ein Sof* (אין סוף) infiniteness or limitlessness, the transcendental par excellence. It refers to the first emanation of the unknown, called *Christos* ("Christ," Χριστος). *Ein Soph Aur* ("the limitless light," אין סוף אור), Emanating Consciousness.

Tzimtzum ("Contraction," צמצום) has a gematria value of 266, same as *Tzelam ke'elehim* ("Image like Elohim," צלם כאלהים).

$$צ\ מ\ צ\ ו\ ם$$
$$40\ 6\ 90\ 40\ 90$$
$$266$$

$$כאלהים \quad צלם$$
$$40\ 10\ 5\ 30\ 1\ 20\ \ 40\ 30\ 90$$
$$266$$

The Greek word *Christos* ("the Anointed," Χριστός) is the Hebrew for *Mashiyach* ("Messiah," משיח).

109 is the 29th prime number, and the sum of the first 29 prime numbers is 1480, the gematria value of *Christos* (Χριστός).

The 109th composite number is 144, and the sum of the first 144 digits of PI (π) equals 666, a significant number in the mathematical structure of the first verse of the Torah, Genesis 1.1.

THE FIRST VERSE OF GENESIS

3.14159265358979323846264338327950288419716939
9375105820974944592307816406286208998628034822
5342117067982148086513282306647093844609550582
231725359

So, *Christos* ("the Anointed," Χριστός) is identified as the perfect circle and the primary being, as 109 is the standard gematria of *Igul* ("Circle," עגול) and it is the ordinal gematria of *Metzuy Roshon* ("Primary Being," מצוי ראשון). The mathematical structure of Genesis 1.1 shows clearly the relationship between 666 and 703. The number 666 is associated with the physical shell and external appearance. At the same time, the core part is spiritual (within the soul) at the center, 703, the standard gematria of *Metzuy Roshon* ("Primary Being," מצוי ראשון).

Christos ("the Anointed," Χριστός) is the "Primary Being," the "first primordial emanation of divine light." *Christos* ("the Anointed," Χριστός), *Mashiyach* ("Messiah," משיח) is *Bekar lekal nivra* ("The firstborn of every creature," בכר לכל נברא). The standard gematria value of *Bekar lekal nivra* (בכר לכל נברא) is 555, which is the sum of 266 for *Tzelam ke'elehim* ("Image like Elohim," צלם כאלהים), *Tzimtzum* ("Contraction," צמצום) and 289 for the five books of the Torah (ordinal gematria). *Mashiyach bekar lekal nivra* ("The Messiah is the firstborn of every creature," משיח בכר לכל נברא) has a gematria value of 913, the same value as *Bereisheit* ("In the beginning," בראשית) the first word in Torah, Genesis 1.1.

משיח בכר לכל נברא
בראשית

913

The remaining six words of the first verse in the Torah total 222 (ברא אלהים את השמים ואת הארץ), which is 37 x 6 and correspond to the standard gematria of *Bekar* ("firstborn," בכר).

THE FIRST VERSE OF GENESIS

GENESIS 1.1 the last six words of ordinal value 222
….. Elohim created the heavens and the earth.
….. *Bara Elohim et hashamayim v'et ha'aretz'*

Created	ברא	23
Elohim	אלהים	41
Aleph Tav	את	23
the heavens	השמים	62
and	ואת	29
the earth	הארץ	44
	=	
the first born	בכר	222

THE FIRST VERSE OF GENESIS

This insight reveals a profound truth: *Mashiyach btzelem haelehim* ("The Messiah is the image of Elohim," משיח בצלם האלהים) is the great secret of *Tzimtzum* ("Contraction," צמצום) for *Tzimtzum haelohim* ("Elohim's Contraction," צמצום האלהים) has a standard gematria of 357, which is the standard gematria of *Mashiyach* ("Messiah," משיח), 358 less 1, and 1 is the gematria value of *Aleph* (א) representing the One Source in the Bible, the origin of all things.

Diving in more deeply, let's analyze the standard and ordinal gematria values of *Mashiyach btzelem haelehim* ("The Messiah is the image of Elohim," משיח בצלם האלהים). Its standard gematria value is 611, the same as the gematria value of *Torah* (תורה) and the Hebrew word *Ashish* ("Foundation," אשיש). Not to mention that the Greek Word *Stoma* ("Mouth" or "Opening," στόμα) is also of numerical value 611. The ordinal value is 165, the same as the gematria value of *Nekudah* ("Point," נקודה) from which everything came into existence, including matter, space, and time. It is the "singularity point," that is *Tzimtzum haelohim* ("Elohim's Contraction," צמצום האלהים).

Let's recall that two other letters of the alphabet construct the inner structure of *Aleph* (א), *Yod* (י), and *Vav* (ו) into a group of three letters: two *Yods* (יי) and a *Vav* (ו). The sum of these letters is 10 + 6 + 10 = 26, the number value of the name *Yahweh* (יהוה).

The number of Hebrew letters of the five books making up the Torah is 26: *Bereisheit* ("Creation," בראשית), *Shemot* ("Names," שמות), *Vayikrah* ("And he called," ויקרא), *Bamidbar* ("In the Wilderness," במדבר), *Hadevarim* ("The Second Word," הדברים). In full gematria, the sum of the inner structure of *Aleph* (א) is two *Yods* (יי) (2 x 20) + a *Vav* (ו) 6 = 52, which is the gematria of *Elohim* (אלהים) using the *Mispar Siduri* method (("ordinal value," Fig 126). The sum is 24 (ם), 10 (י), 12 (ה), 5 (ל) and 1 (א) equals 52. Interestingly, the square root of the number 2701, the standard gematria of the first verse of Genesis in Hebrew, is about 52. This quantity is double the 26 standard gematria of *Yahweh* (יהוה), and it has a natural triangular relationship with *Eve* (יהוה) and *Adam* (אדמ) in Elohim's image. Adam, being at the center of gravity of the mathematical structure of Genesis 1.1, at position 1201, is the centroid counter of the Triangular Number 73. The centroid is where the triangle's internal structure "converges" or "collapses" into a single balanced point. It would naturally correspond to *Tzimtzum haelohim* ("Elohim's Contraction," צמצום האלהים), reflecting the idea that all of existence emerged from the expression of the truth of a "Primary Being" (both physically and spiritually) as the first emanation of the divine light, *Ein Soph Aur* (אין סוף אור), the highest configuration of light from the Infinite *Ein Soph* (אין סוף).

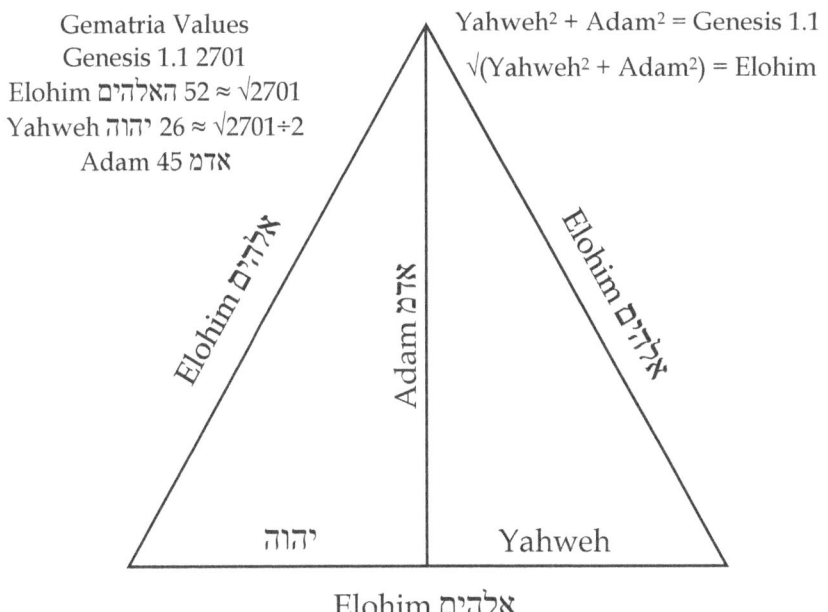

Fig 28.
Triangular relationship between Elohim, Yahweh, and Genesis 1.1.

THE FIRST VERSE OF GENESIS

Coming back to the number 2485, the gematria of the five books of the Torah, it is the 70th triangle number. Its perimeter is 207 dots, the gematria value of *Ohr* ("light," אור). The standard gematria value of *Gevurah* ("Might," "Restraint," גבורה) is 216, which is the difference between 2701 and 2485, for *Gevurah* (גבורה) constricts and encloses the infinite divine light in finite "vessels" and holds the inner part to make it possible for creation to exist.

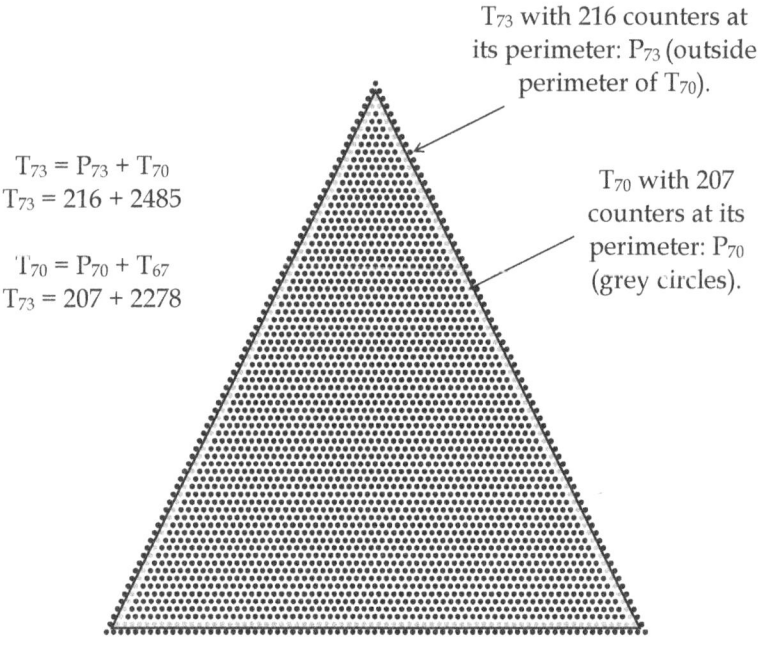

T_{73} with 216 counters at its perimeter: P_{73} (outside perimeter of T_{70}).

$T_{73} = P_{73} + T_{70}$
$T_{73} = 216 + 2485$

$T_{70} = P_{70} + T_{67}$
$T_{73} = 207 + 2278$

T_{70} with 207 counters at its perimeter: P_{70} (grey circles).

Fig 29. Triangular Numbers T_{73} and T_{70}.

"A spark of impenetrable darkness flashed within the concealed of the concealed."

Zohar's parable "The Creation of Elohim."

THE SIGN OF THE COVENANT

The previous chapter uncovers the standard gematria value of *She'Amar Dai L'olamo* ("Who said 'enough is enough' for their Universe," שאמר די לעולמו) is 737, which is also the "perimeter gematria" of *Gevurah* ("Might," "Restraint," גבורה).

So, there is a vital link between *Gevurah*'s function and the value of PI (π) in its essence to constrict and enclose the infinite divine light, as the contracted version of *She'Amar Dai L'olamo* (שאמר די לעולמו) is the holy Name *Sha-dai* (ש-די) with a standard gematria of 314. The perimeter gematria, known as *Ofanim* (אופנים) gematria, uses the last letter of each letter expansion, i.e., *Gevurah* "expanded" (גימל בית ואו ריש הא).

גבורה

Gevurah contracted   216

גִימַל בֵּית וָאו רֵישׁ הַא

Gevurah expanded   1024

ל ת ו ש א

1 300 6 400 30
737

Referring to the story of Noah in Genesis 9, *Ot habrit* ("The sign of the covenant," אות הברית) with a standard gematria value of 1024, was a divine manifestation. "The sign of the covenant" was a resplendent rainbow arcing across the sky, displaying all the spectrum colors, and reaching down to touch the earth.

THE SIGN OF THE COVENANT

"Behold, I, even I, am establishing my covenant with you, and with your seed after you, and with every living creature which is with you .... And I have established my covenant with you, and all flesh shall not be cut off again by the waters of the flood; nor shall there ever again be a flood to destroy the earth. And Elohim said, This is <u>the sign of the covenant</u> which I am about to make between me and you, and every living soul which is with you, for everlasting generations; I have set my bow in the cloud, and it shall be a sign of the covenant between me and the earth. And when I gather clouds on the earth, then the bow shall be seen in the clouds .... And Elohim said to Noah, this is the sign of the covenant which I have established between me and all flesh that is on the earth." (Genesis 9)

As Noah and his family came out of the Ark, they saw a magnificent rainbow, displaying the complete spectrum of colors. Elohim told him this brilliant rainbow was "the sign of the covenant." The word "rainbow" is not used in Genesis 9. The Hebrew text says *kashet* ("bow," קשת). It has a gematria value of 800. "The sign of the covenant" has a gematria value of 1024 – a multiple of 8 (8 x 128 = 1024). There were eight souls saved (Noah's family) from the waters. And Noah stayed 370 days in the Ark, which is 8880 hours. 888 is the gematria value of *Iesous* ("Jesus," Ιησους) in Greek. 8 is a key number about "the sign of the covenant." A rainbow is composed of water and light and only exists in the eye of the beholder. No two people ever see the same rainbow. Seeing a rainbow is a personal experience, no matter how many people may be looking at it. A rainbow is 360 degrees – but we see only 180 degrees from our stance. If we were to multiply 180 degrees by the Great Cubit, which Elohim gave to Ezekiel for building the Temple (1.76'), the product would be 316.8. Throughout the Greek text of the New Testament, the Name *Kyrios Iēsous Christos* (Lord Jesus Christ) has a Gematria value of 3168.

THE SIGN OF THE COVENANT
κυριος Ιησους Χριστος

800   888   1480

Kurios Iesous Christos

3168

To see this relationship more clearly, let's draw a simple diagram — a circle and square whose circumference and perimeter are the same length, 1024 — representing the binding of a covenant between God and Goddess, man and woman. "The sign of the covenant" has a gematria value of 1024.

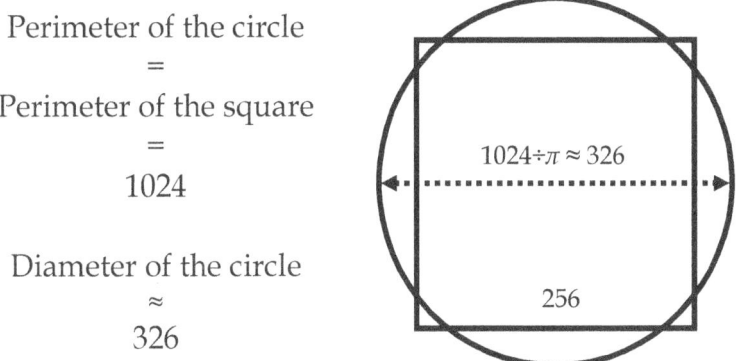

Perimeter of the circle
=
Perimeter of the square
=
1024

Diameter of the circle
≈
326

$1024 \div \pi \approx 326$

256

Fig 30. Sign of the Covenant.

1024 = *Ot habrit* ("The sign of the covenant," אות הברית)
256 = *Nor* ("To give light, to shine, to burn," נור)
  = *Ee leha'ir* ("To illuminate" or "Yod gives light," י להאיר)
Yod (י) is the starting point of the presence of God and Goddess in all things — the "spark" of the Spirit in everything. *Leha'ir* (להאיר) is the 208th word in the Torah when They set the great lights in the firmament of Heaven to give light upon the earth (Gen 1:16-17), and 208 is the sum of *Ohr* ("light," אור) of numerical value 207 and 1 for *Aleph* (א). *YHShinVH* (יהשוה) is the Hebrew Christ name of gematria value of 326.

THE SIGN OF THE COVENANT

1024 is the standard gematria of *Gevurah* expanded (גימל בית ואו ריש הא) which constricts and encloses the infinite light in finite vessels. It would correspond to "the sign of the Covenant," as the rainbow (circle) displays the complete spectrum of light colors. Elohim's design extends the original singularity point, *Nekudah* ("Point," נקודה) into a perfect circle. The covenant was spoken from "Their Opening Mouth," "In the beginning," *Bereisheit* (בראשית). The rainbow symbolizes Elohim's promise, which goes back to Noah and follows up to Abraham in the lineage. "The sign of the covenant" was meant to be "for all future generations" (Genesis 9.12). The Greek word *Iris* (ἰρις) used in the New Testament for "rainbow" has a value of 320. Drop the zeros and multiply (8 x 32); the product is 256. An iris displays 256 unique characteristics, while a fingerprint shows 40. Iris scans are used more for security clearance because they have 256 unique characteristics, while fingerprints have only 40. The top half of the rainbow that we see bears the number 3168 – Lord Jesus Christ. That is a man's-eye-view of it. But an Elohim's-eye-view (viewed from the heavens) is a complete 360-degree circle. Using the same calculations, multiply the 360 degrees by the Great Cubit – 360 x 1.76 = 633.6. Noah's Ark has a full length of 6336 inches when using the Great Cubit for its construction measure. The Ark with this number represents salvation, the promised and sealed covenant through the Lord Jesus Christ. The *Parashat* ("Section," פרשה) *Lech-Lecha* ("Go forth," לך־לך), the third weekly Torah portion in the annual Jewish cycle of Torah reading, comprises 6336 Hebrew letters. In the *Parashat*, Elohim first encounters Abraham (known as Abram), guides him on his journey to Canaan, and witnesses the birth of his son Ishmael. Elohim establishes a covenant with Abraham and his descendants and commands him to circumcise the males of his household. Taking 6336 as the perimeter of a circle, one can calculate its diameter to be approximately 2017, determine the composite order as 2368, and find the standard gematria value of *Iesous Christos* (Jesus Christ) in Greek.

THE SIGN OF THE COVENANT

The promise that Elohim gave to Noah in Genesis 9.11 ("I will establish my covenant," והקמתי את בריתי) has a standard gematria value of 1584, an ordinal gematria value of 162, and a reduced gematria value of 36. A square with sides of 1584 will have a perimeter of 6336. It is an Elohim's-eye view of salvation through the Lord Jesus Christ.

בריתי   את   והקמתי

10 400 10 200 2   400 1   10 400 40 100 5 6

Standard gematria   **1584**

10 22 10 20 2   22 1   10 22 13 19 5 6

Ordinal gematria   **162**

1 4 1 2 2   4 1   1 4 4 1 5 6

Reduced gematria   **36**

Let's recall that 162 refers to the golden ratio (1:1.62). *B'tzelem* ("In the Image," בצלם) in Genesis 1.27, has a gematria value of 162 in the standard gematria system, the golden ratio in nature on a scale of 100. 162 is the sum of the gematria values of the Hebrew words *Adam* (אדמ), *Eve* (חוה), *Yahweh* (יהוה) and the timeless nature of Elohim's existence ("He/She was, He/She is, He/She will be," יהיה היה הוה) which is purely and perfectly divine. The reduced gematria of the timeless nature of Elohim's existence is 45, Elohim's contraction Itself, which is the standard gematria value of *Adam* (אדמ). It could refer to *Tzimtzum* ("Contraction," צמצום), the process at the beginning of creation. The golden spiral is a remarkable blueprint referring to Elohim's Promise from the origins of creation.

THE SIGN OF THE COVENANT

The golden ratio in nature is a reminder of Elohim's Promise and the expression of a profound truth already spoken: "I will establish my covenant" (והקמתי את בריתי). Not only is the rainbow "the sign of the covenant," but it remains perpetually present as a great reminder of the sacred promise between Elohim and Noah. Similarly, the golden spiral observed in nature from microcosm (atoms, cells) to macrocosm (cosmos) begins its pattern from any singularity point in the fabric of the space-time continuum.

The rainbow that Noah saw was a beautiful sight to behold. It displayed all the colors of visible light (white light). It was a complete circle. However, Noah only saw the top half of it. The Great Architect arranged the colors in the order of the spectrum – red at the top, followed by orange, yellow, green, blue, and violet. Indigo is the next level of color, as it combines blue and violet.

The seventh color (Indigo) completes a group of seven visible colors of the rainbow, which is the first display of the sign of the covenant. However, it would belong to the next level of colors. The next level would then consist of 12 colors.

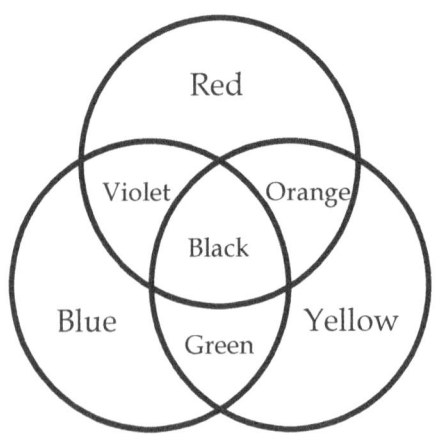

Light begins with three colors — red, yellow, and blue — but they appear as six colors when they overlap.

**Fig 31.
Light and Colours.**

THE SIGN OF THE COVENANT

The colors red, green, and blue each use 8 bits, allowing for integer values ranging from 0 to 255, which results in 256×256×256 = 16777216 possible colors. The number 16777216 would correspond to the volume of a cube of side length 256, the standard gematria value of *Nor* ("To give light, to shine, to burn," נור).

Let's point out that the last three digits of the number 16777216 are 216, the standard gematria value of *Gevurah* ("Might," "Restraint," גבורה), whose function is to constrict and enclose the infinite divine light in finite "vessels." It is fitting that 16777216 is the number of possible light colors from the separation of white light.

The number 777 is the standard gematria value of *Elohim hasamayim hares* ("Elohim the heavens the earth," אלהים השמים הארץ) from the first verse of Genesis. These three Hebrew words are the first verse's 3rd, 5th, and 7th words. The concatenation of 3, 5, and 7 is 357, the standard gematria value of *Tzimtzum haelohim* (צמצום האלהים).

The number 16 is indicated in Hebrew by two letters, *Yod* (י) of gematria value 10 and *Vav* (ו) of gematria 6. *Yod* (י) is a dot, looking like a flame that soars ever higher, representing Elohim's essential power: the One Who is indivisible. *Vav* (ו) signifies "Torah," which descends from heaven to earth through its inherent hook design. These two letters symbolize two hearts joining together as one in love. The interpretation of the sixteenth Hebrew letter *Ayin* (ע) as two eyes united at the optical chiasma reveals its meaning: it serves as the nerve center that receives and interprets visual impulses at the back of the head. Here, it is possible to visualize the full spectrum of all the different colors, 16777216, in the RGB color system. The number 16777216 encodes the information of the light through the triplet (16, 216, 777).

THE SIGN OF THE COVENANT

So, the concatenation of 16, 777, and 216 can be interpreted as the cube that constricts the infinite light (white light) and breaks it into "vessels" to become different colors with Elohim's essential power who descended the Torah (Their Word) from heaven to earth. When light passes through the prism, it separates into its component colors: red, orange, yellow, green, blue, and violet. This process is the full expression of 16777216, a sign of the covenant, shown as the rainbow.

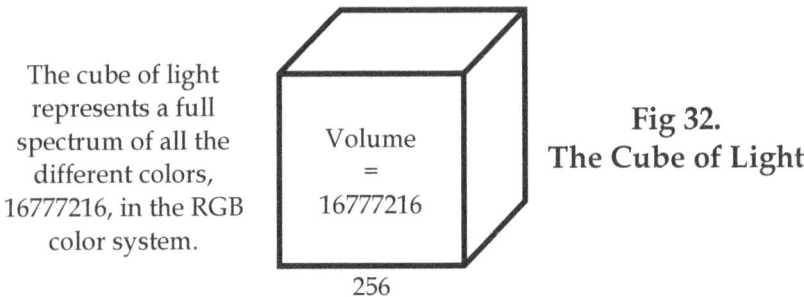

The cube of light represents a full spectrum of all the different colors, 16777216, in the RGB color system.

**Fig 32.
The Cube of Light**

The length of the light wave determines each color of white light. The units commonly used for this measurement are nanometers, denoted by the symbol nm, which equals one thousand millionth of a meter. The table below converts these measures into the British inch and shows the equivalent RGB value.

Colours	nm	Inch	RGB
Red	721.301	0.00000284	(216,0,0)
Orange	629.869	0.00000248	(255,79,0)
Yellow	579.073	0.00000228	(255,255,0)
Green	528.277	0.00000208	(87,255,0)
Blue	477.481	0.00000188	(0,202,255)
Violet	416.326	0.00000164	(114,0,243)
Aggregate (White)		0.00001320	

THE SIGN OF THE COVENANT

When we combine the colors of the spectrum, they produce white light. When you add all the lengths of the light waves (in inches), you get a total of 0.00001320. Interestingly, the Hebrew word *l'vaniym* ("white," לבנים) has a standard gematria value of 132, which serves as evidence of a Great Intelligent Architect. White, bearing the number 132, identifies *YHVH Elohekhem* ("Lord, Elohim of you," יהוה אלהיכם (Joshua 4:5)). The number 132 is also the value of *Kabal* (קבל) which means "to receive" and is the root of the word *Kabbalah* ("Receiving," קבלה).

These three primary colors bear the numbers:
- Red, 284; the standard gematria value of *Theos* ("God," θεος).
- Yellow, 228; the standard gematria value of *Ohr Yah* ("Light of Yah," אוריהו). The Hebrew word *Yah* (יהו) is the first three letters of *Yahweh* (יהוה).
- Blue 188; the standard gematria value of *B'tzelem Yahweh* ("In the Image of Yahweh," בצים יהוה).

The aggregate of these three primary colors is 700, which is also the sum of the gematria values of *Bereisheit* ("In the beginning," בראשית), *Elohim* (אלהים), *Hashmim* ("The heavens," השמים) and *Hartz* ("The earth," הארץ) using the biblical gematria cipher from Genesis 1.1. These Hebrew words are the first, third, fifth, and seventh positions in the first verse (odd numbers).

700 is also the sum of the gematria values of *Haalma* ("The virgin," העלמה), *Hara* ("Child," הרה), Ben ("Son," בן) and *Immanuel* (עמנואל) from Isaiah 7:14, using the Reversal Cipher. A golden rectangle with a long side of 132 will contain a golden spiral measuring 316.8 in length. It's important to note that the number 3168 corresponds to the Greek gematria of *Kýrios Iēsoûs Christós* ("Lord Jesus Christ," Κύριος Ἰησοῦς Χριστός). Additionally, *B'tzelem* ("In the Image," בצלם) has a gematria value of 162 in the standard gematria system, representing the golden ratio in nature on a scale of 100.

THE PRIMARY BEING

The Hebrew plural noun *Dvarim* ("Words" or "spoken," דברים) has a gematria value of 256, and we can connect it intricately to the Greek words *Christos* ("Christ," Χριστος) and *Iesous* ("Jesus," Ιησους), which appear together in 256 Bible verses. Similarly, the Hebrew word *Nor* ("to give light, to shine, to burn" נור), also with a number value of 256, adds another layer of interconnectedness. In Figure 30, the square and the circle symbolize the reconciliation of man (square) to Elohim (circle) through a covenant, further deepening the web of connections.

If we look closely at the structure of *YHWVH* (יהשוה), the Christ name in Hebrew, it is *Yahweh* (יהוה) with the letter *Shin* (ש) placed in the middle. The Hebrew letter *Shin* (ש) is the letter which "gives light" and "shines" like *Eish* ("Fire," אש) and it came after the first letter *Aleph* (א) in the emergence of the building blocks of creation. Let's recapitulate in the image of a man's or woman's body, the consonants of *Yahweh* (יהוה) position themselves vertically, respectively aligning with the head, shoulders, spine, and legs. The position of *Shin* (ש) in the middle corresponds to the spiritual fire at the heart, the innermost part of the soul, and Elohim's divine breath. It is the center of gravity, Elohim's contraction in a man or woman. Here, the crucial and missing 5th element, "ether," is added to the previous formulation, covering the earth, water, air, and fire-manifested elements. The Christ name *YHWVH* (יהשוה) completes the "ground luminosity" element in the "Holy Family," *Yod* (Father י), *Heh* (Mother ה), *Vav* (Son ו), and *Heh* (Daughter ה).

י ה ש ו ה
10 5 300 6 5
326
"Ground luminosity"
The Holy Spirit
The Breath of the Elohim

THE PRIMARY BEING

In Hebrew, the "Holy Spirit" is *Elohim Ruach* ("Elohim's breath," אלהים רוח).

$$\underset{8\ 6\ 200}{רוח} \quad \underset{40\ 10\ 5\ 30\ 1}{אלהים}$$
$$300$$

=

ש 300 Shin / Spiritual Fire

Note that the reverse standard, ordinal, and reduced gematria of *Elohim Ruach* ("Elohim's breath," אלהים רוח) is the numerical blueprint of *Metzuy Roshon* ("Primary Being," מצוי ראשון) respectively 703, 109 and 37. The reverse standard gematria system reverses the gematria system so that the first letter equals the last letter instead (Fig 126).

$$\underset{60\ 80\ 3}{רוח} \quad \underset{10\ 40\ 90\ 20\ 400}{אלהים}$$
$$703$$
Reverse standard

$$\underset{15\ 17\ 3}{רוח} \quad \underset{10\ 13\ 18\ 11\ 22}{אלהים}$$
$$109$$
Reverse ordinal

$$\underset{6\ 8\ 3}{רוח} \quad \underset{1\ 4\ 9\ 2\ 4}{אלהים}$$
$$37$$
Reverse reduced

THE PRIMARY BEING

Let us remind ourselves that everything comes into existence through the expression of the Truth of a "Primary Being," *Bekar lekal nivra* ("The firstborn of every creature," בכר לכל נברא), *Mashiyach* ("Messiah," משיח). The numerical correlation between *Elohim Ruach* ("Elohim's breath," אלהים רוח) *Metzuy Roshon* ("Primary Being," מצוי ראשון) implies that *Mashiyach* ("Messiah," משיח) mirrors the Holy Spirit, "Elohim's breath." *Mashiyach* is *Theos* ("God," θεος (Red 284)), *B'tzelem Yahweh* ("in the Image of Yahweh," בצים יהוה (Blue 188)), and *Ohr Yah* ("Illuminate" or "Light of Yah," אוריהו (Yellow 228)). These three phrases are the simultaneous expression of the first three primary colors defining the famous Trinity, respectively: Father (Red), Son (Blue), and Holy Spirit (Yellow). Interestingly, the ordinal gematria of *Mashiyach* ("Messiah," משיח) is 52, which is also the gematria of *Elohim* (אלהים) in the *Mispar Siduri* method ("ordinal value," Fig 126). 52 is also a numerical blueprint of the first verse of Genesis as the square root of 2701 (stand. gematria of Gen 1.1) is about 52. The number 700, the aggregate of the three primary colors, Red 284 + Blue 188 + Yellow 228, is not far from the number 737. The only number linking these two is 37, the ordinal gematria value of *Chokmah* ("Wisdom," חכמה), the reduced gematria of *Metzuy Roshon* ("Primary Being," מצוי ראשון). 37 is also the standard gematria value of *Haleb* ("The Heart," הלב). The latter follows the same geometric pattern as "Wisdom," based on the Hexagon/Star pair. 19 (Ord. value)/37 (Stand. value) for "The Heart" and 37 (Ord. value)/73 (Stand. value) for "Wisdom."

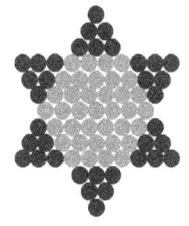

Fig 33.
Hexagon/Star pairs.

37 as Star with
19 as Hexagon

73 as Star with
37 as Hexagon

THE PRIMARY BEING

This insight leads to a more profound truth: that of a "Primary Being," "the firstborn of every creature," *Mashiyach* ("Messiah," משיח) has a Trinity nature, which the three primary colors mirror: *Theos* ("God," θεος (Red 284)), *B'tzelem Yahweh* ("in the Image of Yahweh," בצים יהוה (Blue 188)), and *Ohr Yah* ("Illuminate" or "Light of Yah," אוריהו (Yellow 228)). The expression of the Absolute Truth of Their Being is from "The Heart" with "Wisdom" as 700 + 37 = 737.

Let's recall the sum of the first 165 digits of PI is 737. The number 165 is the standard gematria value of *Nekudah* ("Point," נקודה) from which everything came into existence. So, it is also everything. The number 737 is the standard gematria value of *She'Amar Dai L'olamo* ("Who said 'enough is enough' for their Universe," שאמר די לעולמו). The contracted version is *Sha-dai* (ש-די) of gematria value 314, a direct link to the value of PI (π). The number 737 is also the "perimeter gematria" of *Gevurah* ("Might," "Restraint," גבורה) (Appendix F), the Sephirah of the Kabbalah used to constrict the Yahweh's infinite light in "finite vessels," which allows the white light to split up to produce a spectrum containing all the different colors of visible light. It refers to the cube of light with an edge length of 256 and a volume of 16,777,216, representing the total number of possible colors in the RGB System. Interestingly, there is a relevant Hebrew word whose gematria alone is 737. It is *Shalhevet* ("Flame," שלהבת).

ש ל ה ב ת
400 2 5 30 300
737

THE PRIMARY BEING

Scripture vividly describes the fiery nature of Yahweh's Presence, the spiritual flame, in three terms that add up to 737, the standard gematria value of *Shalhevet* ("Flame," שלהבת) (Ezekiel 1:4). The Hebrew word *Shalhevet* ("Flame," שלהבת) brings a profound sense of enlightenment and connection to every being, highlighting its spiritual significance.

"And I looked and see! a wind - a whirlwind came from the north, a great cloud, and <u>fire</u> ('Eish') intermingled, and a <u>brilliance</u> ('Nogah') encompassed it, and from its midst as an eye of the <u>electrum</u> ('Chashmal') from the midst of the fire."

"וארא והנה רוח סערה באה מן-הצפון, ענן גדול ו<u>אש</u> מתלקחת, ו<u>נגה</u> לו, סביב; ומתוכה--כעין ה<u>חשמל</u>, מתוך האש."

In this verse, there are three aspects of the Spiritual Flame *Shalhevet* (שלהבת): *Eish* ("Fire," אש), *Nogah* ("Brillance," נגה) and *Chashmal* ("Electrum," חשמל). The sum is 737, the same gematria value as *Shalhevet* ("Flame," שלהבת).

	א ש
	1 300
Stand. Gematria	301

	נ ג ה
	50 3 5
Stand. Gematria	58

	ח ש מ ל
	8 300 40 30
Stand. Gematria	378

97

THE PRIMARY BEING

Yahweh's divine love and faith fuel the Spiritual Flame as the One Source of all things and the Absolute Truth of Their singular nature. In Deuteronomy 6:5, the Jewish Prayer *Shema* (שמע) which acts as a "fire holder" to keep the flame burning in the heart of the Jewish People, we realize more deeply how the numerical value 737 relates to the divine love and true faith of the essence of *Yahweh* (יהוה).

"And you shall love Yahweh your Elohim <u>with all your heart, and with all your soul, and with all your strength.</u>"

ואהבת את יהוה אלהיך <u>בכל־לבבך ובכל־נפשך ובכל־מאדך</u>

The Hebrew phrase *Bekol levavka uvkol nafsheka uvkol meodeka* ("with all your heart, and with all your soul, and with all your strength," בכל־לבבך ובכל־נפשך ובכל־מאדך) has a standard gematria value of 737.

$$בכל\ לבבך\ ובכל\ נפשך\ ובכל\ מאדך$$
$$65\ +\ 58\ +\ 450\ +\ 58\ +\ 54\ +\ 52$$
$$737$$

=

Shalhevet "Flame"   שלהבת

=

Three aspects of the "Flame"   אש נגה חשמל

=

בראשית + אלהים + השמים + הארץ + הלב
"In the Beginning + Elohim + The Heavens + The Earth."
+ "The Heart" (with Wisdom)

THE PRIMARY BEING

In response to the Divine Love and Kindness that Yahweh has for all creatures in Their Creation, we invite others to respond with love, with all our heart, with all our soul, and with all our strength, as we proclaim our true faith in the fiery nature of Yahweh's Presence.

Let's look deeper into the root meaning of *Chashmal* ("Electrum," חשמל) one of the three aspects of the Spiritual Flame *Shalhevet* (שלהבת). There is an uncertainty concerning its true meaning. Suggestions vary from "amber" to "electricity" to even a specific angelic entity. However, when we look at the root of the word *Chashmal* ("Electrum," חשמל), it is the combination of two interesting Hebrew words:

- *Chash* ("Silence," חש).
- *Mal* ("Speaking," מל).

Below is an interesting explanation:

"*Chashmal* is a very mystical word that Ezekiel speaks about, which is translated as "everything." It is described as the "speaking silence." One gains a total inner silence. One is able to really listen, and only then one can hear. What people usually ignore in Ezekiel's vision is the very end. The whole vision is a meditation in preparation for hearing the Word." *Aryeh Kaplan, "Conversations in the Spirit," WBAI radio interview, June 6, 1980.*

Chashmal ("Electrum," חשמל) is "the inner silence" that speaks beyond the mind's noise. There is a frontier or veil between the two experiences of the mind:

- The noise fuelled by the physical world and its input of information.
- The inner silence that holds the hearing of the accurate information.

THE PRIMARY BEING

In the image of a candle, we can relate to these subtilities with the three aspects of a flame:
- The visible flame itself *Eish* ("Fire," אש).
- The glow of that flame *Nogah* ("Brillance," נגה).
- The core/innermost, invisible fire of electric nature as it is in everything, *Chashmal* ("Electrum," חשמל).

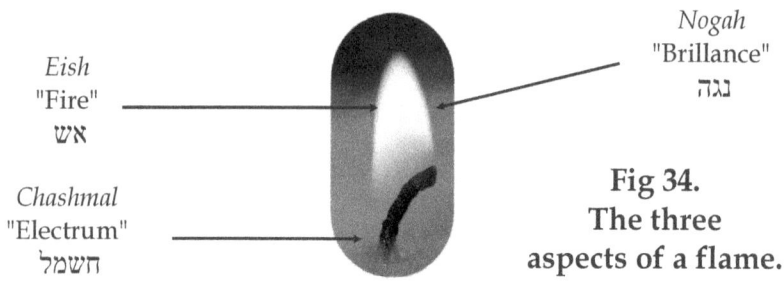

Fig 34. The three aspects of a flame.

The mathematical structure of Genesis 1.1 informs those aspects that present a physical and spiritual nature of our being. The creation took place over 6 days (physical), and then Elohim rested on the 7th day, establishing the *Sabbath* (שבת) (spiritual). The 666 Triangles (and total perimeters) are folded as a "shell" around 703, representing the inner spiritual realm *Sabbath* (שבת), God's and Goddess' Temple, the divine spark that sustains everything. *Sabbath* (שבת) has a standard gematria 702, which, added to *Aleph* (א), 1, or the "center of gravity," "point of convergence," *Yod* (י) 10 by dropping the zero (1), gives a complete structure of 703 (spiritual realm). The "balance point" is the innermost spiritual core, God's and Goddess' breath of divine essence, which vivifies the souls of man and woman, and which grants wisdom and the ability to love "with their heart, and with all their soul, and with all their strength." This center of gravity is also *Tzimtzum haelohim* ("Elohim's Contraction," צמצום האלהים), the door leading to *Chash* ("Silence," חש), the total inner silence. It is by nature a man or woman's soul in the image of Elohim (בצלם האלהים). In this pure and clear space, a man or woman hears their inner voice speaking the Absolute Truth of their being.

THE PRIMARY BEING

The famous palindromic phrase *Echad Usho Echad* ("One and Their Name are One," אחד־ושמו־אחד) from Zecharia 14:9 has a standard gematria value of 378.

אחד־ושמו־אחד
4 8 1   6 40 300 6   4 8 1
378

Like the flame of a candle, the innermost *Chashmal* ("Electrum," חשמל) of the Spiritual Flame *Shalhevet* (שלהבת) represents the total inner silence, which is the "speaking Word of Their Name." The number 378 intimately connects with the number 42. The sum of the first 42 digits in the sequence of prime numbers is 181, and the sum of the first 181 digits in the primes is 378. The last two digits of the first 42 digits are 83, the 23rd prime number, which is the midpoint of 165, the standard gematria of *Nekudah* ("Point," נקודה). Its reduced gematria is 21 with a midpoint of 11. The prime factors of the opening word *Bereisheit* ("In the beginning," בראשית) are the exact midpoints of 165 and 21, which are 83 and 11, and 83 × 11 = 913. Let's bring back to mind *Mashiyach bekar lekal nivra* ("The Messiah is the firstborn of every creature," משיח בכר לכל נברא) also has a gematria value of 913.

According to the Kabbalah, the creation began as *Nekudah Emtzait* ("Middle Point," נקודה אמצעית), which expanded into a perfect circle (with PI (π) 3.14). The "Middle Point" would correspond to the letter *Yod* (י) of *Elohim* (איהלם), a point containing the Tree of Life (the 10 Sephiroth), at the center of the Genesis 1.1 Triangle of 28 letters. Elohim is the third word, and *Yod* (י), the center of gravity, is the 13th letter. Think of the number 13 as the "Seal of Unity" for *Ekhad* ("One," אחד) and *Ahavah* ("Love," אהבה). The second star number forms 13 dots, the six-pointed star symbol.

THE PRIMARY BEING

Interestingly, number 181 is the 42nd Prime Number. For example, 2 3 5 7 11 13 17 19 23 becomes.... 2 3 5 7 1 1 1 3 1 7 1 9 2 3. ∑ (sum of) 42 digits = ∑ (sum of) 2 3 5 7 1 1 1 3 1 7 1 9 2 3 2 9 3 1 3 7 4 1 4 3 4 7 5 3 5 9 6 1 6 7 7 1 7 3 7 9 8 3 = 181. Using the same method, the sum of the first 181 digits in the set of prime numbers is amazingly 378.

It is relevant since there are 181 digits in 111! (factorial), and 111 is the full standard value of *Aleph* (אלף) "One" 1, where it all begins.

111! = 111 × 110 × 109 .... 4 × 3 × 2 × 1 = 1762952551090244663872161047107075788761409536026565516041574063347 3469550872483164365555745984623157731960476628379789131458474971998 71623320096254145331200000000000000000000000000

The Kabbalists understand the first 42 letters of the Torah as the 42 letters of God or Goddess. *Echad Usho Echad* ("One and Their Name are One," אחד־ושמו־אחד) refers to *Yahweh* (יהוה) and *Mashiyach* ("Messiah," משיח) as *Bekar lekal nivra* ("The firstborn of every creature," בכר לכל נברא).

In the beginning God created the heaven and the earth.
Gen 1.1 – 28 letters – Standard Gematria 2701

בראשית, ברא אלהים, את השמים, ואת הארץ

Now the earth was unformed and void...
Gen 1.2 – 14 letters – Standard Gematria 1141

והארץ, היתה תהו וב

Expanding the *Nekudah* ("Point," נקודה) into a perfect circle established the 42-letter name of God or Goddess "In the Beginning" to receive Their creation in a space-time continuum, revealing the number 42 as a foundational number for the origins of creation.

THE PRIMARY BEING

The first 42 letters of Genesis concealed a more profound truth about the full divine expression of *Mashiyach* ("Messiah," משיח) who is called the "Power" and "Wisdom" of Elohim (1 Cor 1:24). The Hebrew word *Kach* ("Power," כח) has a standard gematria value of 28, an ordinal gematria value of 19 and a reduced gematria of 10. The number 28 alludes to the 28 letters of the first verse. The number 19 could allude to the ordinal gematria value of *Haleb* ("The Heart," הלב) or the reduced gematria value of *Igul* ("Circle," עגול). The number 10 could allude to the *Yod* (י) of *Elohim* (איהלם), the center of gravity of the first 28 letters. *Yod* (י) is the center of gravity where the "Power" of Elohim lies. Here we speak of the Power of "Love" and "One". The standard gematria of *Chokmah* ("Wisdom," חכמה) is 73, and the triangular number 73 is 2701, the standard gematria of the first 28 letters.

So, "Power" and "Wisdom" are both concealed in the first verse of Genesis as the absolute truth in the expression of Their Being through *Mashiyach* ("Messiah," משיח), *Bekar lekal nivra* ("The firstborn of every creature," בכר לכל נברא). *Ein Soph Aur* ("The unfathomable light," "Arising Consciousness," אין סוף אור) who is the first emanation of the unknown, called Christos in Greek ("Christ," Χριστος). The Hebrew name *Elohim* (איהלם) has a standard gematria of 86.

The 86th Triangular Number represents the creation process, the sum of all integers from 1 to 86, as follows: $\sum$ (sum of) 1 to 86 = 1 + 2 + ... + 85 + 86 = 3741. Adding Elohim's "Wisdom" and "Power" by which the creation took place: 3741 + 101 = 3842, the total standard gematria of the first 42 Hebrew letters of Genesis.

The 42 letters seem to have played a significant part as the trigger or starting point to form the creation; the earth was originally unformed and void after that. Is 42 the ultimate answer to life, the universe, and everything, as Douglas Adams stated*?

* The Hitchhiker's Guide to the Galaxy

THE PRIMARY BEING

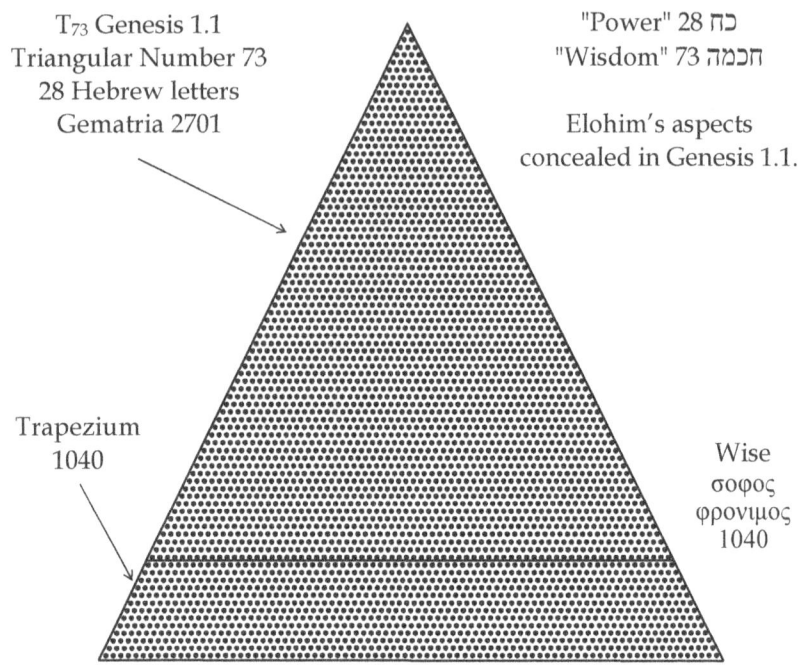

Fig 35. Elohim's Triangle.

Elohim אלהים 86
Triangular Number 86
$T_{86} = (86 \times 87) \div 2 = 3741$
$T_{86} = 2701 + 1040 = 3741$

Genesis 1.1　　בראשית ברא אלהים את השמים ואת הארץ
Genesis 1.2　　והארץ היתה תהו וב

1.1 In Wisdom, Elohim created the heavens and the earth,
1.2 And the earth was without form, and void (…).

The total standard gematria of the first 42 Hebrew letters of Genesis is 3842. The intricate relationship between Elohim and Their attributes involved in the craft of the creation:

$3842 = T_{86}$ (Elohim's Triangle) + Power + Wisdom
$3842 = T_{73}$ (Genesis 1.1) + Wise + Power + Wisdom
$3842 = 2701 + 1040 + 28 + 73$

THE PRIMARY BEING

The sum of the 181 digits in the factorial of 111 is 693, the standard gematria value of *Vayikra, el-misheh* ("And the Lord called Moses," ויקרא, אל-משה) from Leviticus 1.1. The small *Aleph* (א) of the first word, *Vayikra* (ויקרא) corresponds to the contraction of *Aleph* (א) within itself, the *Alufo Shel Olam* ("Master of the Universe," אלופו של עולם) opening a space where finite and independent realms can co-exist, the start of everything. It's about Elohim making room for something other than itself, which is the first step of creation *Tzimtzum* ("Contraction," צמצום). There is a contracting or concealing of Elohim, an inward drawing, creating a nothingness and a separation, so there is room for another process to unfold.

Call to mind, the Hebrew gematria revealed a profound truth: *Mashiach btzelem haelehim* ("The Messiah is the image of Elohim," משיח בצלם האלהים) is the great secret of *Tzimtzum Tzimtzum* ("Contraction," צמצום) here *Aleph* (א) for *Tzimtzum haelohim* ("Elohim's Contraction," צמצום האלהים) in Hebrew standard gematria, is 357, which is the standard gematria of the *Mashiyach* ("Messiah," משיח), 358 less 1, the gematria value of the first letter of the Hebrew Alphabet, *Aleph* (א), *Elohim* (אלהים), the origin of all things. *Mashiach btzelem haelehim* ("The Messiah is the image of Elohim," משיח בצלם האלהים) refers to *Nekudah* ("Point," נקודה) from which everything came into existence, that is all spaces and dimensions. It is the "singularity point," *Tzimtzum haelohim* ("Elohim's Contraction," צמצום האלהים).

Notice that there are 26 zeros at the end of the factorial, 111. The standard gematria value of *Yahweh* (יהוה) is 26. The sum of the digits in the prime numbers through 349, the 70th prime number, is 699. There is a total of 181 digits counted, the 42nd prime number. The sum of the Hebrew standard gematria value of *Vayikra, el-misheh* ("And the Lord called Moses," ויקרא, אל-משה) 639 and the value of the Hebrew letter *Vav* (ו) 6, is 699. *Vav* (ו) corresponds to Elohim's staff, which Moses used to begin the plagues and split the sea. The 70th triangular number is 2485, the standard gematria of the Hebrew names of the five books of the Torah. 2485 = 2701 (Triangular number 73 Genesis 1.1) - 216 (Perimeter of T73), the gematria value of *Gevurah* ("Might," "Restraint," גבורה), a sephirah of the Kabbalah, whose function is to embody the inner core in a finite vessel (physical body). The perimeter of the triangular number 70 is 207, the gematria value of *Ohr* ("light," אור).

The inner structure identifies *Yahweh* (יהוה) 26 and *Elohim* (אלהים) 52, with *Aleph* (א). When we add 699 to the numerical value of *Aleph* (א) 1, it results in 700:

$$700 = א + ו + ויקרא, אל-משה$$

700 communicates a sense of "fullness," "completeness," or "wholeness" with Yahweh's Presence (*Aleph* (א) on its own). The image of the visible light corresponds to the aggregate of the three primary colors, bearing a total sum of 700 (Red (284), Yellow (228), and Blue (188)).

Only one biblical verse has a standard gematria value of 700: "Splendor and majesty are before him; strength and joy are in his place." (Chroniques I 16:27)

הוד והדר לפניו עז וחדוה במקמו.

Seven is the number of Sephiroth corresponding to the seven days of the week. Sephiroth composed *Zeir Anpin* ("Lesser Countenance," זעיר אנפין) and *Malkuth* ("Kingdom," מלכות, the physical world). *Zeir Anpin* ("Lesser Countenance," זעיר אנפין) is an aspect of Elohim comprising the six emotional sephirot attributes: *Chesed* ("Kindness," חסד), *Gevurah* ("Might," גבורה), *Tiphereth* ("Beauty," תפארת), *Netzach* ("Eminence," נצח), *Hod* ("Majesty," הוד), and *Yesod* ("Foundation," יסוד).

THE PRIMARY BEING

Each Sephira is composed of 10 Sephiroth. The number 100 (10 x 10) is the number symbolizing *Shleimut* ("Wholeness," שלמות). The standard gematria value of *Shleimut* (שלמות) is 776, the same as *Nekudah Emtzait* ("Middle Point," נקודה אמצעית) where Elohim's creation began.

ש ל מ ו ת
400 6 40 30 300
776

The 776th prime number is 5897, appearing strictly at location 10 of PI (π): 3.1415926535897. The center of gravity of the first verse of Genesis is the 13th Hebrew letter *Yod* (י) 10, a "Point," which represents Elohim's "Power" and "Wisdom."
Only one biblical verse has a standard gematria value of 776: "Trust in the Lord forever, for the Lord is Elohim, an everlasting Rock." (Isaiah 26:4).

בטחו ביהוה, עדי-עד: כי ביה יהוה, צור עולמים.

In Hebrew, the "Holy Spirit" is *Elohim Ruach* ("Elohim's Breath," אלהים רוח). This phrase has a standard gematria value of 300, corresponding to the numerical value of the Hebrew letter *Shin* (ש) "Spiritual Fire." *Shin* (ש) denotes the trinity fiery nature of Elohim (combined by three Hebrew letters *Vav* (וו) so three sixes), like the light of a candle described by the three levels: *Eish* ("Fire," אש), the glow of that flame, *Nogah* ("Brilliance," נגה) and the core or innermost, invisible fire, *Chashmal* ("Electrum," חשמל) or the three primary colors of the visible light (Red (284), Yellow (228) and Blue (188)).
It is interesting to note that 3 x 100 = 300 = *Shin* (ש). The number 100 is the standard gematria value of the inner vital breath in Hebrew *Ch'i* ("Qi," צי, 氣 in Chinese).

THE PRIMARY BEING

צ׳י
10 90
100

The ordinal gematria value of *Ch'i* ("Qi," צ׳י, 氣 in Chinese) is 28, the standard gematria value of *Kach* ("Power," כח), an aspect of Elohim concealed in the first verse of Genesis (28 letters). It is the same "Power" used to create and establish Their creation. It comes through the center of gravity of the triangular number 7, "a Point," *Yod* (י) of value 10. The number 10 is, interestingly, the reduced gematria value of *Ch'i* (צ׳י) the inner vital breath. *Yod* (י) is a dot, looking like a flame that soars ever higher, representing Elohim's essential power.

There is a deep meaning of the words *Lekh-Lekha* (לך-לך). Genesis 12.1 translates them as "Go, Leave, Travel." What they mean is: "Journey (*Lekh* לך) to yourself (*Lekah* לך). In other words, the invitation urged Abraham to leave behind all external influences that make him a victim of circumstances beyond his control, prompting him to travel inward to the self. The standard gematria value of *Lekh-Lekha* (לך-לך) is 100. We attain true freedom only in the core of our soul, the center of gravity, where we achieve deliverance. The Spiritual Flame *Shalhevet* (שלהבת) sustains this freedom, remaining ever-present in all dimensions and accessible to every soul that immerses itself in total inner silence, for Elohim created man and woman in Their Image.

ל ך - ל ך
20 30 20 30
100

THE PRIMARY BEING

The 19th Hebrew letter *Kuf* (ק) of value 100 enlightens the lowest worlds. "Going inward" surpasses our animalistic nature, "monkey," the full form of *Kuf* (קוף). It activates the 100 Sephiroth within, accessing and seeing the Great Image, our divine nature, Elohim, Yahweh. The Great Image will be the focus of the next chapter.

Three times (3x)

Ch'i ("Qi," צ'י, 氣 in Chinese) = 100

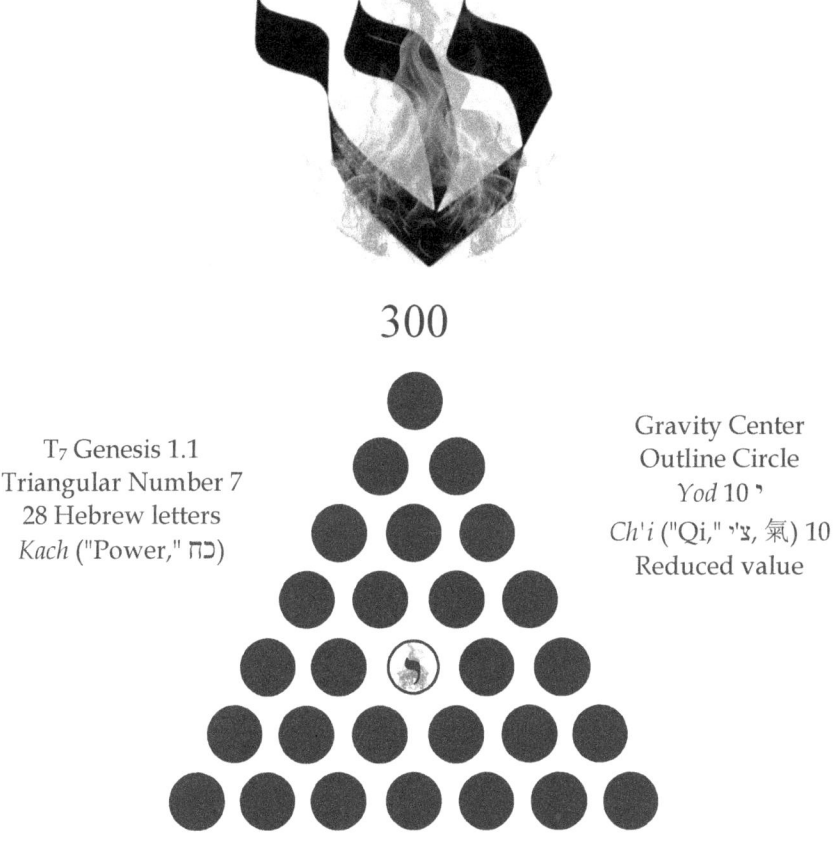

Fig 36.
Threefold of Elohim's *Ch'i* (צ'י).

THE GREAT IMAGE

The Great Image is the unification between the feminine and the masculine principle, encompassing the four aspects within every man and woman: Faher *Yod* (י), Mother *Heh* (ה), Son *Vav* (ו) and Daugher *Heh* (ה), which is Yahweh's signature ("Lord," YHVH, יהוה).

In the Tree of Life, Kabbalah (קבלה) the first letter of the *Tetragrammaton* YHVH, *Yod* (י), is attributed to the sphere of *Chokmah* ("Wisdom," Father, חכמה). The second letter, *Heh* (ה), belongs to *Binah* ("Understanding," Mother, בינה). The third letter, *Vav* (ו), belongs to the realm *Zeir Anpin* ("Lesser Countenance," זעיר אנפין), comprising the six emotional Sephirot attributes: *Chesed* ("Kindness," חסד), *Gevurah* ("Might," גבורה), *Tiphereth* ("Beauty," תפארת), *Netzach* ("Eminence," נצח), *Hod* ("Majesty," הוד), and *Yesod* ("Foundation," יסוד). The last letter, *Heh* (ה), appears in the sphere of *Malkut* ("Kingdom," מלכות) representing Daughter.

In the Torah, the first letter of the word *Bereisheit* ("In the beginning," בראשית) is the Hebrew letter *Beit* (ב), the point of creation in the beginning, which is symbolized by the "Mouth" with a dot in the center, a sound/frequency out of the "Mouth" (ב). The Hebrew letter *Beth* (ב) has a numerical value of 2, the feminine principle.

In the *Kabbalah* (קבלה), there are two feminine aspects: the mother in the sphere of *Binah* ("Understanding," בינה) and the daughter in the sphere of *Malkuth* ("Kingdom," מלכות). These two aspects represent the *Shekinah* ("Divine Presence," שכינה) eternally present in all spheres and often discussed at the feminine side of God (Goddess).

The Kabbalah teaches us that the first step in revealing the Great Image of Elohim, Yahweh, is to unite the feminine and masculine aspects of the lower levels: the daughter, the bride, with the son as the groom. The son represents the six emotional spheres, attributed to the Hebrew letter *Vav* (ו) of numerical value 6.

THE GREAT IMAGE

As the seventh (the bride) is independent of them, the 7th and the group of six represent the bride and groom, respectively. The broom (son) calls to rectify the six spheres of emotions by joining the two feminine aspects: the mother and the daughter. Thus, with understanding, the son becomes the groom in this alchemical process, and the daughter becomes the bridge with the mother's help. The son and daughter are unified, and the son joins the two "females." The groom and bride's marriage equals 42, as the product is six by seven. The marriage is celebrated with a quality of "Emotional Understanding" gained. This level of "Understanding" leads to the next level, the Sephirah *Chokmah* ("Wisdom," Father, חכמה).

The connection between the number 42 and the number 378 is significant, as 378 is the gematria value of *Chashmal* ("Electrum," חשמל). This term represents one of the three aspects of *Shalhevet* (Spiritual "Flame," שלהבת), which embodies the invisible and innermost aspect of total inner silence. Analog to the "speaking Word of Their Name," as *Echad Usho Echad* ("One and Their Name are One," אחד־ושמו־אחד (Zecharia 14:9)).

So, there is a clear relationship between the marriage of the bride (daughter) and groom (son) of the lower spheres with the opening and access to the higher spheres. Those higher levels reveal the 42-letter name of God or Goddess. *Chibur* ("joining," "connection from heaven to earth," חבור), then establishes itself. The standard, ordinal, and reduced gematria values of *Chibur* (חבור) in its absolute state are, respectively, 216, 36, and 18, the same values as the Sephirah of *Gevurah* ("Might," "Restraint," גבורה) referring on some levels to the number 737, standard gematria value of *Shalhevet* (Spiritual "Flame," שלהבת) and the value of PI (π) as an Important Key, a bridge between heaven and earth.

THE GREAT IMAGE

Interestingly, the term *Nukveh* ("Female," נקבה) has a standard gematria value of 157, and that for the six sefirot making up the groom *Zeir Anpin* ("Lesser Countenance," זעיר אנפין) has a standard gematria value of 478. The "joining" and "connection" of the two female aspects, mother and daughter, by the son corresponds to the product between these two: 157 × 2 = 314. The sum of the term *Nukveh* ("Female," נקבה) of value 157 and the groom *Zeir Anpin* (זעיר אנפין) 478, equals 635. The word *Elohim* (אלהים) appears in 635 verses in the Hebrew Bible. The Hebrew word *Musarot* (מוסרות), the plural form of *Moserah* (מוסרה) which comes from the root *Asar* ("to bind" or "to tie," אסר) can mean "correction," or "bonds." The standard gematria of *Musarot* (מוסרות) is 712.

$$\text{מ ו ס ר ו ת}$$
$$400\ 6\ 200\ 60\ 6\ 40$$
$$712$$

Now, the Hebrew word *Ulam* (אולם) could carry the idea of something "bound" or "joined together:" vault, arch, hall, in most architectural terms. The entrance hall of Solomon's Temple is called *Ulam* (אולם) in 1 Kings 6:3. The standard gematria value of *Ulam* (אולם) is 77. Think of the two sevens as the two female aspects bounded. When we add 77 to 635, which is the sum of the term *Nukveh* ("Female," נקבה) of value 157, and the groom *Zeir Anpin* (זעיר אנפין) 478, it results in 712. Diving more profoundly in the Simple English Gematria, the numerical value of "Christ" in English ordinal gematria is 77.

$$\text{C H R I S T}$$
$$3\ 8\ 18\ 9\ 19\ 20$$

THE GREAT IMAGE

The number 712 has two interesting meanings in this context. The groom corrects the emotions of the lower levels, hence "correction," and connects the two females, thereby "bonding" the mother with the daughter. There is a more profound truth about the essence and function of the two feminine aspects within the Tree of Life, and their union leads to the value of PI (π), the Key to bridging heaven and earth.

Remember, the contracted version of *She'Amar Dai L'olamo* ("Who said 'enough is enough' for their Universe," שאמר די לעולמו) is the Holy Name *Sha-dai* (ש-די) with a standard gematria of 314. The expanded version, *She'Amar Dai L'olamo* (שאמר די לעולמו) has a standard Gematria 737. The expanded version of *Gevurah* (גימל בית ואו ריש הא) has a standard gematria value of 1024, referring to the cube of light 16,777,216, the number of possible colors in the RGB system (a square of perimeter 1024 leads to a cube of edge length 256).

Squaring the circle with such a square, the radius of the circle is 326, the standard gematria value of *YHSVH* (יהשוה) the Hebrew Christ-name. It reveals a more profound truth about our divine nature with a fifth aspect through the letter *Shin* (ש) well placed in the middle between the Father and Mother aspects of the higher levels and the Son and Daughter aspects of the lower levels of the Tree of Life. *Elohim Ruach* ("Elohim's breath," רוק אלהים) has a standard gematria of 300, the same as the Hebrew letter *Shin* (ש). It is naturally the bridge between heaven and earth, the Holy Spirit breathed and infused in the innermost of every man or woman's soul. Man or woman was created "in the Image of Elohim," encompassing the four aspects as "Lord" (YHVH) with the fifth aspect, "Spirit" *YHSVH* (יהשוה) the Great Image. The Hebrew term *Androginiyut* ("Androgyny," אנדרוגניות) has a standard gematria value of 730 = 73 x 10. The number 730 is the term *Chokmah* ("Wisdom," 73, חכמה) multiplied by the 10 Sephiroth or *Yod* (י), a "Point," the number of perfection.

THE GREAT IMAGE

The number 10 is also the reduced gematria value of *Ch'i* ("Qi," צ'י, 氣 in Chinese), the inner vital breath, while 100 is the standard gematria value. *Androginiyut* ("Androgyny," אנדרוגניות) also has an ordinal gematria value of 100, the number symbolizing *Shleimut* ("Wholeness," שלמות) and *Ch'i* ("Qi," צ'י, 氣 in Chinese). The fifth aspect is the Hebrew letter *Shin* (ש), the spiritual fire embodying the trinity aspect with the three *Vavs* (ווו) in its construction. It is Elohim's breath, as 300 is three times 100. It's also Elohim's power as the ordinal gematria value of *Ch'i* ("Qi," צ'י, 氣 in Chinese) is 28, the standard gematria value of *Kach* ("Power," כח). "Power" and "Wisdom" are concealed in the first 28 Hebrew letters, an aspect of Elohim hidden in the first verse of Genesis (28 letters) and the first 42 letters of Genesis conceal a more profound truth about the full divine expression of *Mashiyach* ("Messiah," משיח), who is called "Elohim's Power and Wisdom" (1 Cor 1:24), our "christic" nature revealed on the Path to the One. Jesus' message was to reveal and embody the full expression of "Christ" buried in every person's heart. Everyone has the potential to connect deeply with this innate aspect.

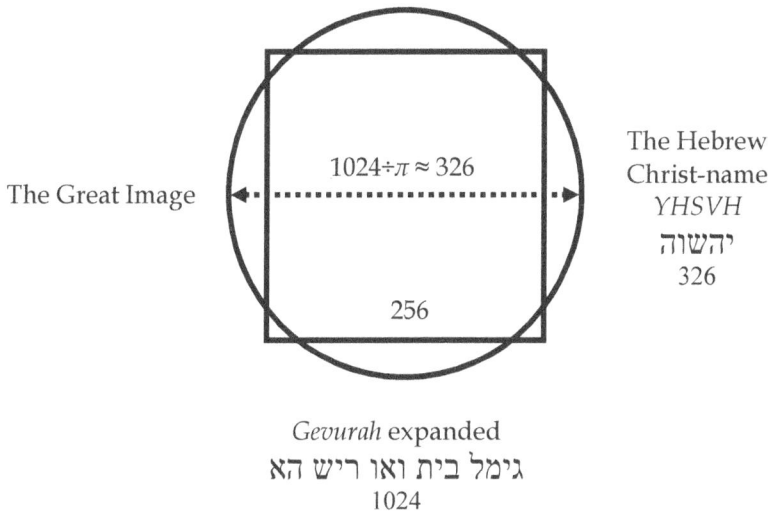

Fig 37. The Great Image

THE RINGS OF YOD

The first verse of Genesis uniquely arranges itself in a triangular number, known as "The Triangle of *Yod*." This arrangement signifies that the Hebrew letter *Yod* (י) of *Elohim* (אִיהֹלִם) the 13th letter, occupies the center of gravity of the "Triangle." The "Triangle of *Yod*" organizes the total of 28 letters in the first verse into three concentric rings of 9 each, with *Yod* (י) "a Point," symbolizing the origin of everything through the "Power" and "Wisdom" of Elohim's Spirit. We can refer to this innovative arrangement as "The Rings of *Yod*" or "The Spiral of *Yod*."

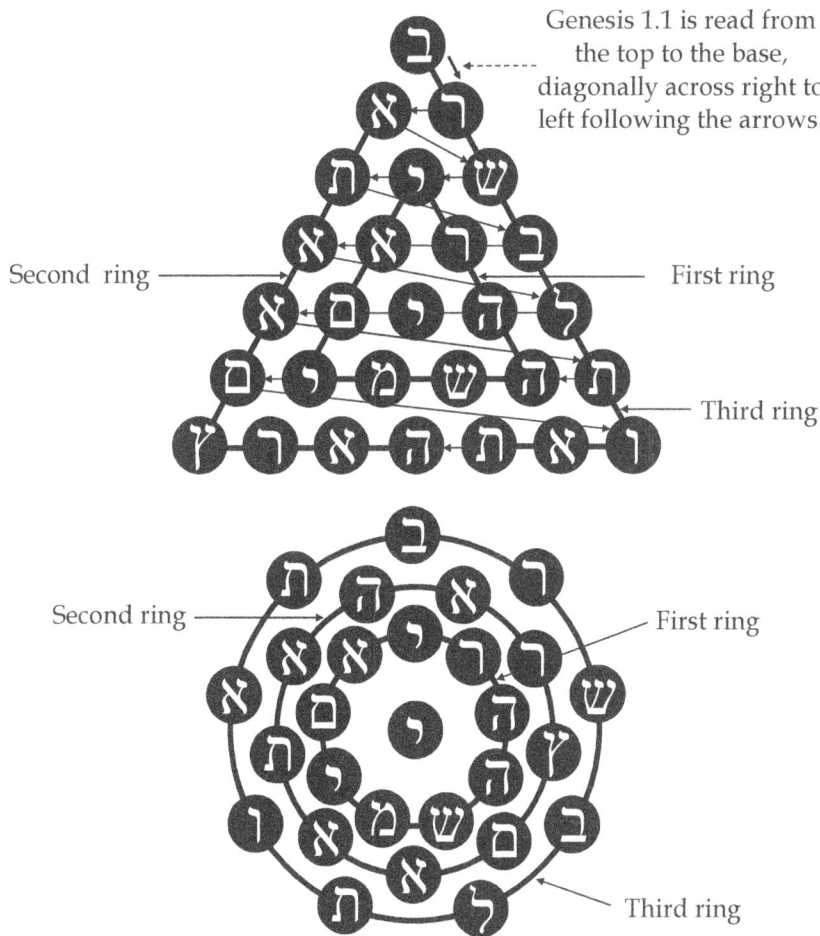

Fig 38. The Triangle and Rings of *Yod* (י).

THE RINGS OF YOD

Torah has a lot more to reveal between the lines. There are different levels of interpretation that the reader can explore and discover—Shiv'im *Panim laTorah* ("The Torah has 70 faces," שבעים פנים לתורה). There is much more than just reading the words and letters linearly. For example, this new arrangement, "The Rings of *Yod*," is one way to read and meditate on the first verse of Genesis with multiple meanings between the lines. Geometry and gematria are the tools required to discern and perceive the depth of the various levels. It is shocking to perceive the multiple facets of the Torah and acknowledge here the Intelligence and Elegance of a great Designer and Artist.

"The Rings of *Yod*" was built from "The Triangle of *Yod*." The first circular ring features the inner triangle made up of 9 letters: ירההשמימא. It starts with *Yod* (י) at the top and moves clockwise through the following 8 Hebrew letters: רההשמימא. The Great Architect constructed the second and third circular rings with the outer triangular ring consisting of 18 Hebrew letters, ברשבלתואתהארץמאאתא, by starting from the top *Beit* (ב) and then going clockwise for the following 17 Hebrew letters: שבלתואתהארץמאאתא. The first nine letters build the outside ring, and the subsequent nine construct the middle ring. Thus, "The Rings of *Yod*" has three rings with different standard gematria values in ascending order, *Yod* (י) being the center of gravity:

- The center *Yod* (י) has a numerical value of 10.
- The first ring has a standard gematria value of 611.
- The second ring has a standard gematria value of 739.
- The third ring has a standard gematria value of 1341.

The first verse of Genesis describes a being composed of three circular rings with a center of gravity. It refers to the threefold nature of Their Expression, with a core, an inner layer (the first circular ring), and an external layer (the last two circular rings).

THE RINGS OF YOD

The total sum is 2701 = 37 (The Heart) x 73 (Wisdom). Interesting Hebrew words attribute the different layers to their numbers, tying them all together well with the essence of Elohim. We can mention the number 10 at the core; it is the numerical value of the word *Ohad* ("United," אהד) or *Azab* ("to shine, blooming, blossoming," אזב). The number 10 is considered perfection, often referring to completion, law, and responsibility.

Consider, for instance, the following:

- On the first day of creation, Elohim created 10 things; on the sixth and final day, They created another 10 things.
- There were 10 generations from Adam to Noah and another 10 generations from Noah to Abraham.
- 10 plagues struck Egypt before God freed the Hebrews from slavery.
- Elohim gave 10 commandments on Mount Sinai (Exodus 20:1-17).
- 10 lepers called out to Yeshua (Jesus) for healing, and He sent them to the priests so they could be declared clean (Luke 17:12-14).
- In the Gospel of John, Yeshua (Jesus) highlighted the ten patterns by making 10 "I Am" declarations.

1. I am the Bread of Life (6:35, 48);
2. I am the Bread that came down from heaven (6:41);
3. I am the Living Bread (6:51);
4. I am the Light of the world (8:12);
5. I am One that bears witness of Myself (8:18);
6. Before Abraham was, I am (8:58);
7. I am the Door of the sheep (10:7, 9);
8. I am the Good Shepherd (10:14);
9. I am the Way, the Truth, and the Life (14:6); and
10. I am the True Vine (15:1, 5).

THE RINGS OF YOD

The number 611 is the standard gematria value of the word *Torah* (תורה). Same as the Hebrew word *Ashish* ("Foundation," אשיש). The Greek Word *Stoma* ("Mouth" or "Opening," στόμα) has a numerical value of 611. Yahweh spoke the first ring, manifesting all matter (atoms). Thus, the most significant foundation holding everything together is "Their Word," "for no word of God, shall be void of Power" (Luke 1:37).

The number 739 is the standard gematria value of *Besher dvar veyhei* ("And the Word became flesh," בשר דבר ויהי (John 1:14)) who is *Christos* ("Christ," Χριστός), *Bekar lekal nivra* ("The firstborn of every creature," בכר לכל נברא), *Mashiyach* ("Messiah," משיח).

ויהי   דבר   בשר
10 5 10 6   200 2 4   200 300 2
739

Its ordinal value is 100, the number symbolizing *Shleimut* ("Wholeness," שלמות). Its reduced value is 28, the number of Hebrew letters in the first verse of Genesis. The "Word" is the Living Torah clothed in flesh; thus, the second ring is part of the physical manifestation of the inner circular ring *Torah* (תורה). The concept of "clothing" is also the concept of *Tzimtzum haelohim* ("Elohim's Contraction," צמצום האלהים), which is the standard gematria of *Mashiyach* ("Messiah," משיח), 358 less 1, the first letter of the Hebrew Alphabet, *Aleph* (א) who is *Yahweh* ("Lord," יהוה) and *Elohim* ("The Mighty Ones," אלהים) when we look at the inner structure of *Aleph* (א).

Livsh Yahweh ("Yahweh clothed," לבש יהוה) in standard gematria is exactly 358, the Gematria of *Mashiyach* ("Messiah," משיח). Elohim reveals themselves to their creation in the lower worlds through Their "clothes."

THE RINGS OF YOD

The number 1341 is the standard gematria of the Hebrew phrase: "Elohim the Father created Adam, the only living creature with a body and a spirit."

אלהים אב ברא אדם יחיד חי נפש עם עצם רוח

The Greek word *Aioniou* ("Eternal," αιωνιου) has a standard gematria value of 1341. It shares the same numerical value as the Greek word *Homoioma* (ομοιωματι, which means "likeness," "made like to," or "that which has been made after the likeness of something").

So, the numerical and geometrical structure of Genesis 1.1 expressed through "The Rings of *Yod*" with Gematria reveals deeper truths regarding the Foundation of Elohim's creation in the beginning. We can express this concisely as a simple yet beautiful mathematical equation incorporating numbers and their gematria meanings:

10
Ohad ("United," אהד)
Oneness - Perfection - Center of gravity

611
Torah (תורה), "The Word"
First Ring/Inner Layer

739
("And the Word became flesh," בשר דבר ויהי (John 1:14))
Second Ring/External Layer (The Word is clothed)

1341
"Elohim the Father created Adam the only living creature with a body and a spirit."
אלהים אב ברא אדם יחיד חי נפש עם עצם רוח
("Eternal," αιωνιου), ("that which is made like," ομοιωματι)
Third Ring/External Layer (Adam is clothed)

$\sum$ (sum of) 10, 611, 739, 1341 =

2701 = 37 × 73

Haleb ("The Heart," הלב) × *Chokmah* ("Wisdom," חכמה)
"The Heart of Wisdom," Genesis 1.1.

THE RINGS OF YOD

The external layer is the sum of the second and third circular rings: 739 + 1341 = 2080. It is also considered the external perimeter of "The Triangle of *Yod*." The number 2080 is the product between 80 and 26. The Hebrew letter *Peh* (פ) has a numerical value of 80 and represents the body part connected to speech since *Peh* (פה) means "Mouth." The signature of 80 is in number 2080 with its last two digits. Another remarkable fact is that the number 28, a second signature of 2080 by dropping the zeros, is the standard gematria value of *Kach* ("Power," כח). The number 28 alludes to the 28 letters of the first verse, referring to the entire design within the verse, here "The Rings of *Yod*." Elohim gave *Adam* the power of speech "In Their Image."

Appropriately using the mouth, from the heart with wisdom, can benefit any man or woman. Otherwise, it can be detrimental, even causing illness or death. In the words of the Hebrew idiom (based on Proverbs 18:21), "Life and death are in the hands of speech."

The standard gematria of *Moach* ("Mind," מח) is 48, and *Lev* ("Heart," לב) is 32. When we add these two, we get 80, which is the same numerical value as *Yesod* ("Foundation," יסוד) the euphemism for the flesh. Clothed with a heart and mind, Adam uses the power of speech through his mouth.

If we look at the full form of *Peh* (פה) of numerical value 85, the part of the body from which Elohim's power comes, the "mouth." The last two digits of 2080 have become 85, and the number is now 2085. Interestingly, 2085 corresponds to the external layer added to one of the Hebrew letters *Heh* (ה) of the first ring/inner circular layer of "The Rings of *Yod*," as 2080 + 5 = 2085, with 5 the numerical value of *Heh* (ה). The function of the feminine aspect, linking the internal to the external layers, lies in the gematria value of 2085.

The Hebrew letter *Heh* (ה) is like linking the external layer of *Adam* made of flesh (mind, heart, and mouth) to the inner layer, "The Word," with no skin (flesh or clothing). The letter *Heh* (ה) represents the feminine aspects of *Yahweh* (יהוה), the Daughter and Mother, corresponding respectively to the Sephiroth *Malkuth* ("Kingdom," מלכו, the physical world) and *Binah* ("Understanding," בינה).

The function of the feminine aspect, linking the internal to the external layers, lies in the gematria value of 2085. The number 2085 corresponds to the Hebrew phrase as follows:

"After Elohim created the flesh of Adam. He breathed into his nostrils the breath of life, creating Adam in Their image."

אחר אלהים ברא בשר אדם נפח אף נשמה חי ברא אדם צלם

The ordinal value of this phrase is 132, which is also the standard gematria value of the Hebrew word *l'vaniym* ("white," לבנים). This word is also a sort of white garment (linen) referring to "clothing," here "clothed with light."

The following Greek words have a standard gematria value of 2085: *omoiosomen* ("like/make like/in the likeness of/to be made like," ομοιωσωμεν) and *agaponton* ("love/beloved/to be well pleased," αγαπωντων).

Elohim created Adam in the image of a spirit and imparted that spirit into Adam's flesh when He "breathed into his nostrils the breath of life." The inner vital breath, referred to in Hebrew as *Ch'i* ("Qi," צי, 氣 in Chinese), has a standard gematria of 100, the same as the ordinal value of "Androgyny."

THE RINGS OF YOD

The first Hebrew letter, *Heh* (ה), occurs in Genesis 1.1 in the third word *Elohim* (אלהים). Elohim has 5 Hebrew letters; the middle is *Heh* (ה) with a numerical value of 5. In the name *Yahweh* (יהוה) there are two *Heh* (ה). The Hebrew letter *Heh* ((ה) means "to behold." *Heh* (ה) also means "breath, sigh, look, reveal," and "revelation" from the idea of showing an incredible sight by pointing it out. Therefore, the Hebrew letter *Heh* (ה) is a picture of *Ruach HaKodesh* ("Holy Spirit," רוח הקודש). The breath of the mouth represents the spirit. Elohim breathed into Adam, transforming and filling him with the Holy Spirit. This act embodies the feminine aspects of Elohim, the fabulous *Shekinah* ("Divine Presence," שכינה), the Divine Feminine aspect of God (Goddess), as she gives birth to live.

It is very appropriate to add the value of 5 to the number 2080, which represents the external layer of Adam. After being "filled with the Holy Spirit," he clothed himself with "a heart and mind." The Hebrew letter *Heh* (ה) of the inner ring/inner layer represents the "breath of Elohim's Mouth," the "Word," or "The Living Torah." Elohim filled *Adam* with "Their Holy Spirit" through the "breath of Their Mouth" or "Their Spoken Word." Thus, Adam is "in the Image of Elohim."

It is interesting to note that the sum of the gematria values for the first 12 Hebrew letters of Genesis 1.1 is 1152, up to the Hebrew letter *Heh* (ה), the middle letter of *Elohim* (אלהים).

אלה	ברא	בראשית
36	203	913

1152

The speed of sound in the air, 1152 ft/s or 351.13 m/s, corresponds to an environment with a temperature of 33°C in dry air. Here, sound in the air refers to "Power of Speech," "Elohim's breath," making a sound.

THE RINGS OF YOD

Looking back, the total value for the "Rings of *Yod*" is 2701. By subtracting 2085, meaning "After Elohim created the flesh of Adam. They breathed into his nostrils the breath of life, creating Adam in Their image", the remaining value is 616, the standard gematria value of *Ha-Torah* ("The Torah," התורה). The text refers to the "center of gravity," *Yod* (י), added to the eight Hebrew letters of the inner circular ring/inner layer (רההשמימא). *Heh* (ה) connects the inner circular ring to the second and third circular rings/external layer.

ה ת ו ר ה
5 200 6 400 5
616

The standard gematria value of *Besher dvar veyhei* ("And the word became flesh," בשר דבר ויהי), 739, is the same gematria value as the second circular ring. This process comes naturally after infusing the breath with the Hebrew letter *Heh* (ה) closing the first ring. In the geometrical and numerical structure of "The Rings of *Yod*," other interesting numbers between the rings can be attributed to relevant meanings with gematria. It is like reading between the lines of the first verse of Genesis.

For example, there is a difference of 601 between *Yod* (י), "the center of gravity," of value 10, and the first circular ring of value 611. 601 is the standard gematria value of *Ashsh* ("to be powerful, strong, to make strong, firm, to establish," אשש). Derivatives include *Ish* ("to glow, to burn," איש), a form of *Eish* ("Fire," אש).

אשש
300 300 1
601

THE RINGS OF YOD

This insight strengthens Elohim's Fiery nature from the "center of gravity," *Yod* (י), to the first circular ring of numerical value 611 associated with "Torah." Let's remember that *Eish* (אש) is one of the three aspects of the Spiritual Flame *Shalhevet* (שלהבת). 601 is the 110th prime number, and 110 = 37 + 73, the signature number of the first verse of Genesis, as 2701 = 37 × 73. *Bereisheit bara Elohim* ("In the beginning, Elohim created," בראשית ברא אלהים) which has a standard gematria value of 1202, which is the double 601. The difference between the second circular ring (739) and the first circular ring (611) is 128. In 1 Samuel 16:13-14, the Hebrew root *Tzade Lamed Chet* (צלח) has a standard gematria value of 128. It conveys the idea of spirit endowment (Elohim's Spirit) and expresses the action "to rush upon/leap forward," as seen in 1 Sam 11:6.

"And the spirit of Elohim rushed (ותצלח) upon Saul (…)"

ותצלח רוח אלהים על שאול

The Hebrew root *Mem Peh Chet* (מפח) also has a standard gematria value of 128. It means "breathing out," which is only constructed in Job 11:20, as breathing out of life means expiring. Between the first and second circular rings, the "Word" became "flesh" with "Elohim's breath." In other words, "Elohim's Spirit" rushed upon "flesh" to succeed in "Their Work."

The difference between the second circular ring (739) and the third circular ring (1341) is 602. 602 = 7 × 86, and let's remember that *Elohim* (איהלם) has a standard gematria value of 86. It is also the standard gematria value of *Theiotēs* ("Godhead," θειοτης (Rom. 1:20)). There is a sense of completion here with the number 7, similar to "Elohim's Work of Creation" completed in six days with the seventh day as *Sabbath* (שבת) day of rest and contemplation.

THE RINGS OF YOD

We now bring to light the meaning of the third circular ring: "Elohim the Father created Adam, the only living creature with a body and a spirit." It represents the completion of Adam's creation through the unification between the physical and spiritual realms. Thus, the first verse of Genesis with the gematria value of 2701, visualized geometrically by the Triangular Number 73 (T73), 2701 = 666 x 3 + 703, is another sight of "The Rings of *Yod*." It consists of the triangular outer physical shells (3 x 666), "flesh" clothed, and the inner spiritual core (703) represented by Elohim's breath, the "rush of Their Spirit upon flesh." Elohim gave Adam the power of speech "In Their Image." The number 602 insists on the power of speech as the Hebrew phrase *Shma Yahva Kol Yehuda* ("Hear, Yahweh (Lord), the voice of Judah," שמע יהוה קול יהודה (Deuteronomy 33.7), has a standard gematria value of 602. Their "Power" and "Wisdom" were concealed within the 28 Hebrew letters of Genesis 1.1 as a completion of Their Design, "The Rings of *Yod*." Summing up all the numbers between the rings (601 + 128 + 602) results in 1331, a perfect cube as 11^3 = 1331, the gematria value of *Mashiyach* ("Messiah," משיח) with the *Mispar Kidmi* method, meaning "primordial number," a Kabbalistic method of calculating the numerical value of a word or phrase by summing the values of each letter, where each letter's value is the sum of all letters from *Aleph* (א) to itself. The Hebrew phrase *Elohim av nati roch yahad ekhad hay nepesh Adam* ("Elohim the Father gave a spirit to only one living creature, Adam," אלהים אב נתן רוח יחד אחד חי נפש אדם) has a standard gematria value of 1331.

Remarkably, "The Rings of *Yod*" embodies our Christ nature as the total sum between the rings. Every descendant of Adam, man and woman, has a spirit "in the image of Elohim." In the numerical structure 1331, the first two digits are 13, the standard gematria value of *Ekhad* ("One," אחד) and *Ahavah* ("Love," אהבה). The mirror is 31, the gematria of *El* ("The Strong One," אל).

THE RINGS OF YOD

601

The first ring (inner) **611** minus the "Center of gravity" **10**
Torah (תורה) emerged out of the "center of gravity"
"The Word" is *Ashsh* "to strengthen, establish" (אשש)
Ish "to burn, glow" (איש)
from *Shalhevet,* Elohim's Spiritual "Flame" (שלהבת)

128

The second ring (outer) 739 minus the first ring (inner) 611
"The Word (The Living Torah) became flesh" (בשר דבר ויהי)
Tzade Lamed Chet (צלח) "to rush upon/leap forward"
"breathing out" to "rush" upon Adam with Their Spirit
Notion of "flesh" or "clothing" from the Holy Spirit of Elohim
Tzimtzum haelohim ("Elohim's Contraction," צמצום האלהים)

602

The third ring (outer) 1341 minus the second ring (outer) 739
Shma Yahva Kol Yehuda ("Hear, Yahweh (Lord), the voice of
Judah," שמע יהוה קול יהודה) (Deuteronomy 33.7)
7 x *Elohim* (86) (אלהים)
"Godhead" (Theiotēs) in Greek θειοτης (Rom. 1:20)
Unification of Physical and Spiritual Realm
Unification of the square and circle (PI () encoded)
Power of Speech with Words
Notion of Completion with 7

$\sum$ (sum of) 601, 128, 602 =

1331
11^3

Mashiyach ("Messiah," משיח)
equivalent to *Christos* ("Christ," Χρίστος)
Christ Blueprint in every man and woman
Completed Design

THE RINGS OF YOD

When we add the digits of the numerical values assigned to each layer, starting from the gravity center *Yod* (י) to the third circular ring, we get the digits 1, 8, 1, and 9.

10
Ohad ("United," אהד)
Reduced value : 1 + 0 = **1**

611
Torah (תורה), "The Word"
First Ring/Inner Layer
Reduced value : 6 + 1 + 1 = **8**

739
("And the Word became flesh," ויהי דבר בשר (John 1:14))
Second Ring/External Layer (The Word is clothed)
Reduced value : 7 + 3 + 9 = 19 and 1 + 9 = 10 = **1**

1341
"Elohim the Father created Adam the only
living creature with a body and a spirit."
אלהים אב ברא אדם יחיד חי נפש עם עצם רוח
("Eternal," αιωνιου), ("that which is made like," ομοιωματι)
Third Ring/External Layer (Adam is clothed)
Reduced value : 1 + 3 + 4 + 1 = **9**

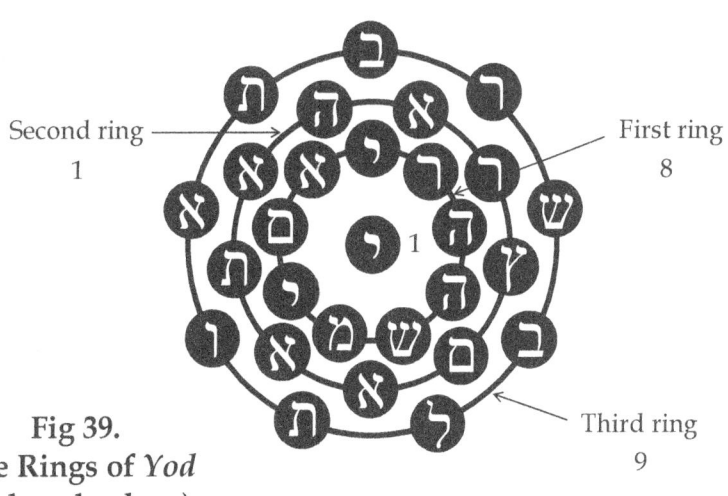

Fig 39.
The Rings of *Yod*
(Reduced values).

THE RINGS OF YOD

The digits 1, 8, 1, 9 form the number 1819, which matches the full standard gematria of the first word of Genesis 1:1, *Bereisheit* ("In the beginning," בראשית).

$$\begin{array}{cccccc} \text{ב} & \text{ר} & \text{א} & \text{ש} & \text{י} & \text{ת} \\ 2 & 200 & 1 & 300 & 10 & 400 \end{array}$$

913

$$\begin{array}{cccccc} \text{בֵּית} & \text{רֵישׁ} & \text{אָלֶף} & \text{שִׁין} & \text{יוֹד} & \text{תָו} \\ 412 & 510 & 111 & 360 & 20 & 406 \end{array}$$

1819

The third star number traces to the number 1819. The third star number is 37, which has 19 counters made of a hexagon, its inner layer. The external layer consists of 18 counters of six triangles, with three counters per triangle. Thus, the first word of Genesis, *Bereisheit* ("In the beginning," בראשית), has the signature number 37. Note that the sum of 18 and 19 results in 37. The system formulates the standard gematria of *Bereisheit* (בראשית) 913 as:

$$18 \times 37 + 13 \times 19 = 913$$
18 Star numbers 37 + 13 Hexagons of 19 counters

The number 13, the standard gematria value of *Ekhad* ("One," אחד) and *Ahavah* ("Love," אהבה) is the second star number which lies within the hexagon of 19 counters. So, all the numbers linked to the second- and third-star numbers are present in the formula for the first word of Genesis 1.1, geometrically speaking. The standard gematria value of the Hebrew word *Chai* (חי) meaning life, is 18. The numbers 19 and 37 stand for the Hebrew word *Chokmah* ("Wisdom," חכמה) respectively reduced and ordinal values. The concatenation of 18 and 19 is 1819, symbolizing wisdom in life.

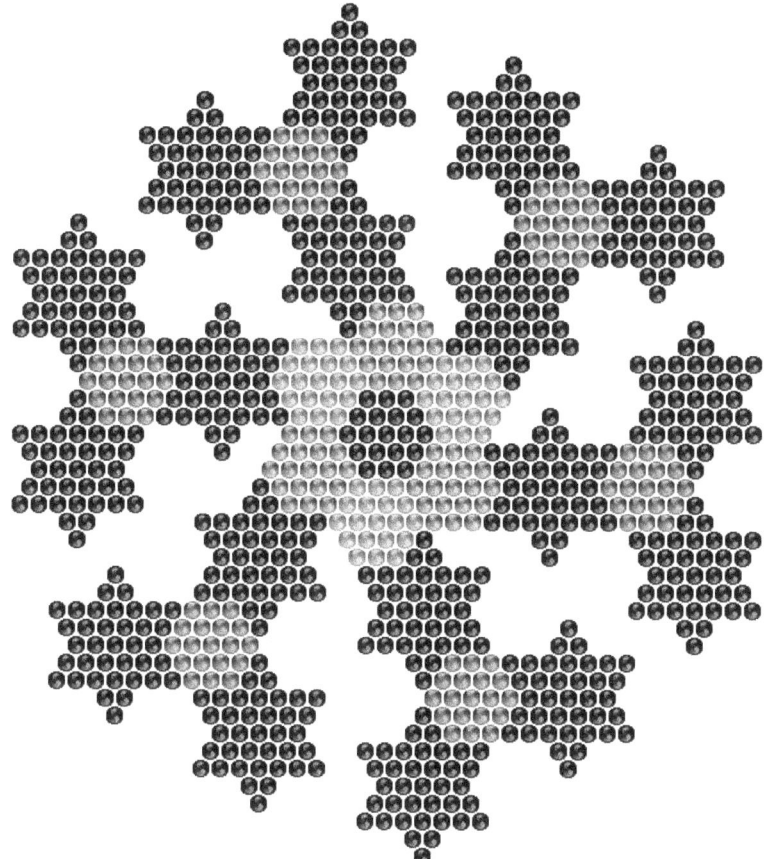

Fig 40. The First Word
(18 Hexagram 37 and 13 Hexagon 19).

There are 17 letters in the full form of *Bereisheit* ("In the beginning," בראשית), and interestingly 17 × 107 = 1819. The signature of the number 17 is present in its divisors. The number 153 is the 17th triangular number, and the number 5778 is the 107th. The number 153 is the number of fish in Peter's catch (John 21:11). It represents a primary key number linking the solar cycle in a year and moon cycle in a month, as follows:

$$365.2423 = \sqrt{153} \times 29.53$$

Number 153 can be represented geometrically within the Pythagorean Triple (5,12,13) by drawing the line from the vertex joining 12 and 13 to the point joining 2 and 3 within the side of edge length 5.

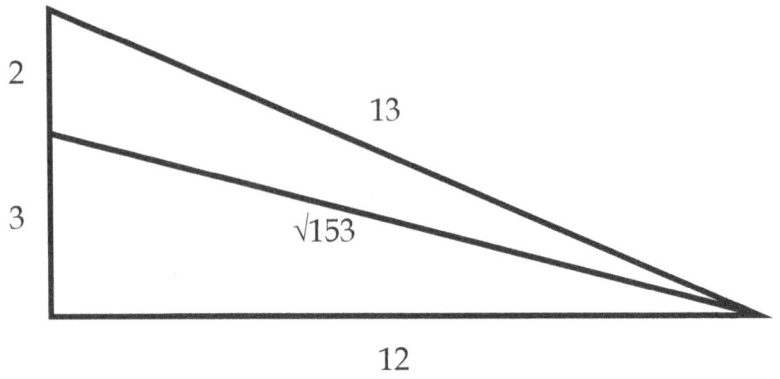

Fig 41. Square root of 153 within the Triangle 5 - 12 - 13.

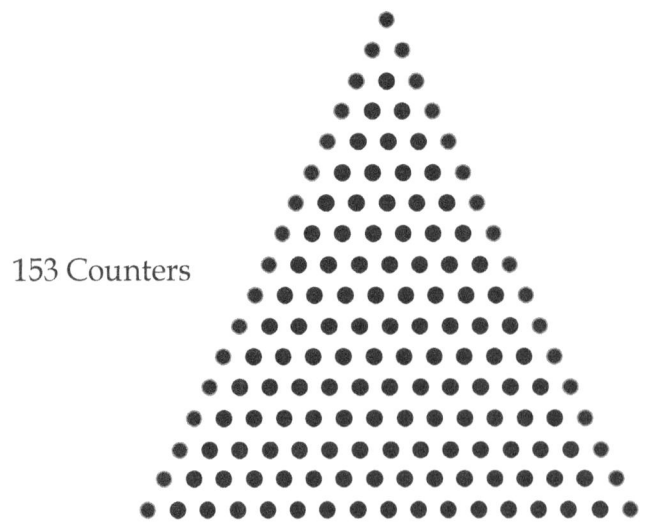

Fig 42. Triangular Number 17.

THE JESUS CODE

THE JESUS CODE

The number 5778 is fascinating. It is known to be the Sun's average surface temperature in Kelvin and has a strong affinity with the golden ratio PHI (Φ) observed in nature: 1.61803399. The formulation of the number 5778 can occur as follows:

$$\Phi^{18} + \Phi^{-18} = 5778$$

We can interpret this simple mathematical expression as the presence of two physical quantities involved in the Sun's energy source. The first factor, Φ^{18}, could be electric, and the other factor, Φ^{-18}, could be magnetic. The number 5778, in this context, represents a unique harmony in the Sun's energy system, a concept that resonates with the biblical idea of life and creation. Remember that 18 is the standard gematria value of *Chai* ("Life," חי).

Number 5778 connects not only with the Sun on a macrocosmic scale but also with 1839, which plays an essential role within the atomic structure. Neutrons weigh 1839 times more than electrons. The mathematical relationship showing this natural connection is the circle with the value of PI (π):

$$\pi \times 1839 \approx 5778$$

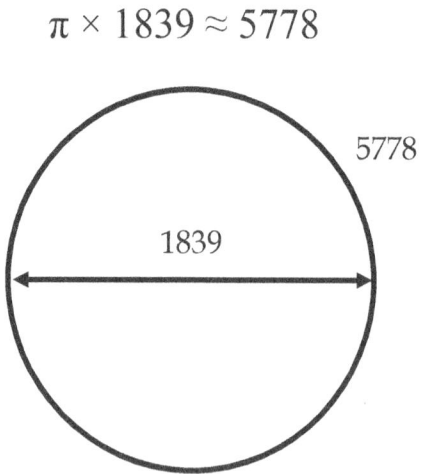

Fig 43. The Macroscopic and Microscopic connection.

The number 5778 corresponds to the date, 21st September 2017, in the Hebrew Calendar. The number 2017 has an affinity with 6336 (full length of Noah's Ark in inches) as it approximates the formula of a circle:

$$\pi \times 2017 \approx 6336$$

The number 6336 refers to "the sign of the Covenant" viewed from the heavens in Elohim's-eye-view, a full 360-degree circle. Half of this (180) is the rainbow viewed on earth by Noah and his family as they came out of the ark, which bears the name of *Kýrios Iēsoûs Christós* ("Lord Jesus Christ," Κύριος Ἰησοῦς Χριστός, 3168).

Following the thread of the numbers linking each other, 2017 would refer to a vital marking time for Elohim's Promise to Noah (Genesis 9:1-19), Abraham (Genesis 12:1-3), and potentially the return of Jesus Christ. 2017 is an anagram of 2701, the standard gematria of Genesis 1.1. A simple permutation of the digits leads to each other. The number 2017 can be uniquely found in Genesis 1.1 with the sum of the standard gematria values of the first, fourth, sixth, and seven words: "In the beginning (*Aleph Tav* את) and the earth":

בראשית את ואת הארץ
296 407 401 913
2017

All seems to point out that the year 2017 is part of a great jigsaw in Elohim's design/plan, a time marker, which was already established "In the beginning," signed by Them (*Aleph Tav* את) to lay out Their Promise on the earth ("and the earth"). It is work already completed through the power of Their Word with wisdom. Their design succeeds, and nothing can act against Their Will.

THE JESUS CODE

The number 2017 is the composite (non-prime) order of 2368, the standard gematria value of *Iesous Christos* ("Jesus Christ," Ἰησοῦς Χριστός) in Greek.

$$
\begin{array}{cc}
\text{Iησους} & \text{Χριστος} \\
888 & 1480 \\
\multicolumn{2}{c}{2368}
\end{array}
$$

More interestingly, the third layer of the first verse of Genesis (a notion of Trinity here), after the second layer with a value of 1819, is the full standard gematria value of 3368, signature number of "Lord Jesus-Christ" in Greek.

ת י ש א ר ב
400 10 300 1 200 2
913

First layer

תָו יוֹד שִׁין אָלף רֵיש בֵית
406 20 360 111 510 412
1819

Second layer

בֵית יוֹד תָו רֵיש יוֹד שִׁין אָלף למד פֵה
85 74 111 360 20 510 406 20 412
שִׁין יוֹד נוּן יָוד וו דלת תָו וו
12 406 434 12 20 106 20 360
3368

Third layer

136

THE JESUS CODE

It comes after a reiteration of the second layer of *Bereisheit* ("In the beginning," בראשית) with a value of 1819 (בית ריש אלף שין יוד תו). There is a notion of Trinity through the *Milui* ("filling," מלוא) process of *Bereisheit* (בראשית). The first Word of the Torah is associated with "Lord Jesus Christ."

The different spellings for *Kurios Iesous Christos* (Lord Jesus Christ) don't add to the same number. There are two different ways to write "Lord:" Κυριος or Κυριου. Each of these spellings carries a unique numerical value, adding another layer of complexity and depth to the numerical and theological connections we are exploring.

$$\begin{array}{ccc} \text{Κυριος} & \text{Ιησους} & \text{Χριστος} \\ 800 & 888 & 1480 \\ & 3168 & \end{array}$$

$$\begin{array}{ccc} \text{Κυριου} & \text{Ιησους} & \text{Χριστος} \\ 1000 & 888 & 1480 \\ & 3368 & \end{array}$$

In the geometric structure of Genesis 1.1, the triangular number 73 has a total of 2701 counters. The analysis will show that the signature number, the Greek gematria of the name "Lord Jesus Christ," 3368, is beautifully encoded with remarkable symmetry. Researchers endorse remarkable facts that the signature numbers 888, 2368, and 3368 encode the Triangular Number 73, the creation code, respectively, based on the names "Jesus," "Jesus-Christ," and "Lord Jesus-Christ." Beginning from the base of the triangular number 73 as the foundation of creation, the first five Hebrew words of Genesis 1.1, *Bereisheit Bara Elohim Et Hashmim* ("In the beginning, Elohim created (*Aleph Tav* את) the heavens," בראשית ברא אלהים את השמים) add up to 1998. We can visualize it geometrically as a trapezoid with a bottom base of 73 counters, two legs of 36 counters each, and a top base of 38. Next, the last two words *Ve'at hartz* ("and the earth," ואת הארץ) add up to 703, the triangular number 37. Joining the base of this triangle with the top base of the trapezoid forms the geometric structure of Genesis 1.1, the triangular number 73 (Fig 44). The intricate connection between the numerical and geometrical codes of Jesus in Genesis 1.1 shows how the Master Plan is harmoniously complete in divine order.

Starting from the top, triangular number 37 has a center of gravity at position 313, while triangular number 73 has a center of gravity at position 1201. The distance between the centers of gravity of the 37th and 73rd triangles is exactly 888 = 1201 - 313 (number of grey circles), the standard gematria value of Iesous ("Jesus," Ιησους). The central spot is the point between the two centers of gravity, located at position 685, the intersection of the 37th row and the 73rd column. Interestingly, the number 685 is a multiple of 137 as 137 x 5 = 685, and it is the 205th semiprime, 205 being the ordinal gematria value of *Iēsous Christos* ("Jesus Christ," Ἰησοῦς Χριστός).

Jesus' signatures, 888 as "Jesus," 2368 as "Jesus Christ," and 3368 as "Lord Jesus Christ," are all amazingly encoded in the Triangle of Genesis 1.1 (Fig 45). Notice that the middle row (37th row) and column (73rd column) consist of 37 counters each. Some significant numbers emerge from the central spot 685. Its horizontal count from the base is 2017, the composite order of 2368, the Greek gematria value of *Iesous Christos* ("Jesus Christ," Ἰησοῦς Χριστός). Its vertical count from either corner at the base is 1351, and the total counters of the Triangular Number 73 is 2701, an anagram of 2017. The sum is 2017 + 1351 = 3368, the Greek standard gematria of *Kyriou Iesous Christos* ("Lord Jesus Christ," Κύριου Ἰησοῦς Χριστός) using the second version of the word for "Lord" (Κυριου). It is located precisely at the middle point of the two gravity centers, revealing Jesus (888).

THE JESUS CODE

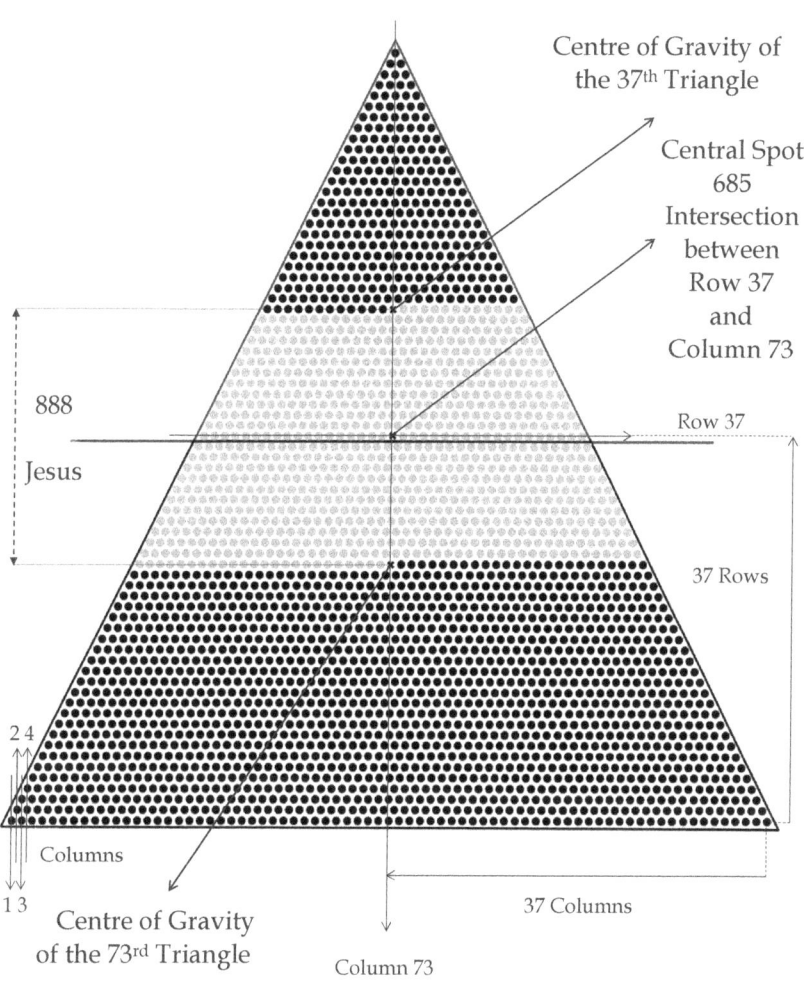

**Fig 44.
Jesus' name decoded in Genesis 1.1.**

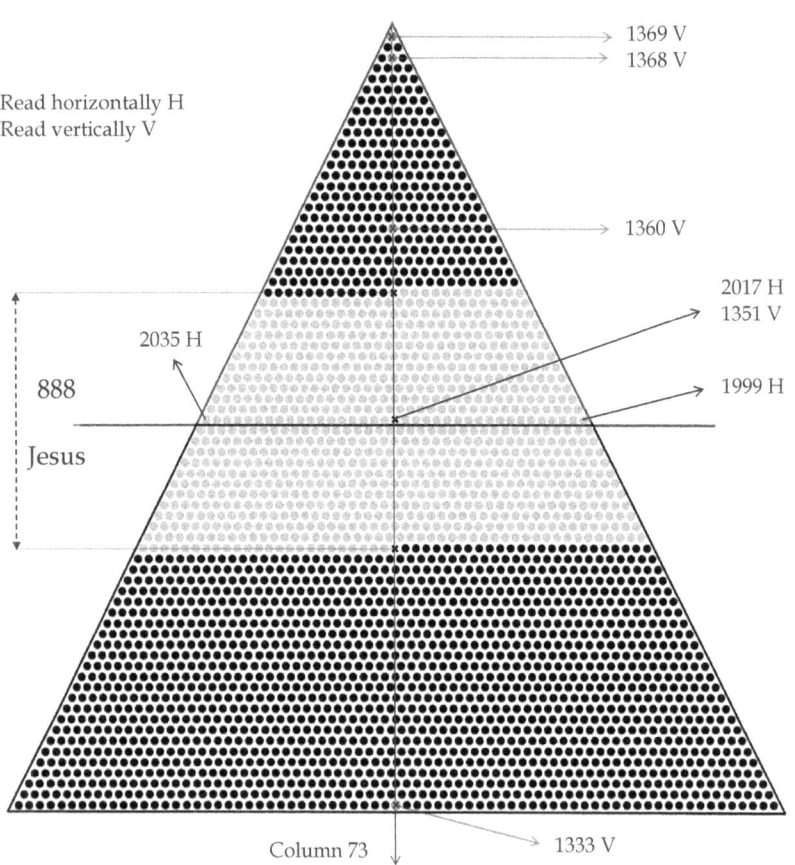

**Fig 45.
Interpretation of Triangular Number 73.**

THE JESUS CODE

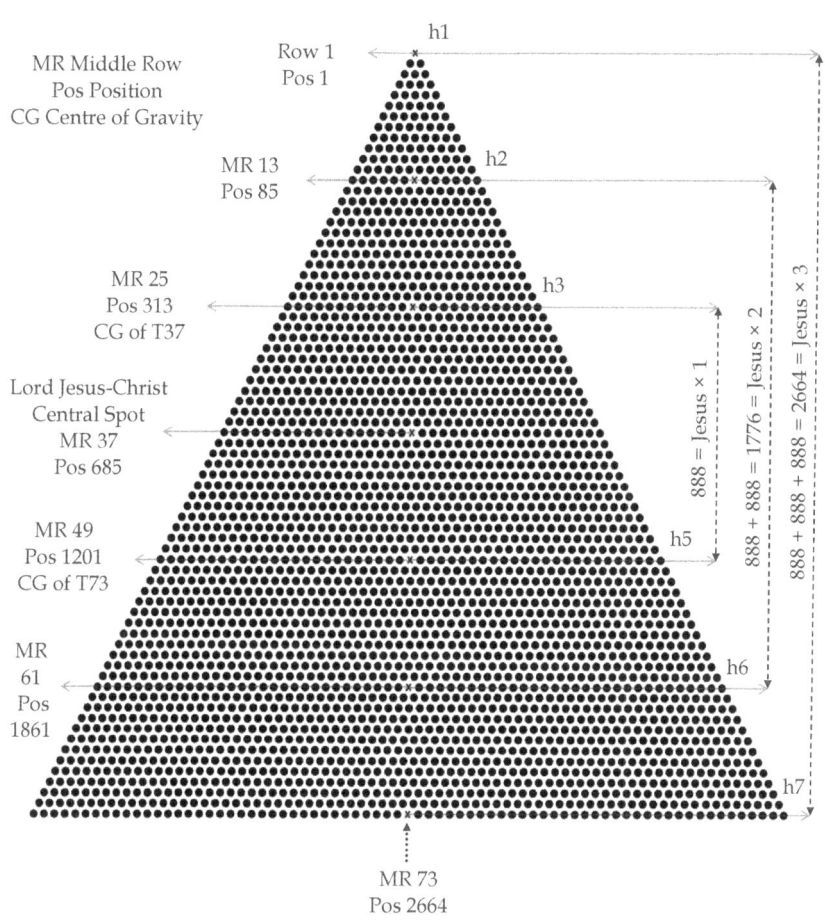

**Fig 46.
Jesus' Code.**

THE JESUS CODE

The coding of Jesus' signatures shows clear evidence that there is an Intelligent Architect and Designer of the Triangle 73, Genesis 1.1. As we move away from the Lord Jesus-Christ (LJC) center along the vertical axis, an interesting numerical pattern emerges, revealing 888 "Jesus" under the form of the Trinity through the perfect number 6, as 1 + 2 + 3 = 6 and 1 × 2 × 3 = 6. Seven points, p1 to p7, are evenly distributed on the vertical axis (Fig 46); each adjacent pair spaces seven counters apart. In each counting from opposite adjacent (h3 to h5, h2 to h6, and h1 to h7) away from the LJC center, the number 888 "Jesus" is added to the distance between each pair of points.

$$h5 - h3 = 1201 - 313 = 888 = \text{Jesus} \times 1$$
$$h6 - h2 = 1861 - 85 = 888 + 888 = 1776 = \text{Jesus} \times 2$$
$$h7 - h1 = 2665 - 1 = 888 + 888 + 888 = \text{Jesus} \times 3$$

The 37th Hebrew word of Genesis 1 is in the fourth verse, *Hohr* ("The light," האור) starts with the 137th Hebrew letter, *Heh* (ה) of value 5. In the "Rings of *Yod*," *Heh* (ה) is "Elohim's breath," referring to the Holy Spirit, bridging the inner layer to the outer layer with "clothing" and "flesh."

"And Elohim saw the light that it was good, and Elohim separated between the light and the darkness" (Genesis 1.4).

וירא אלהים את-האור, כי-טוב; ויבדל אלהים, בין <u>האור</u> ובין החשך

The number 137 corresponds to the gematria value of the word *Kabbalah* ("Receiving," קבלה). It refers to a fundamental number in Physics, the inverse ratio of which is the fine structure constant *Alpha* (α) governing the interaction between matter and light.

$$\text{Alpha } (\alpha) = 1 \div 137 = 0.00729927 \approx 0.0073$$

Notice that the numerical value approximates ten-thousandth of 73, with a mirror number of 37. These two numbers are the key gematria values of the first verse of Genesis. The standard gematria value of Genesis 1.4 is 1776, the double 888, the Greek standard gematria of Jesus. The fourth verse of Genesis is also encoded in the Triangular Number 73 with the unfolding code of Jesus in the form of the Trinity. 1776 is the distance between points h2 and h6. It is part of the creation story involving "the light" focused as the spot center 685 between the two centers of gravity of the Triangular Numbers 37 and 73. At this spot, the geometry of the Triangle shows that the full signature of Jesus, "Lord Jesus Christ," has a gematria value of 3368 in Greek. Unfolding the full name values of each Hebrew letter, it is also the gematria of Genesis 1.1 with 46 letters on the third layer using the *Mispar Shemi* Method.

The standard Hebrew gematria of *Hohr* ("The light," האור) is 212.

ה ו א ר
200 6 1 5
212

A circle of 212 in diameter has a circumference of 666. This geometric relationship points out that the number 666 is intrinsically connected with the expression of the light. Not to mention that 666 is an excellent part of the mathematical structure of the Triangle Creation: 666 × 3 + 703 = 2701.

Fig 47.
Light connection with 666.

The exact value of the fine structure constant is 137.035999, which is about 137.036. The Triangular Number 36 has a total of 666 counters. Looking at the fourth verse of Genesis, the 36th Hebrew word is *Ben* ("Between," בין) and has a standard gematria value of 62. 137.036 can be read as the 36th Hebrew word followed by the 137th letter of the 37th word, *Ben Hohr* ("Between the light," בין האור). This phrase has a standard gematria value of 274, which is double of 137. The information is, therefore, still present within the 36th word.

$$בין\ האור$$
$$212\quad 62$$
$$274$$

The value of the fine structure constant as 1÷137 is only valid at atomic scale energies. At higher energy levels, the fine structure constant changes from 1÷137 to 1÷127 at the Z or boson mass, i.e., 90 GeV. 0127 is an anagram of 2701 and 2017. The seven words of Genesis 1.1 can create 127 unique word combinations: $2^7 - 1 = 127$. The middle number between 127, the 31st prime number, and 137, the 33rd prime number, is 132, standard gematria of *l'vaniym* ("white," לבנים). The primary colors are red, yellow, and blue; the secondary colors are orange, green, and violet. 132 refers to the aggregate of the six colors of light, i.e., white. When we add all the lengths of the light waves (in inches), the result is 0.00001320. Secondly, 132 takes the root of the word *Kabbalah* ("Receiving," קבלה) as it is the value of the word *Kabal* ("to receive," קבל).

Looking at the Triangle Creation (Fig 44), the center spot of Lord Jesus Christ, located at position 685 from the top, is a multiple of 137 as $685 = 137 \times 5$. So, it carries the information of *Hohr* ("The light," האור) with the fine structure constant *Alpha* (α), $α = 1 ÷ 137 = 5 ÷ 685$.

Remarkably, 685 divided by Euler's number *e* approximates 252. The base of the natural logarithm is the mathematical constant *e*, which we use in problems of exponential growth or decay. The number 252 is the product of 12 and 21, two mirror numbers; respectively, the mirror primes 37 and 73 in the list of prime numbers. The prime numbers 37 and 73 are both signatures of Genesis 1.1 in their gematria value (37 x 73 =2701) and identify the Lord Jesus Christ. Interestingly, the standard gematria of *Hamaohr* ("Luminary," המאור) in Genesis 1:16 is 252.

$$ה מ א ו ר$$
$$200\ 6\ 1\ 40\ 5$$
$$252$$

HYPERDIMENSIONAL LIGHT

In this chapter, we delve into the profound significance of 685, a key that unlocks the intricate relationship between critical mathematical constants and geometry within the creation triangle. Position 685, the midpoint of row 37 or the intersection between row 37 and column 73, serves as a gateway to a higher dimension. It marks the spot center, the meeting point of the center of gravity of the Triangular Number 37, and the center of gravity of the Triangular Number 73. This location is not just a point but a bridge to a higher dimension, connecting the fundamental constant in Physics 137, the interaction between matter and light, and the creation triangle.

The number 685 is not just a numerical value; it carries information from a higher dimension than the third dimension. Let's consider 685 as the volume of a hyperdodecahedron (120 cells) in four dimensions. The dodecahedron is the fifth platonic solid in the third dimension. For a hypervolume of 685, let's see what it involves mathematically and geometrically. We chose the dodecahedron because it is the only Platonic solid with a strong relationship with the number 5. Indeed, its faces are pentagonal. The dodecahedron is also associated with the fifth element, the ether, corresponding to the heavens. This firmament is displayed as the 12 zodiac signs along a circle or projected into a sphere. Thus, the 12 pentagonal facets of the regular dodecahedron fit perfectly with the design of the firmament.

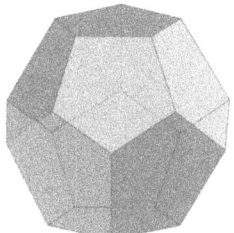

**Fig 48.
The regular dodecahedron.**

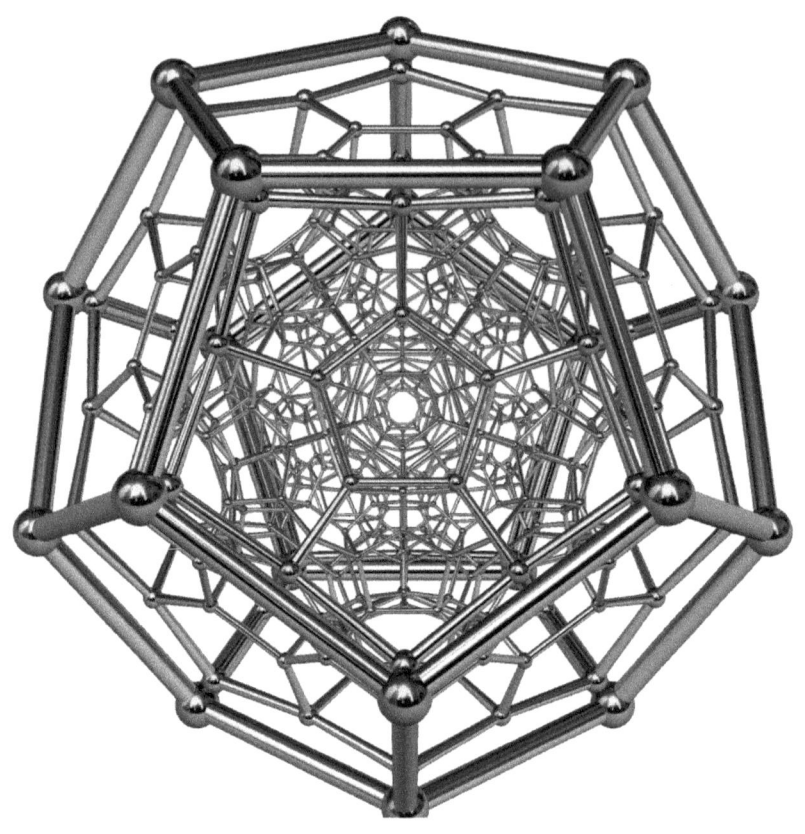

Fig 49. Hyper dodecahedron in four dimensions.
Image Source: Robert Webb's Stella Software.
https://www.software3d.com/Stella.php

The figure above represents the four-dimensional analog of the regular dodecahedron. The 120-cell, a stunning object, is composed of 120 dodecahedra, joined 3 to an edge, meeting at 720 pentagons, 1200 edges, and 600 vertices. It is a masterpiece of geometry, the equivalent of the three-dimensional regular dodecahedron and the dual of the 600-cell.

HYPERDIMENSIONAL LIGHT

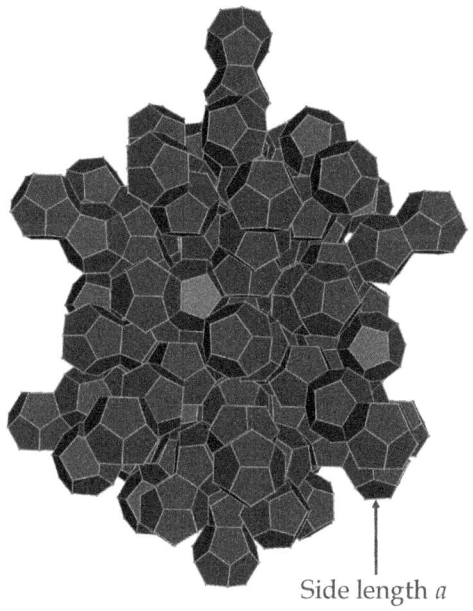

Side length a

Fig 50. 120 dodecahedral cells.
Image Source: Robert Webb's Stella Software.
https://www.software3d.com/Stella.php

We can't find the volume of a hyperdodecahedron, also known as the 120-cell, by simply adding up the volumes of its 120 dodecahedral cells. These cells overlap and share faces, edges, and corners in four-dimensional space. While calculating the volume of shapes in three dimensions is straightforward, four-dimensional geometry presents more complexity. Each dodecahedral cell influences the total volume, rendering a simple addition formula ineffective. This complexity arises from the curvature and connections of the 120-cell in four dimensions.

If we calculate the combined volume of 120 separate, non-intersecting dodecahedra, we are looking for the side length of a single dodecahedron respecting the following equation:

$$120 \times V_{dodecahedron} = 685; \text{ Therefore}$$
$$V_{dodecahedron} = 685 \div 120 = 5.7083333+$$

HYPERDIMENSIONAL LIGHT

This total volume calculated differs from the hypervolume of the 120-cell in four dimensions, as the dodecahedra are arranged in 4D space and intersect. In three dimensions, the formula for the volume of a dodecahedron with a side length of a is as follows:

$$V_{dodecahedron} = [(15 + 7\sqrt{5}) \div 4] \times a^3 \approx 7.6631\ a^3$$

The following equation determines the side length a:

$$V_{dodecahedron} = [(15 + 7\sqrt{5}) \div 4] \times a^3 = 5.7083333+$$

The value of the side length a of a dodecahedra cell is:

$$a \approx (5.7083 \div 7.6631)^{(1 \div 3)} \approx 0.9065$$

Before we discuss the implications of this final value, we note that the numerical value of the volume of a dodecahedron cell, 5.7083333+, provides essential information from the Science of Gematria. When we match this value with the side length of a cube, we find that its cubic volume is 186.

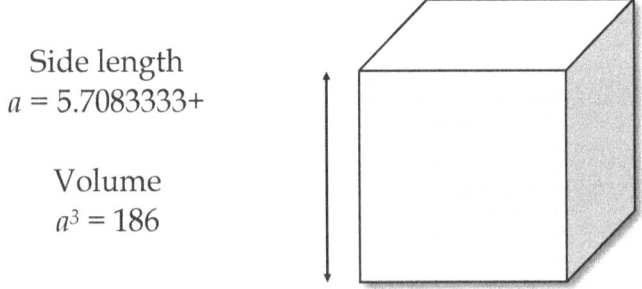

Side length
$a = 5.7083333+$

Volume
$a^3 = 186$

**Fig 51.
The Cube of Light.**

HYPERDIMENSIONAL LIGHT

Position 186 is where 294 first appears in PI (π).

```
3.14159265358979323846264338327950288841971693
9937510582097494459230781640628620899862803482
5342117067982148086513282306647093844609550582
2317253594081284811174502841027019385211055
5964462294
         -----↓
         186th digit
```

On the fourth day of creation, Elohim made two great lights, and set them in the firmament (Gen 1:16-17):

16. And <u>Elohim</u> made the two great lights: <u>the greater light</u> to rule the day, and the lesser light to rule the night; and the stars.
17. And Elohim set them in the firmament of the heaven to give light upon the earth,

ויעש <u>אלהים</u>, את שני המארת הגדלים: את <u>המאור</u> <u>הגדל</u>, לממשלת היום, ואת המאור הקטן לממשלת הלילה, ואת הכוכבים.

ויתן אתם אלהים, ברקיע השמים, להאיר, על הארץ

Hamaret hagdal ("The greater light," המארת הגדל) has a gematria value of 294. The 186th word in the Torah is *Elohim* (אלהים) when they made two great lights in Genesis 1:16. The number 186 shows the numerical signature of Elohim in its digits, as 86 is also the Hebrew standard gematria of *Elohim* (אלהים).

המאור הגדל
42   252
294

HYPERDIMENSIONAL LIGHT

The speed of light is 186000 miles per second. The number 186 is a natural harmonic number referring to *Ohr* ("Light," אור) as shown in Genesis 1:16; the greater light here is the Sun, the source of life on Earth.

The number 186 is the Hebrew standard gematria of *Makom* ("Place," מקום), the name of God or Goddess, connoting that They are the "Place" of the world. It is the same as the gematria of squares of *Yahweh* ("Lord," YHVH, יהוה).

$$5 \times 5 + 6 \times 6 + 5 \times 5 + 10 \times 10 = 186$$

מ ק ו ם
40 6 100 40
186

186 is also the sum of the standard and ordinal gematria of the Hebrew word *Nekudah* ("Point," נקודה).

Standard: 165
Ordinal: 21
Total: 186

Let's not forget this is the original "Point" from which everything emanated. The product of their midpoints 83 and 11 is 913, the Hebrew standard gematria value of *Bereisheit* ("In the Beginning," בראשית), the first word of the Torah in Genesis 1.1.

The second Hebrew letter of *Nekudah* ("Point," נקודה) and *Makom* ("Place," מקום) is the 19th letter in the Hebrew Alphabet. It is called *Kuf* (ק) and equals 100 in Hebrew gematria. Added with the standard Hebrew gematria of *Elohim* (אלהים) 86, the result is 186.

The number 685, the full form of *Kuf* (קוף), originally meant "the back of the head" or "the eye of a needle," signifying descent into the lower world and the ability to ascend from there. This Hebrew letter has the particularity to illuminate the lower Sephirah of the Kabbalah, *Malkuth* ("Kingdom," מלכות), the physical world. The illumination of living matter is definitely from "the light," not only from a physical point of view but there is also a spiritual aspect, with "Wisdom" and "The Heart" as *Kuf* (ק) is the 19th Hebrew letter having a numerical value of 100. 19 is the reduced gematria value of *Chokmah* ("Wisdom," חכמה) and the ordinal value of *Haleb* ("The Heart," הלב), a perfect geometric fit between the hexagon/star pairs: 19/37 and 37/73 (Fig 33).

Baseline אבגדהוזחטיכלמנסעפצקרשת

Kuf's long left leg is below the baseline

Remember that "Going inward" surpasses our animalistic nature, "monkey," the full form of *Kuf* (קוף). It activates the 100 Sephiroth within, accessing and seeing the Great Image, our divine nature, *Elohim* (אלהים) and *Yahweh* (יהוה). The number 100 is the standard gematria value of *Ch'i* ("Qi," צ'י, 氣 in Chinese), the inner vital breath in Hebrew.

Thus, the number 186 reveals the nature of light as the source of life. In the image of the Sun, Elohim has supernaturally supplied the universe's light, which is always ever-present. They began creating from the original "Point" and extended it to a perfect circle with the constant PI (π) 3.14. It became the space continuum, a container of existence for every creature, beginning with the first pristine emanation of light, "Christ," and emerging from the *Ein Soph* (סוף אין).

THE ROOT OF THE ROYAL CUBIT

In the previous chapter, we calculated a dodecahedra cell's side length a, about 0.9065. This value has profound implications and leads to other critical mathematical constants, including the ancient Egyptian royal cubit. The significance of this cubit, the earliest attested standard measure from the Old Kingdom pyramids of Egypt, is genuinely fascinating. To determine its value, we must allocate the side length of 0.9065 to the height h of a *Vesica Piscis*, as shown below.

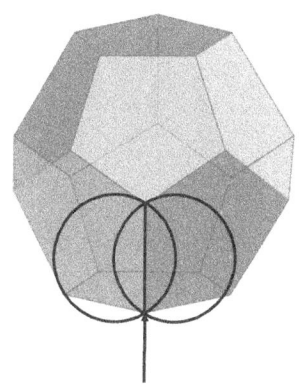

Side length a = Height h = 0.9065

Fig 52. The geometric origin of the Royal Cubit.

The relationship between the width w and height h of a *Vesica Piscis* is formulated with the square of 3, as follows:

$$w = h \div \sqrt{3}$$

The width w result is approximately the ancient Egyptian Royal Cubit in meters, 0.5234.

Fig 53. *Vesica Piscis* and Royal Cubit.

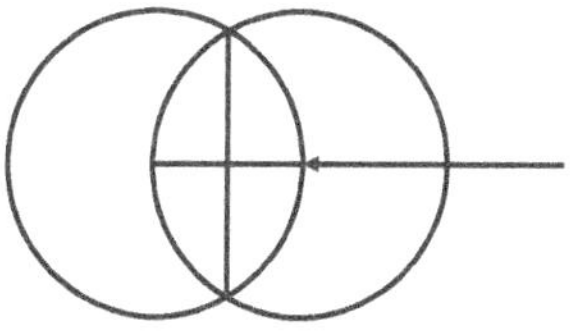

Width w = 0.5234

THE ROOT OF THE ROYAL CUBIT

The Hieroglyph of the Royal Cubit was called *meh niswt* in Ancient Egypt. In the Figure below, we have three symbols — papyrus, a wavelength, and an arm. The Hieroglyph may indicate that the Royal Cubit is a sacred proportion within the human body.

Fig 54. Hieroglyph of the Royal Cubit.

The Royal Cubit measures the forearm's ratio to the humerus's deltoid tuberosity (1:√2). This triangular area on the anterolateral (front side) lies proximally about a third of the way to the elbow. It serves as an attachment point for the deltoid muscle. This ratio is a key concept in understanding the royal cubit's measurement, as it is a fundamental proportion within the human body.

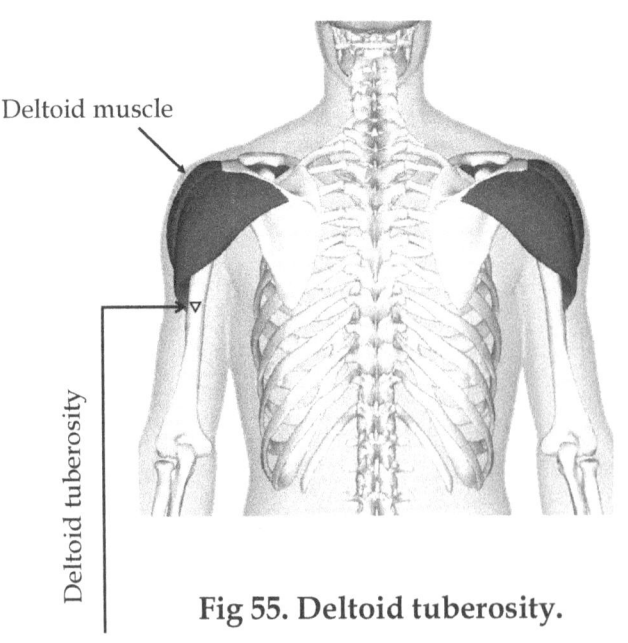

Fig 55. Deltoid tuberosity.

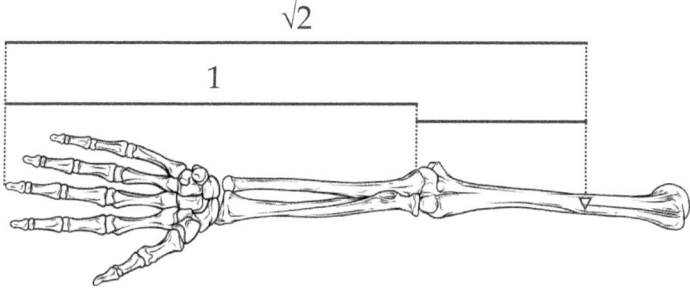

Fig 56. The 1:√2 ratio in the arm.

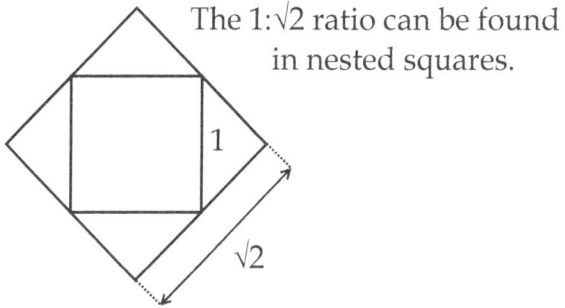

The 1:√2 ratio can be found in nested squares.

Fig 57. The 1:√2 ratio in the square.

With its essential relationship with the Sun, the Egyptian Royal Cubit demonstrates its universal nature. When a circle's circumference equals a square's perimeter (squaring the circle), then the heaven (circle) and the earth (square) somehow balance, transcending the space and time continuum. This definition involves the value of PI (π) 3.14, which the Great Designer set as transcendental *Bereisheit* ("In the beginning," בראשית). The transcendental nature of PI (π) proves that no ruler and compass construction can square the circle, connecting us to the divine through mathematics.

In parallel to those who seek within, the soul calls to reach the total inner silence *Chashmal* ("Electrum," חשמל) to be the bridge between heaven and earth, the link between God or Goddess and man or woman, a luminous bridge between *Malkuth* ("Kingdom," מלכות) and the higher sphere *Kether* ("Crown," כתר) of the *Kabbalah* ("Receiving," קבלה).

From this critical relationship (squaring the circle) and by repeating the same pattern of nested squares in a fractal manner drawn from the midpoint of their parents, it appears to show a fantastic pattern (the Lotus) creating 45-degree spirals that regress far beyond our visual faculties. The beauty and complexity of this Lotus pattern, with its elegant 45-degree spirals, is truly awe-inspiring.

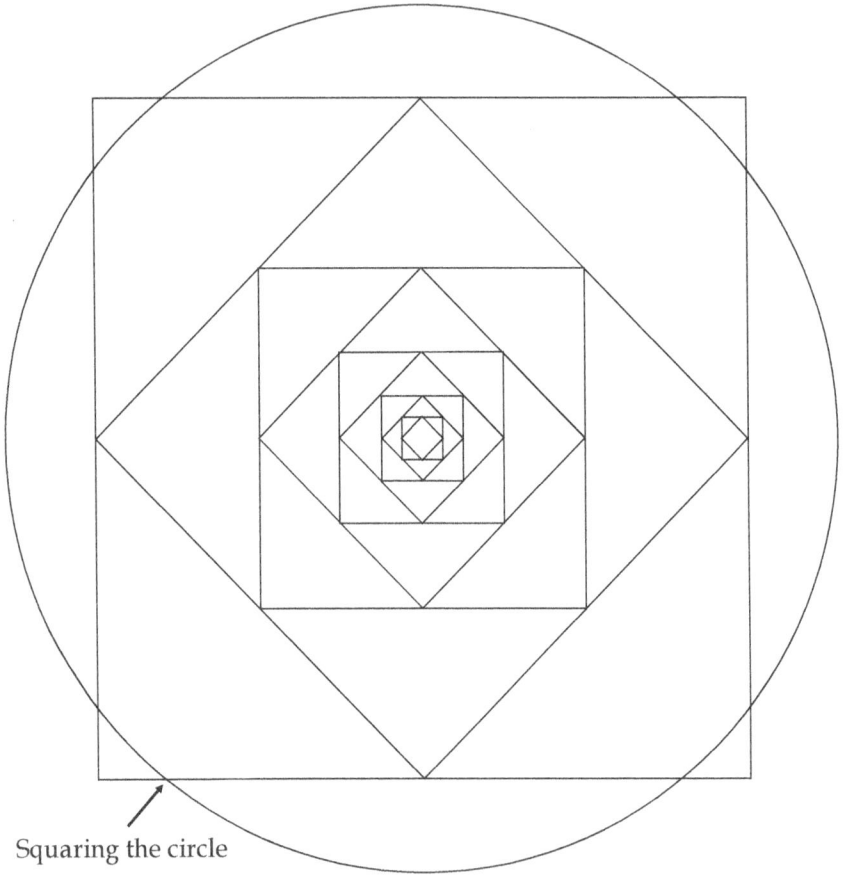

Squaring the circle

Fig 58. The Royal Cubit and the Sun.

Consider the circle as the Sun's circumference, which equals the square's nearly 4.4 million km perimeter. Therefore, the square's sides approach 1.1 million kilometers. When we nest this geometric shape 42 times within itself, we get a side length of 0.5237 kilometers.

The result is 1000th times the Egyptian royal cubit, 0.5237 meters (see Appendix A for further details of the calculations). The circle represents a specific layer of the Sun, marking the transition between the chromosphere, which is roughly 4000 km thick, and the Sun's Corona, which extends millions of kilometers into outer space. The bright light of the Sun's surface usually hides the Corona, but observers can view it during a total solar eclipse.

Fig 59. The visible Corona in a Solar Eclipse.

At the top of the chromosphere, the temperature increases rapidly with height, up to two million degrees of the Corona.

The hidden part of the Sun (Corona) recalls the invisible aspect of the candle, the core/innermost, invisible fire of electric nature as it is in everything, *Chashmal* ("Electrum," חשמל) of standard gematria value 378. The chromosphere would represent then *Nogah* ("Brillance," נגה) of value 58, the glow of the flame. Below the chromosphere, the photosphere would be the visible flame itself, *Eish* ("Fire," אש), with a value of 301.

THE ROOT OF THE ROYAL CUBIT

The total standard gematria of the first 42 Hebrew letters of Genesis is 3842, close to 4000, the distance in km between the upper chromosphere (brilliance) and the lower Corona (electrum). The innermost *Chashmal* ("Electrum," חשמל) meaning "Electrum," of the Spiritual Flame *Shalhevet* (שלהבת) embodies the total inner silence while simultaneously expressing the speaking Word of Their Name.

Remember that the 42-letter name of God or Goddess was established "In the Beginning" by expanding the *Nekudah* ("Point," נקודה) in a perfect circle to receive Their creation in a space-time continuum. So, the transitional layer of the Sun at 3842 km recalls the number 42 as a foundation for the origins of creation.

Impressive, the fractal of nested squares is done 42 times with a final value of 0.5237 km, a thousand times the royal cubit. This value is approximately the same as that calculated for the width w of a *Vesica Piscis* (99.952% accuracy) having a height of 0.9065 h, the dodecahedron cell's side of the 120-cell (hyperdodecahedron).

$$w = h \div \sqrt{3} = 0.5234 \approx 0.5237$$

The Royal Cubit is a harmonic partial of the Sun's length and correlates numerically with the hyperdodecahedron. Could it be the bridge between the Royal Cubit and the Sun? The Sun's length is the circumference of the circle, the actual transitional layer between the top of the chromosphere and the lower Corona.

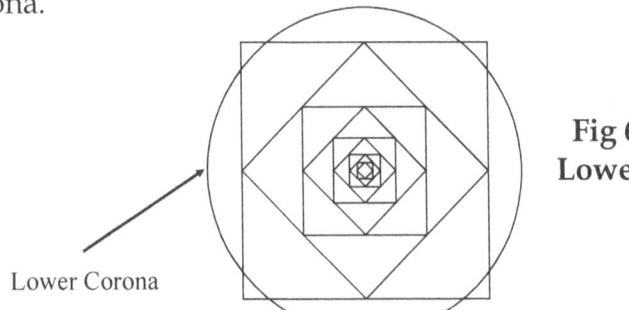

Fig 60. Sun's Lower Corona.

Other fundamental constants naturally appear from the *Vesica Piscis* with a width w equal to 0.5234, close to the Royal Cubit, and a height h of 0.9065, the dodecahedron cell's side of the 120-cell (hyper dodecahedron). Multiplying 0.9065 by the square root of 3 equals 1.5702 and approximates half of PI (π). Geometrically, the height of the first *Vesica Piscis* becomes the width of a bigger *Vesica Piscis* in a fractal manner. The new height h_2 multiplied by 2 is thus an approximation of PI (π).

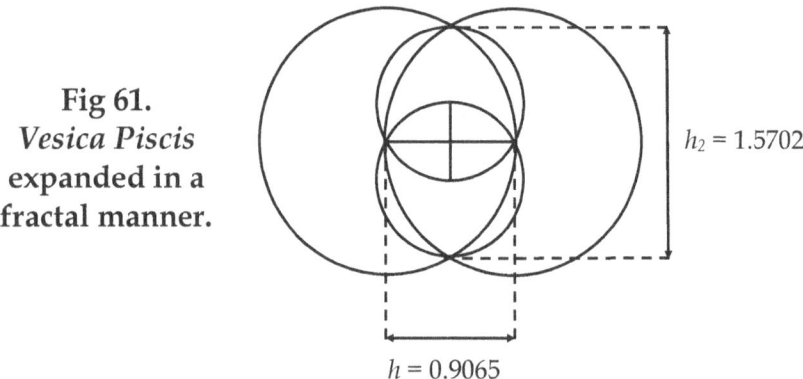

Fig 61.
Vesica Piscis **expanded in a fractal manner.**

$h_2 = 1.5702$

$h = 0.9065$

Continuing the same fractal pattern, the new height of the bigger *Vesica Piscis* h_3 from the previous one approximates 2.72, a close value to another fundamental constant e equal to 2.718. The beauty of these mathematical relationships is genuinely fascinating.

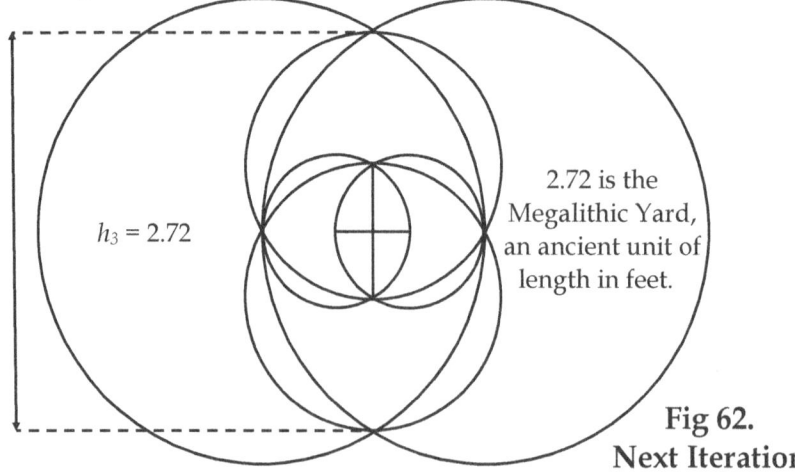

$h_3 = 2.72$

2.72 is the Megalithic Yard, an ancient unit of length in feet.

Fig 62. Next Iteration

KEY 117

The *Vesica Piscis* has a special relationship with three different square roots. If A to B is 1, the radius of both circles, then C to D equals $\sqrt{3}$, E to G to $\sqrt{5}$, and E to A to $\sqrt{2}$.

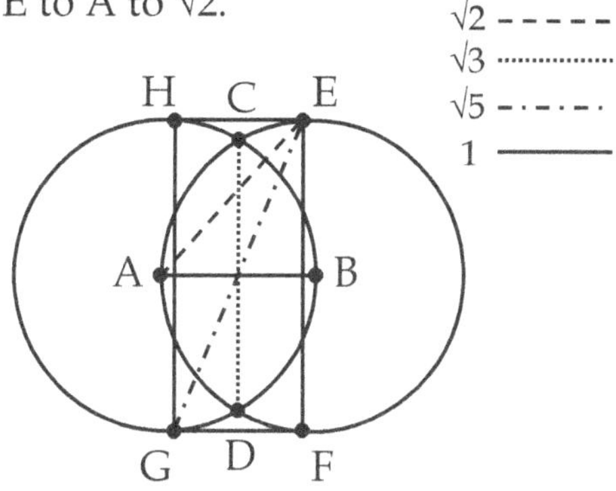

$\sqrt{2}$ - - - - -
$\sqrt{3}$ ....
$\sqrt{5}$ -·-·-·
1 ———

Fig 63. Numerical Values of the *Vesica Piscis*.

Scaling up the above *Vesica Piscis* to a width w equals to 0.5234 for the radius of both circles (A to B), close to the Royal Cubit 0.5237, leads to interesting results for the other line segments CD, EA and EG.

- The line segment CD is the value of a dodecahedra's cell side length a calculated previously.
- The line segment EA is $w\sqrt{2}$, about 0.74.
- The line segment EG is $w\sqrt{5}$, about 1.17.

The numerical values 74 and 117, part of the measurements of the *Vesica Piscis* on a scale of 100, have both important meanings in gematria. The standard gematria of *Yasad* ("founded," לסד) is 74. It means "to set; to be found; to set down; to appoint; to assign; foundation, beginning" - also a variant spelling of the name of the ninth Sephirah, *Yesod* ("Foundation," לסוד). The number 117 is significant in the Bible Code. The 117th word in the Bible is Elohim (אלהים) in Genesis 1.11: "And Elohim said, Let the earth bring forth grass, the herb yielding seed, and the fruit tree yielding fruit after his kind."

ד ס י
4 60 10
74

KEY 117

The Hebrew word *Yasad* ("founded," לסד) appears in Proverbs Chapter 3, verse 19:

The LORD (Yahweh) by wisdom <u>founded</u> the earth; by understanding He established the heavens.

יהוה בחכמה <u>יסד</u> ארץ; כונן שמים, בתבונה.

This verse reveals the nature of this foundation as "Wisdom," which strengthens the feeling that we could potentially translate the opening word of Genesis 1.1 *Bereisheit* ("In the beginning, בראשלת) as "In Wisdom;" "At first" (with Wisdom); or "In Principle" (with Wisdom).

Thus, the *Vesica Piscis*, which refers mainly to the geometry used in God's and Goddess' Creation, is founded with Wisdom. Its measurements are a key, calling us to look deeper into the science of gematria.

The ordinal gematria of Jesus in English is 74. It is only one unit more than the prime number 73 (the 21st prime and the fourth star number), a foundation number in the coding of Genesis 1.1, as the standard gematria of the first verse in Hebrew is 2701, the product of the prime number 37 (the 12th prime and the third star number) and 73.

J e s u s
10 5 19 21 19
74

The number 117 is quite significant in the Bible Code. The 117th word in the Bible is *Elohim* (אלהים) in Genesis 1.11: "And <u>Elohim</u> said, Let the earth bring forth grass, the herb yielding seed, and the fruit tree yielding fruit after his kind."

KEY 117

The standard gematria value of *Yahweh Halaim* ("Yahweh is Elohim," יהוה האיהלם) is 117. In English, the ordinal gematria of "YHVH is God" or "God the Father" is 117. Three interesting English words with the ordinal value of 117 can be highlighted in some verses of the Bible, all three referring to YHVH's expression: Image, Breath, and Voice:

- "YHVH's Image" (117) from the verse "And Elohim said, Let us make man in our image" (Gen 1:26)
- "YHVH Breath" (117) from the verse "the Lord (Yahweh) Elohim breathed into his nostrils the breath of life." (Gen 2:7)
- "YHVH Voice" (117) from the verse "And the Lord (Yahweh) spoke to you out of the midst of the fire: and you heard a voice." (Deut 4:12)

The first three books of the Torah, Genesis, *Bereisheit* ("Creation," בראשית), Exodus, *Shemot* ("Names," שמות) and Leviticus, *Vayikrah* ("And They called," ויקרא) have 117 total chapters.

The Hebrew word *Sabbath* (שבת) is used 117 times in the Old Testament. *Sabbath* (שבת) is the 7th day, a day of rest and contemplation after achieving the six days of Elohim's creation.

The number 117 concatenates the two prime numbers, 7 and 11. They are scaled-down measurements of the Great Pyramid of Egypt, respectively, its height and the side length of its base. As we will discuss further, the Great Pyramid is part of a geometric diagram that has appeared in the arts, architecture, and literature of cultures worldwide. It encodes the ideal patterns and proportions toward which nature's forms strive to represent the universe's complete order on every scale. This diagram appears microcosmically in the designs of cosmic temples and sacred spaces worldwide.

THE NEW JERUSALEM DIAGRAM

THE NEW JERUSALEM DIAGRAM

Its dimensions are described as the Heavenly City in The Book of Revelation, as seen in Stonehenge, the Lady's Chapel of Glastonbury Abbey, and Plato's ideal city Magnesia. The design features a central "squared circle" plan that reflects the sizes and relationships among the Earth, Sun, and Moon. The Great Pyramid of dimensions 11 and 7, referring to the number 117 when concatenated, is a significant key to this geometric diagram of universal harmony.

John Michell, the author of the celebrated book "City of Revelation," described this geometric design as the New Jerusalem. In this book, we will focus only on the original proportions of the Lady's Chapel, whose foundations of the first wattle church were erected by Joseph of Arimathea, with his companions and potentially the carpenter Jesus himself. We will further explore how the science of gematria plays an integral part in understanding the knowledge and wisdom of this universal design, prompting us to investigate John Michell's research more deeply, as presented in his book "New Light on the Ancient Mystery of Glastonbury." The Great Pyramid faces the four points of the compass and lies at the center of gravity for all of Earth's land. The cosmic and terrestrial forces unify, serving as a cosmic instrument of Alchemy that bridges the physical and spiritual realms, which the square and circle respectively represent. The design of the Great Pyramid based on the ratio 7:11 is a perfect approximation of "squaring the circle." This ratio equals 1.571, a recall of the term *Nukveh* ("female," נחבה) with a gematria value of 157 in the kabbalist context of the marital union between the groom (male) and bridge (female). In the following diagram, we place the slope angle apparent at ground level of 51.84° over the plan of its square base, and we add a circle with a radius equal to the Pyramid's height. The union of the male and female geometrically interprets as the equal perimeters or areas of the square and circle, which naturally involves PI (π) 3.14.

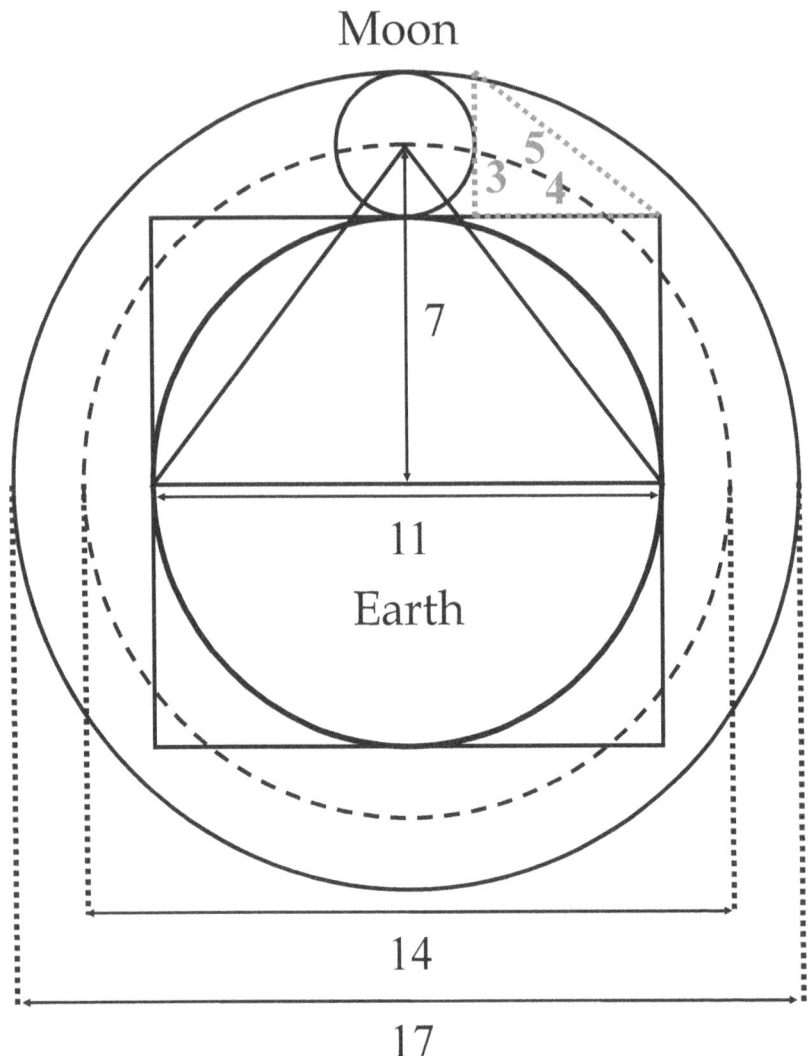

Fig 64. The Diagram of the New Jerusalem with Key 117.

This diagram shows the dashed line circle as the squared circle and the relative circles of Earth and Moon constructed from the 3, 4, and 5 triangles. The diameter of the outermost circle is 17, and it shares the same center as the square. The diameter of the circle (Earth) inscribed in the square is 11. The squared circle has a circumference, if $\pi = 22 \div 7$, of 44, which is also the perimeter of the square.

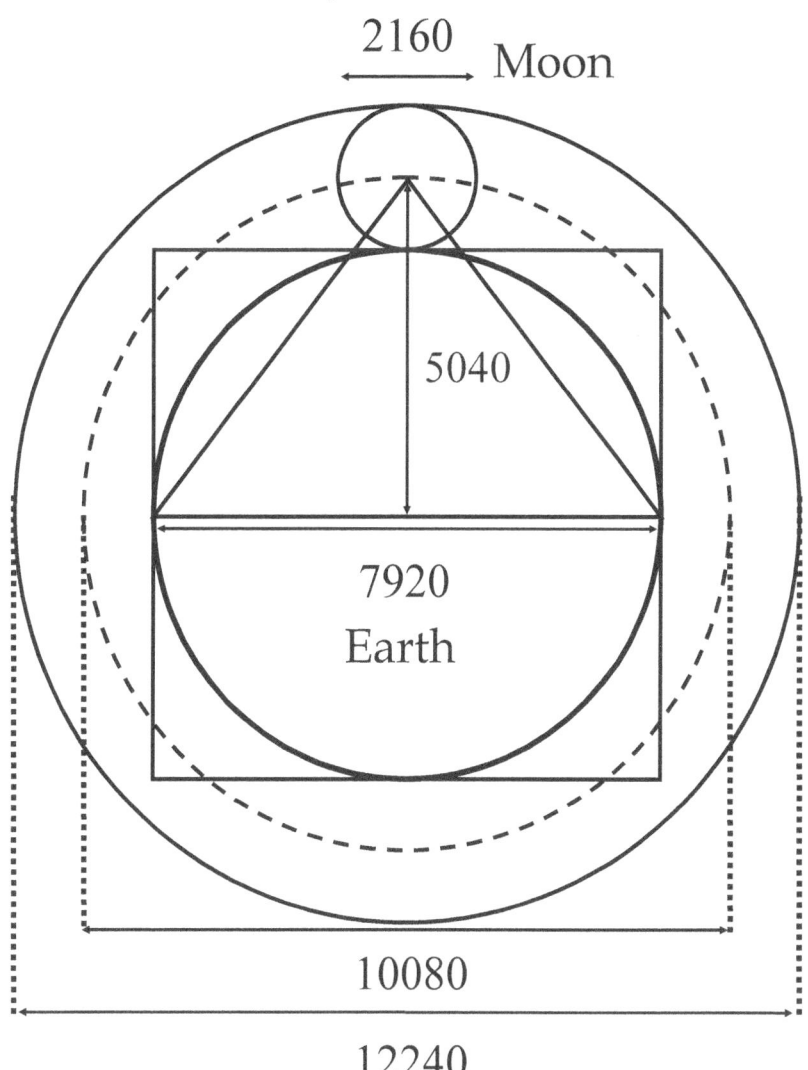

Fig 65. The Celestial City described by John Michell.

John Michell argues that the canonical numbers he discovered in the spheres of Earth and Moon describe the Celestial City, which he expresses in miles. The circumference of the squared circle in dashed lines is 31680 miles, the same value as the perimeter of the square containing the Earth. The standard gematria value of *Kurios Iesous Christos* ("Lord Jesus-Christ," Κυριος Ιησους Χριστος) is 3168.

THE NEW JERUSALEM DIAGRAM

This universal design is a numerical and geometric blueprint of Genesis 1.1. When we double the scaled-down measurement of the first diagram, we can see a numerical pattern: 22 as the diameter of the Earth and six as the diameter of the Moon. The squared circle in dashed lines has a diameter of 28, and its circumference is 88, the same value as the perimeter of the square. There are 8 points of intersection between the square and the squared circle.

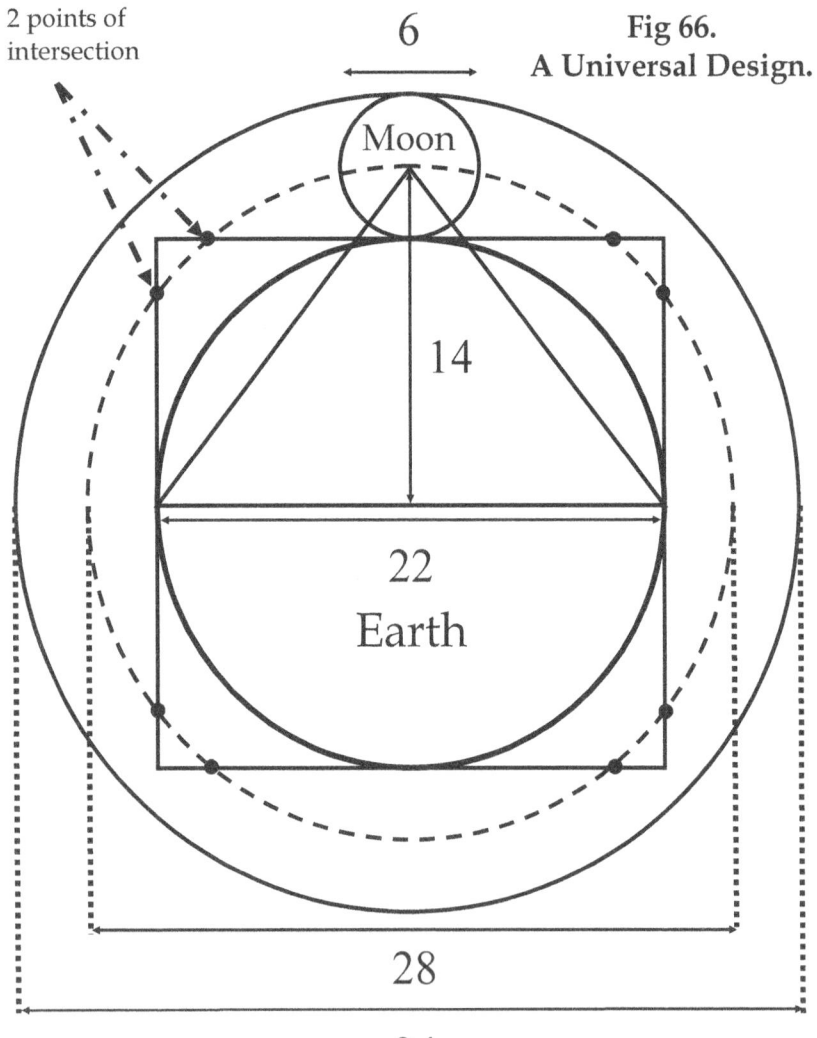

Fig 66. A Universal Design.

- Kabbalistic teachings suggest that 22, the number of Hebrew letters that supposedly "heaven and earth made," is not just a numerical value but a divine inspiration. Elohim intentionally designed these letters to convey the essence of creation, a fact that fills us with awe and reverence for the divine inspiration behind this universal design.
- 28 is the number of letters in the first verse of Genesis.
- The approximative value of Pi (π), as the division of 22 by 7, is encoded in the first verse through the science of gematria. The sum of gematria values of the first letter in each word is 22 (average per first letter is $22 \div 7 = 3.14+$).

בְּרֵאשִׁית, בָּרָא אֱלֹהִים, אֵת הַשָּׁמַיִם, וְאֵת הָאָרֶץ

ב ב א ה ו ה
2 2 1 1 5 6 5
22

- The number of letters in the first word of Genesis *Bereisheit* ("In the beginning," "In Principle," "In Wisdom," or "At First," בראשית) is 6. It is not just a numerical fact but a perfect number as the sum of its factors is 6; $1 + 2 + 3 = 6$. The design incorporates two perfect numbers, including 6, which fills us with admiration for the perfection embedded in this universal design.

The building of the complete pattern continues by drawing 12 circles with a diameter of 6 units. The squared circle (dashed line) with a diameter of 28 contains the centers of these 12 circles, which touch the inner circle with a diameter of 22. The Great Architect situated four of these circles according to the points where the square is tangent to the inner circle and placed the other eight circles according to the 8 points of intersection between the square and the squared circle.

THE NEW JERUSALEM DIAGRAM

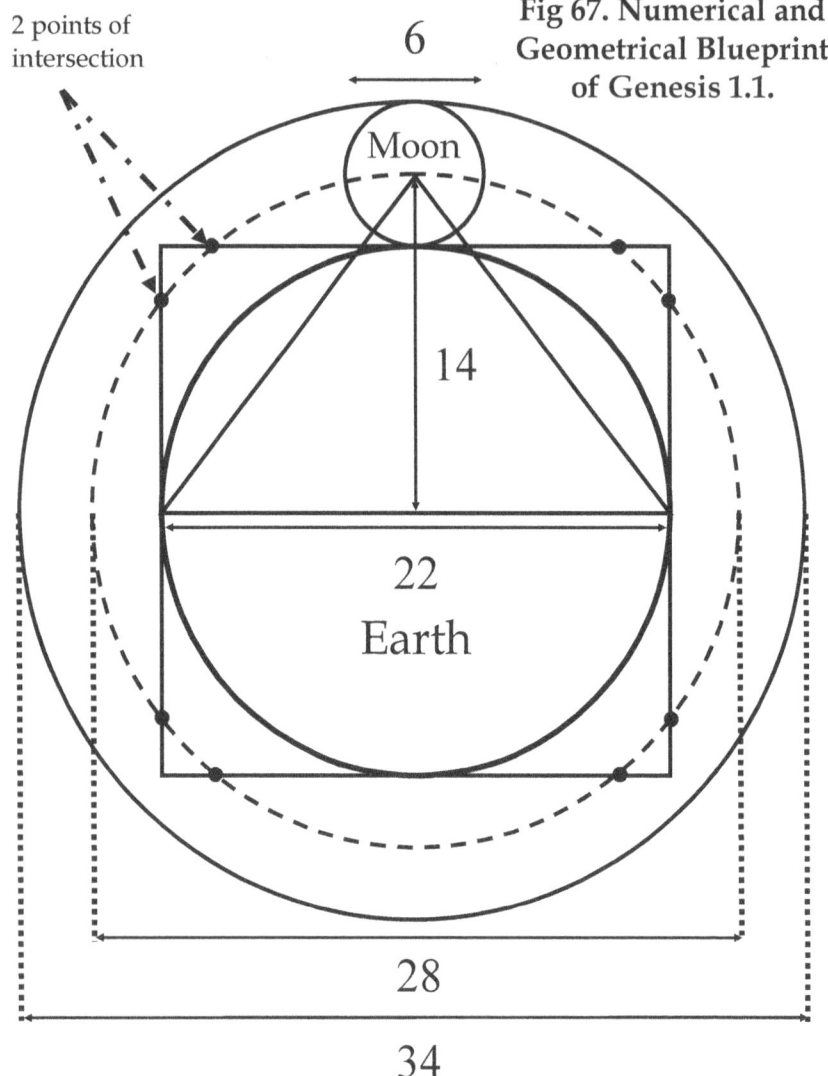

Fig 67. Numerical and Geometrical Blueprint of Genesis 1.1.

- 28 is the second perfect number as the sum of its factors is 28; 1 + 2 + 4 + 7 + 14 = 28. The design incorporates two perfect numbers, including 6. In Hebrew, the standard gematria of the first verse of Genesis totals 2701, which signifies 28 as 27 plus 01 equals 28.
- The standard gematria value of *Belev* ("In the Heart," בלב) is 34 — the same value as *Koach* ("Force," כוח).

THE NEW JERUSALEM DIAGRAM

- This geometric design could be a blueprint of the ether, God's or Goddess' Particle.
- This construction squares the circle, the union of spirit and matter, the bridge between Heaven and Earth.
- It divides the squared circle (dashed) into 28 sectors, which refers us back to the 28 Hebrew letters of the first verse of Genesis as a numerical blueprint.
- It reflects the ratio 22:7, which approximates PI (π) 3.14+.
- It reflects the Golden Ratio PHI (φ) 1.618034+; The ratio of the hypotenuse of the Great Pyramid to its half base is the golden ratio.
- Finally, it reflects the ratio of 22:6, which is also the exact accurate ratio between the diameter of the Earth and the Moon.

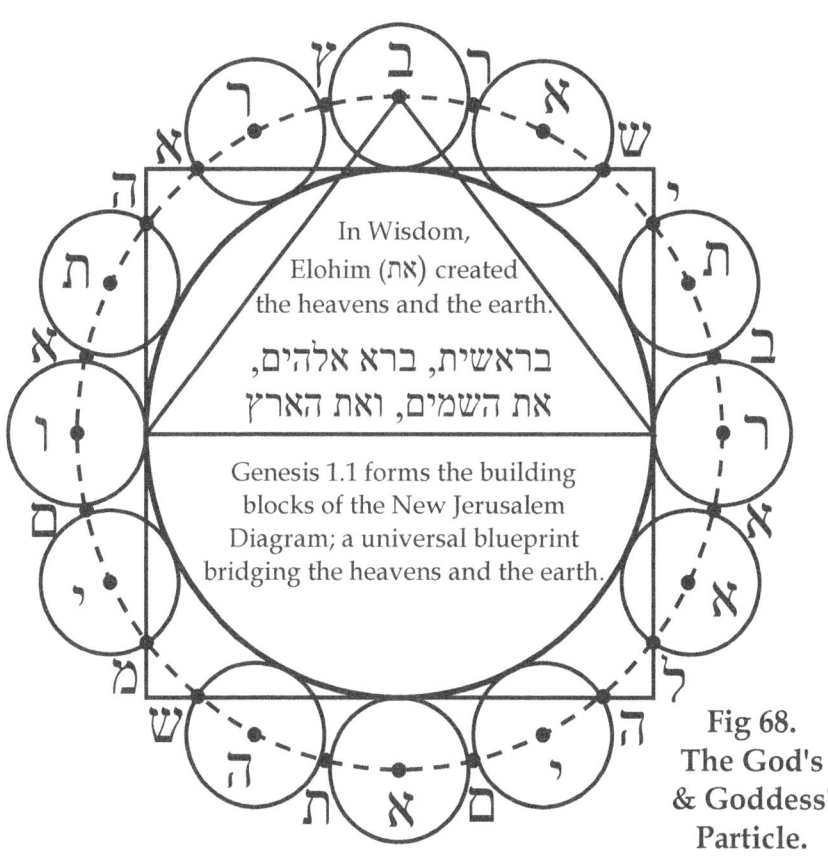

Fig 68. The God's & Goddess' Particle.

ST. MARY'S CHAPEL OF GLASTONBURY ABBEY

A further investigation into John's Michell research into the original proportions of the first church built by Joseph of Arimathea, his missionaries, and possibly Jesus himself on the grounds of what we call today "Glastonbury Abbey" is undertaken and presented in this chapter. Astonishingly, after studying and more profound research into the original proportions presented by John Michell in his book "New Light on the Ancient Mystery of Glastonbury," it concluded that the Science of Gematria is the key and that the first church was laid out and made with wisdom and knowledge. It seems that the builders knew how to apply the coding of these sacred numbers in the foundation of the first church by sacred geometry at the root of the core of Elohim's Creation. The design follows the same principle in Elohim's eye: creating the heavens and the earth in Genesis 1.1. Their Creation was made "In Wisdom". Gematria will ultimately lead the seeker of the Grail to the precise location of Joseph of Arimathea's grave, which constitutes another essential element discussed herein. However, Historians identified a specific site south of Mary's Chapel at Glastonbury Abbey in the 14th century as the location of Joseph's grave. While we might not dispute any previous discoveries, the research in this chapter invites readers to reconsider the location of Joseph's grave in light of new insights derived from gematria and sacred geometry, which may illuminate a highly probable site for Joseph's final resting place.

After John Michell, we can examine a site or building using multiple geometry schemes. We can analyze Saint Mary's Chapel through the Seal of Solomon, a hexagon, or the Seal of Melchizedek, an octagon (Fig 67). Thus, the first number involved in the geometric foundations of the chapel is 6, the first perfect number, referring to the first six letters of Genesis *Bereisheit* ("At first," or "In Wisdom," בראשלת).

ST. MARY'S CHAPEL OF GLASTONBURY ABBEY

8 represents resurrection and regeneration, a new beginning, meaning a new order or creation. The two figures below show a hexagon and an octagon with sides of equal length, both containing the rectangular chapel.

Fig 69. The hexagonal/octagonal layout of the rectangular Mary's Chapel of Glastonbury Abbey.

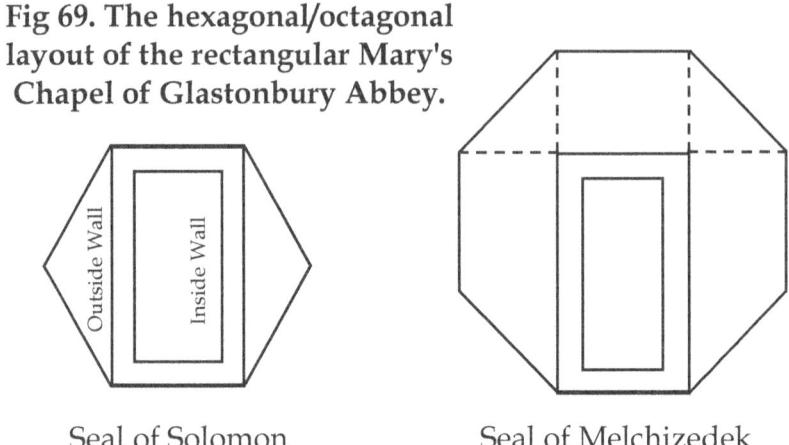

Seal of Solomon   Seal of Melchizedek

According to John Michell, the width of the chapel is a microcosm of the Heavenly City, the New Jerusalem outlined by the Earth and Moon. The Earth has a radius of 3960 miles, and the builders wisely defined the width of the chapel as 39.6 feet, which is one-hundredth of Earth's dimensions in miles, with 1 mile equivalent to 1 foot. The length of the chapel is the product of 39.6 feet by the square root of 3, a theoretical value of 68.6 feet. The rectangle of the chapel is a natural construction of sacred geometry, a ratio of $1:\sqrt{3}$.

Bligh Bond discussed the analysis of the chapel's hexagonal proportions. A circle with a diameter of 79.2 feet inscribes the hexagon. Geometric construction forms a *Vesica Piscis* in the chapel using two other circles of the same

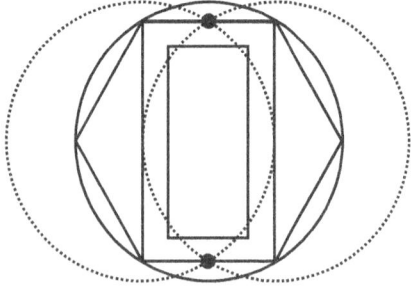

Fig 70. Geometric discussion by Bligh Bond.

ST. MARY'S CHAPEL OF GLASTONBURY ABBEY

With this geometrical interpretation, one could only locate St Joseph's circular wattle church at the center of the rectangle. An inner circle represents it within the rectangular chapel, whose diameter is half the diameter of the circle that contains the rectangle. It is a microcosm of the New Jerusalem Plan.

The diameter of the inner circle is 39.6 feet, and the outer circle is 79.2 feet. The perimeter of the square containing the outer circle is 316.8 feet. 3168 is the Greek standard gematria value of *Kyrios Iēsous Christos* ("Lord Jesus-Christ," Κύριος Ἰησοῦς Χριστός).

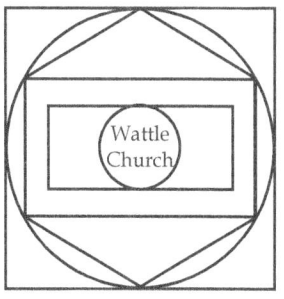

Fig 71. Wattle Church Circle in Elohim's Particle.

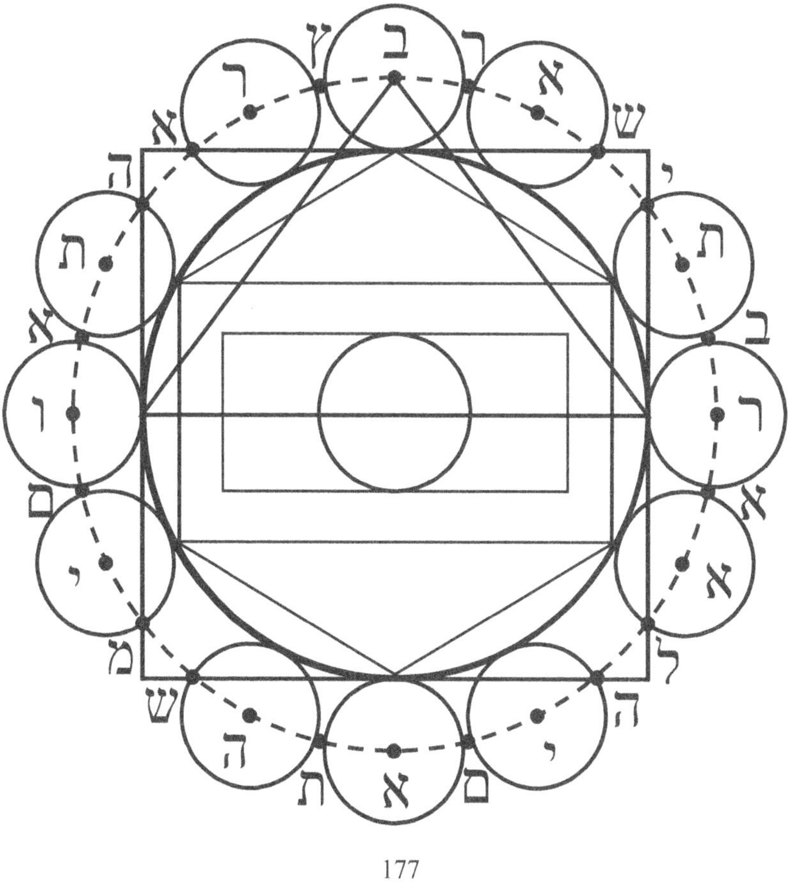

ST. MARY'S CHAPEL OF GLASTONBURY ABBEY

The rectangular chapel overlaid upon the New Jerusalem Diagram shows the possible layout of the Wattle Hut and the cells of Joseph's followers. The squared circle (dashed line) has a circumference of 316.8 ft, the same value as the perimeter of the square. Each cell would correspond to one of the 12 circles with a diameter of 21.6 feet, considering that the circle's diameter in the Macrocosm for the Heavenly City is the diameter of the Moon of 2160 miles.

By examining the gematria of the Hebrew letters from the first verse of Genesis in each cell, we can highlight important information about the New Jerusalem and its purpose.

Each cell is a circle with a center associated with a Hebrew letter. At the top of the diagram (Fig 71), reading clockwise, the first triplet is *Rava* ("Great," "Master," and "Leader," רבא), and it derives from the compound *Rav Ava* (רב אבא). The Aramaic word *Ava* (אבא) means "a father". The standard gematria of *Rava* (רבא) is 203, the same value as Bara ("created," ברא), the second word of the first verse of Genesis. The ordinal gematria of *Rava* (רבא) is 23, the ninth prime number. 23 is also said to be one of the numbers that, when we add up its digits, results in the prime number 5, which is the reduced gematria of *Rava* (רבא). The reverse standard gematria of *Rava* (רבא) is 703, the Triangular Number 37 (T37) representing the inner spiritual core and fitting in the exact center of the Triangular Number 73 (T73) of Genesis 1.1 with a total counter of 2701 (Fig 25). The standard gematria of *Et hartz* ("and the earth," את הארץ) is also 703, the sum of the 6th and 7th words of Genesis 1.1. The first triplet also forms another interesting Hebrew word, *Be-er* (באר), which means "to explain" from a teacher or master. This word appears in the first chapter of Deuteronomy, verse 5. Would it refer to the Master/Teacher Lord Jesus Christ encoded in the first verse of Genesis?

ST. MARY'S CHAPEL OF GLASTONBURY ABBEY

On this side of the Jordan, in the land of Moab, began Moses to explain law, saying:

בעבר הירדן, בארץ מואב, הואיל משה, באר את -התורה
הזאת לאמר

We can interpret the second triplet as *Atar*, which means "place," "site," or even "room," (אתר). For example, we can tell *Atar kadosh* ("Sacred site," אתר קדוש) in this context. It is also *eter* (ether) the fifth element, a potential reference to the "Elohim's Particle" reflecting the Plan of the New Jerusalem. It could also evoke the idea of a non-physical or energetic field surrounding or permeating that site. As a verb, it translates to *itur* ("to localize," "to identify," "to locate," אתר) as well as ("to confine," "to delimit," and "to circumscribe") in geometric terms. *Itur* (איתור) refers to localizing, identifying, or locating a position. The standard gematria value of the second triplet *Atar* (אתר) is 601, the same value as the Hebrew word *Ashsh* ("to be powerful, strong, to make strong, firm, to establish," אשש). Its derivatives include *Ish* (איש), a form of *Eish* ("Fire," אש) or "to glow, to burn," strengthening Elohim's fiery nature from the "center of gravity," *Yod* (י) to the first circular ring (Torah) in the "Rings of *Yod*" (Fig 37). The ordinal gematria of the second triplet *Atar* (אתר) is 43, the 14th prime number and the smallest number with a rare mathematical property: 43 = 4 × prime(4) + 3 × prime(3) = 4 × 7 + 3 × 5. Interestingly, the only other number possessing this unique property is 127, which represents the number of unique word combinations we can create from the seven words of the first verse of Genesis: $2^7 - 1 = 127$.

At the bottom of the diagram (Fig 71), reading clockwise, we can interpret the third triplet as *Yaeh* ("to be becoming," יאה), reminding every man or woman to do their alchemical inner work to become the bridge between the heavens and the earth.

ST. MARY'S CHAPEL OF GLASTONBURY ABBEY

However, our Christic Blueprint is already within. To unearth and discover it, one must possess the intent, belief, and will to do so through righteousness, as every man and woman aspires to become the best version of themselves, Yahweh's blueprint (YHWVH, *Yehoshua*, Christ's Hebrew name, יהשוה).

The standard gematria of the third triplet *Yaeh* ("to be becoming," יאה) is 16, the same value as the ordinal gematria. As we remember, the two Hebrew letters, *Yod* (י) with a value of 10 and *Vav* (ו) with a value of 6, indicate the number 16. *Yod* (י) is a dot, looking like a flame that soars ever higher, representing Elohim's essential power: the One Who is indivisible. The "Rings of Yod" center houses the dot. *Vav* (ו) signifies that the Torah descends from heaven to earth in its inherent hook or chute design. *Yod* (י) and *Vav* (ו) symbolize two hearts joining together as one in love.

Fig 72. Love 16 (וי).

The full standard gematria of the third triplet (יאה) is 137.

The number 137, the 33rd prime number, beginning with 13, gematria value for for *Ekhad* ("One," אחד) and *Ahavah* ("Love," אהבה) corresponds to the standard value of the word *Kabbalah* ("Receiving," קבלה).

The last and fourth triplet is the Hebrew root *Tav Yod Vav* (תיו) which is the full form of *Tav* (ת). The final letter in the Hebrew Alphabet serves as a mark, a seal, or a signature—essentially, something that completes or affirms the whole. It symbolizes a conclusion, the finality of a process, or the achievement of a goal. The last triplet *Tav Yod Vav* (תיו), therefore, "marks" the completion of the letters of "Elohim's Word" or "Covenant," and at the same time represents the "Whole of the Covenant" or "the Mark of the Covenant." *Tav* (ת) literary means a "mark, sign, omen, or seal." In its Paleo-Hebrew form, it looks like a cross.

י א ה
יוד אלף הא
20   111   6
137

It is the symbol of truth, perfection, and completion. It also represents *Tikkun* ("restoration," repair," "amendment," תיקון), and in the context of *Tikkun olam* ("repairing the world," "making the world a better place," תיקון עולם). We accept the Covenant ((Torah תורה beginning with *Tav* (ת)) as our sign and seal that Elohim is with us.

One possible combination of the root *Tav Yod Vav* (תיו) can be associated with words like *Tivuch* (תיווך), meaning "mediation" or "intercession," which involves the concept of a bridge, an intermediary or the act of connecting two things.

The standard gematria of the fourth triplet is 416, the same value as the standard gematria of *Iaréd* ("Jared," "to descend," Ἰάρετ) in Greek, a sixth-generation descendant of Adam and Eve.

Ἰ ά ρ ε τ
10 1 100 5 300
416

His etymology derives from the Hebrew root *Yod Reish Daleth* (ירד), which forms words relating to descending. In the book of Revelations, John of Patmos depicts the New Jerusalem descending to reunite heaven and earth. Another possible interpretation explains that it derives from the Hebrew root *Reish Dalet Heh* (רדה), which forms words related to ruling. It also means "Rose," possibly referring to the Virgin Mary, since the Wattle Church dedicated itself to Jesus' Mother.

The sum of standard gematria values of the four triplets *Rava* (רבא), *Atar* (אתר), *Yaeh* (יאה), and *Tav* (תיו) is 1236.

רבא אתר יאה תיו
203   601   016   416
1236

"A great place (location) to be becoming (*Tav* תיו)"

Astonishingly, the gematria value of the meaning of the name *Immanuel* in Greek, *Meth' imón Theós* ("God with us," Μεθ' ἡμῶν Θεός), adds up to 1236, which is twice the golden proportion 618 (2 × 618 = 1236).

Matthew said, "The virgin will conceive and give birth to a son, and they will call him Immanuel" (which means "God with us") (Matthew 1:23).

Μεθ' ἡμῶν Θεός
54   898   284
1236

The ordinal gematria is 127, a numerical signature of Genesis 1.1, and the reduced gematria is 66. The 66th prime number is 317, the standard gematria value of *Vayikrah* ("And he called," ויקרא), the third book of the Torah, Leviticus. It is also the gematria value of *Parzel* ("Iron," פרזל).

ST. MARY'S CHAPEL OF GLASTONBURY ABBEY

"Therefore the Lord Himself shall give you a sign: the virgin will be with child and will give birth to a son, and will call him Immanuel." (Isaiah 7:14).

In Hebrew, the standard gematria value of *Immanuel* (עמנואל) equals 197. The centroid of the Triangular Number 73 (Genesis 1.1) is at 1201, the 197th prime number. 197 is the 45th prime number referring to *Adam* (אדם, gematria value of 45).

Position 1201 is the center of gravity of *Metzuy Roshon* ("Primary Being," מצוי ראשון), who spoke with *Chokmah* (Wisdom," חכמה). *B'tzelem Metzuy Roshon* ("in the Image of a Primary Being," בצים מצוי ראשון), *Adam* (אדם) was made and was the intermediary between Them and the entire creation. Here is the last *Adam*, *Immanuel*, as a sign and seal of Elohim's Covenant.

Jesus is the branch that would grow out of the root of David. Isaiah calls him *Shoresh meretz tizyah* ("A Root out of dry ground," שרש מרץ ציה) of standard gematria value of 1236.

$$\begin{array}{ccc} \text{שרש} & \text{מארץ} & \text{ציה} \\ 800 & 331 & 105 \\ & 1236 & \end{array}$$

66 is the standard gematria value of Ben David ("The son of David," בן דוד), the reduced value of *Meth' imón Theós* ("God with us," Μεθ' ἡμῶν Θεός), the meaning of *Immanuel*.

Peter mentions Jesus, at His return, as "The Chief Shepherd" in I Peter 5:4. In Greek, this translates to *Archipoímenos* (Ἀρχιποίμενος) and has a standard gematria value of 1236. And when the Chief Shepherd appears, you will receive the crown of glory that will never fade away. (I Peter 5:4)

ST. MARY'S CHAPEL OF GLASTONBURY ABBEY

Thus, the number 1236 is an essential numerical blueprint within the New Jerusalem Diagram, encoded in the first verse of Genesis, the four triplets corresponding to the 12 cells of Joseph's followers. This number bears the name of Immanuel, Jesus, as a promised ruler, a sign and seal of Elohim's Covenant. The original foundations of the Wattle Church and the 12 cells held important information, such that the science of gematria is the only way to decipher lost and forgotten wisdom and knowledge for humanity.

The study of Mary's Chapel through the Seal of Solomon (hexagonal layout) shows enough remarkable gematria numbers underlying a great design about the first verse of Genesis, the names of Jesus-Christ, and amazingly mapping out the Heavenly New Jerusalem Master Plan by the Moon and Earth dimensions. The Great Architect applied those dimensions to the earth, using a ratio of 1:100, where 1 mile corresponded to 1 foot. As above, so below. The original ground of the Wattle Church and its 12 cells would have carried a wonderful message, a universal harmony representing the marriage between the heavens and the earth — a perfect model for preserving life for men and women living in society.

The study of Mary's Chapel through an octagonal architectural plan, the Seal of Melchizedek, will reveal much more than its hexagonal layout. These two geometry schemes are complementary, bringing essential information.

"(...) The width of the chapel being 39.6 ft, its theoretical length is 68.6 feet if its proportions are hexagonal, or 67.6 feet if they are octagonal. The slight projection of the chapel's corner towers accounts for the difference." John Michell, New light on the ancient mystery of Glastonbury, p 133.

ST. MARY'S CHAPEL OF GLASTONBURY ABBEY

In addition to the canonical numbers and cosmological proportions of the Heavenly New Jerusalem about sacred sites, particularly Stonehenge, one of the evidences for the reconstruction of the foundation pattern of St. Joseph's Church is the information on the dimensions of the Old Church given on the plaque attached to St. David's pillar, excavated and discovered by Frederick Bligh Bond in 1921 at the Abbey Ruins. John Michell expanded his work to reveal the appropriate measurements of the original building, using the whole numbers of 60 feet in length and 26 feet in width as essential pieces of the puzzle.

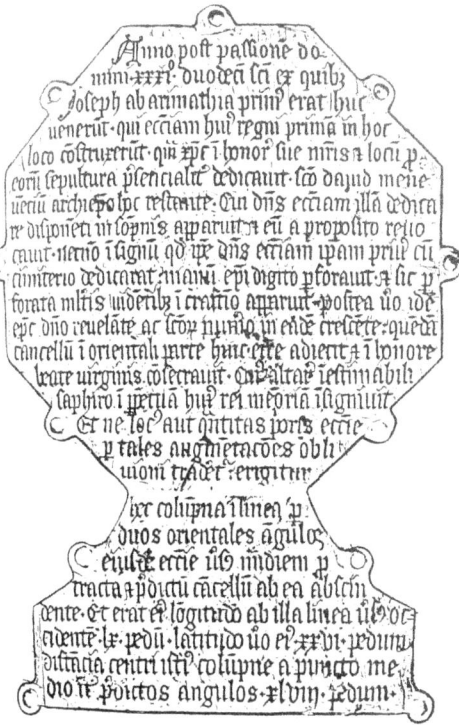

Fig 73.
Spelman's illustration of the plaque from Glastonbury Abbey describes the Old Church's history.

The translation by John Goodall is on the next page.

ST. MARY'S CHAPEL OF GLASTONBURY ABBEY

"The 31st year after the Passion of the Lord twelve saints, among whom Joseph of Arimathea was the first, came here. They built in this place that church, the first in this realm, which Christ in honour of his mother, and the place for their burial, presently dedicated. St David, archbishop of Menevia (i.e., Wales), rested here. To whom the Lord (when he was disposed to dedicate that church), appeared in sleep and recalled him from his purpose, also in token that the same Lord had first dedicated that church with the cemetery: He pierced the bishop's hand with his finger, and thus pierced it appeared in the sight of many on the morrow. Afterwards indeed the same bishop as the Lord revealed, and the number of the saints in the same grew: added a chancel to the eastern part of this church and consecrated it in honour of the Blessed Virgin. The altar whereof, of priceless sapphire, he marked the perpetual memory of these things. And lest the site or size of the earlier church should come to be forgotten because of such additions, he erected this column on a line drawn southwest through the two eastern angles of the same church, and cutting it off from the aforesaid chancel. And its length was 60 feet westward from that line, its breadth was truly 26 feet; the distance from the centre of this pillar from the midpoint between the aforesaid angles, 48 feet."

Frederick Bligh Blond uncovered the remains of St. David's pillar north of the Lady Chapel. It rested on a more ancient circular foundation (late 15th century) to replace something older that marked the eastern extremity of the Old Church.

Using the Seal of Melchizedek (octagonal scheme), it has been possible to locate the position of St. David's pillar, where the measurements indicated on the plaque are 48 feet from the center of St Mary's Chapel. Archaeologists discovered two pyramidal structures south of St. Mary's Chapel, both positioned significantly within the octagonal layout. These positions were not arbitrary, as the evidence will demonstrate.

ST. MARY'S CHAPEL OF GLASTONBURY ABBEY

According to John Michell, the graves of King Arthur and his Queen were found between these two pyramids.

"Bond also discovered the rectangular footings of another monumental structure outside the south porch of the chapel. This he believed to have been one of the two 'pyramids' between which or pillar crosses between which the tomb of King Arthur and his Queen was excavated in 1190." John Michell p 124, New light on the ancient mystery of Glastonbury.

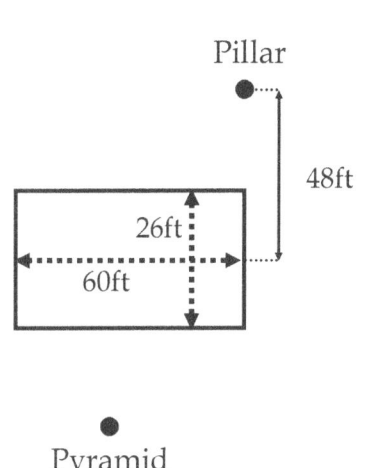

Fig 74. Bligh Bond's discoveries.

In the left diagram, the measurements in whole numbers are those stated on the plaque discovered by Bligh Bond. The positions of his discoveries, St. David's Pillar, and the "pyramid" are also illustrated.

The builders enclosed the Round Wattle Church of St. Joseph of Arimathea in a rectangular wooden building for better protection. The text on the plaque does not specify any of the inner measurements of the wooden church. Still, according to John Michell (p. 130), they would have been 54 by 24 feet by the masonic proportions (an acceptable ratio between outer and inner dimensions is 1:10).

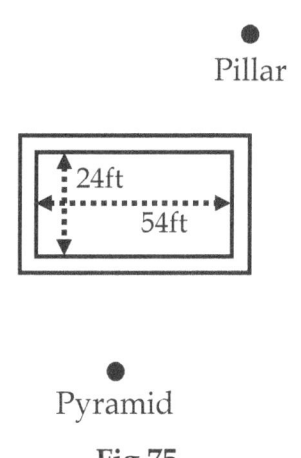

Fig 75. The outer enclosure.

ST. MARY'S CHAPEL OF GLASTONBURY ABBEY

The circular St. Joseph's Wattle Church, representing the heavens, would have stood on a square platform representing the earth. This design resembles the Chinese Ming T'ang Architecture. According to John Michell (p. 130, New light on the ancient mystery of Glastonbury), the ratio between the widths of the square and circle was 3:2. This is a construction of the *Vesicae Piscium* in the form of a Rose, as shown in the diagram below.

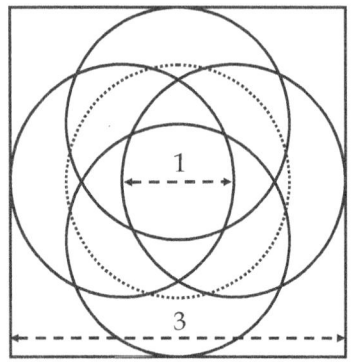

The intersection of two circles forms the *Vesicae Piscium* with the same width radius 1; a *Vesica Piscis* constructed vertically and horizontally. The square of width 3 contains these circles. The dashed circle is the same circle of radius 1 representing the heavens.

Fig 76.
The Vesicae Piscium.

Suppose the width of the square was 36.9 feet, one-hundredth of the radius of Earth, 3690 miles, with 1 mile associated with 1 foot. Then, the outer diameter of the Wattle Church Circle was 26.4 feet, a difference of 2.4 feet with 24 feet in the inner diameter. The width of 2.4 feet is one-tenth of 24 feet; this is coherent with the masonic proportions. Another square sharing a *Vesica Piscis*, a third of the square with a width of 13.2 feet, determined the western limit of the rectangle by a second circle of 26.4 feet touching the first circle. The depth of this result is that the new measurements presented by John Michell come naturally from the original blueprint of sacred geometry itself, creating the Rose Pattern with perfect and balanced proportions. The length of the rectangle was, therefore, 59.4 feet, with an interior length of 52.8 feet, a hundredth part of a mile; see diagram on the next page.

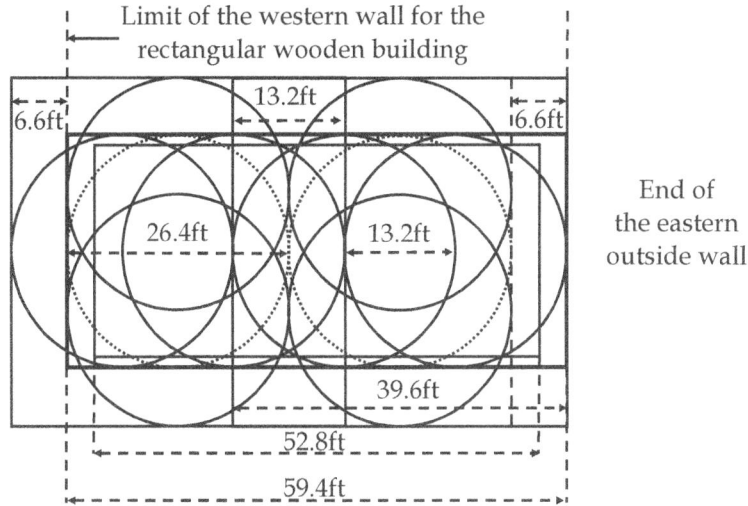

Fig 77. Detailed measurements of the original building.

The design leaves 6.6 feet on the eastern part of the outside wall, which represents one-fourth of the width of the church circle. The western part of the outside wall starts beyond the limit for the rectangular wooden building with a width of 6.6 feet, bringing the total to 66 feet. However, this measurement does not accommodate the full theoretical length of the outside rectangular chapel, which should be 67.6 feet within an octagonal scheme. An additional 1.6 feet is needed to complete the rectangular chapel. The architects expect the total width of the western outside wall to be 8.2 feet. They may have used the length of the *Vesica Piscis*, calculated as $13.2 \times \sqrt{3} = 22.86$ feet, as a reference for the church's inner dimensions. Adding the value of PI ($\pi = 3.14$) means they arrive at 26 feet for the outside measurements, as stated on the plaque. Surprisingly, the difference between 26.4 and 22.86 feet is about 3.537 feet, a ratio of 1:1.547 for one-tenth of the length of the *Vesica Piscis* (2.286 feet). A higher octave of this ratio is astonishingly 396 ($256 \times 1.547 = 396$, another reference to the earth's radius of 3960 miles). The difference between 26.4 and 2.286 is about 24 feet if taken as a whole number, potentially confirming John Michell's findings for the inner width of the church circle.

ST. MARY'S CHAPEL OF GLASTONBURY ABBEY

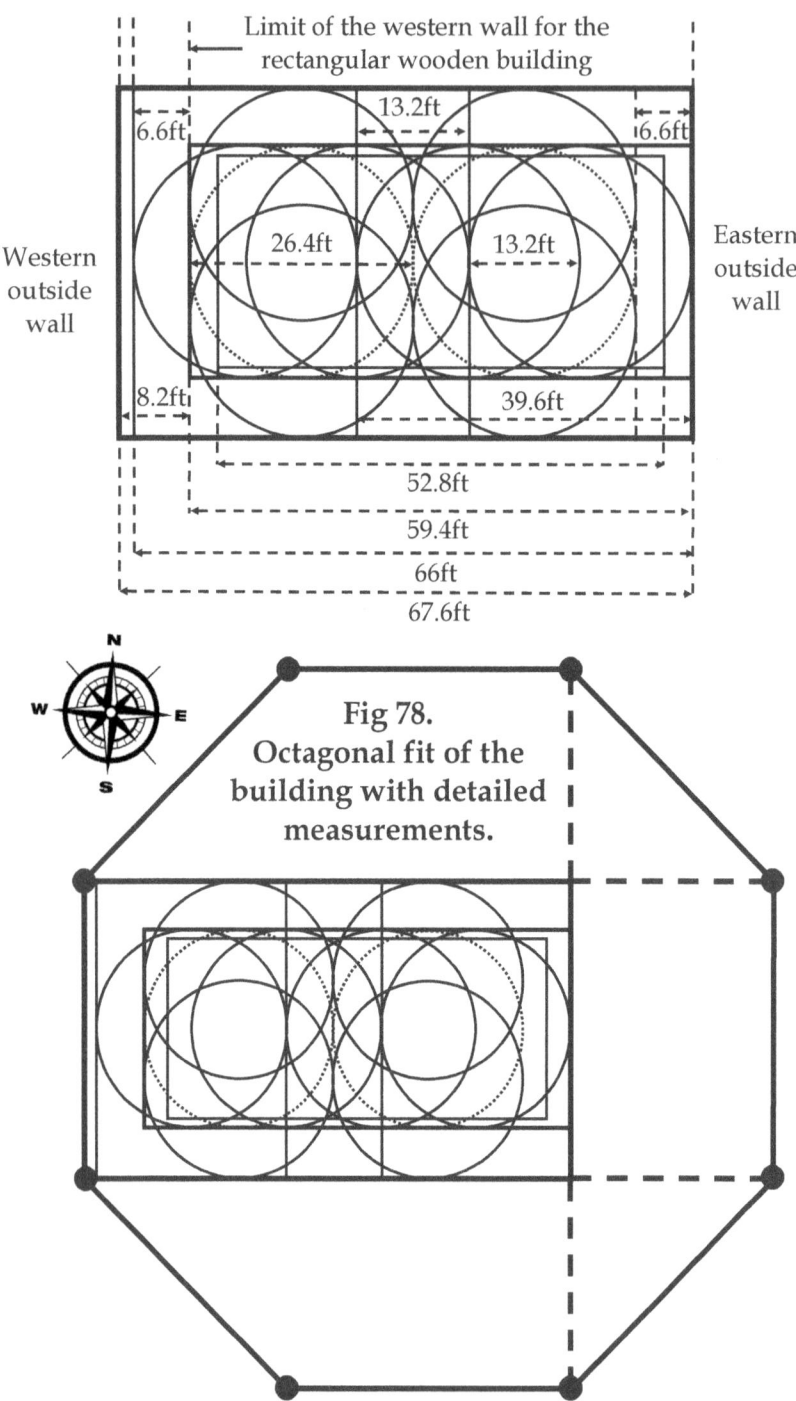

Fig 78. Octagonal fit of the building with detailed measurements.

ST. MARY'S CHAPEL OF GLASTONBURY ABBEY

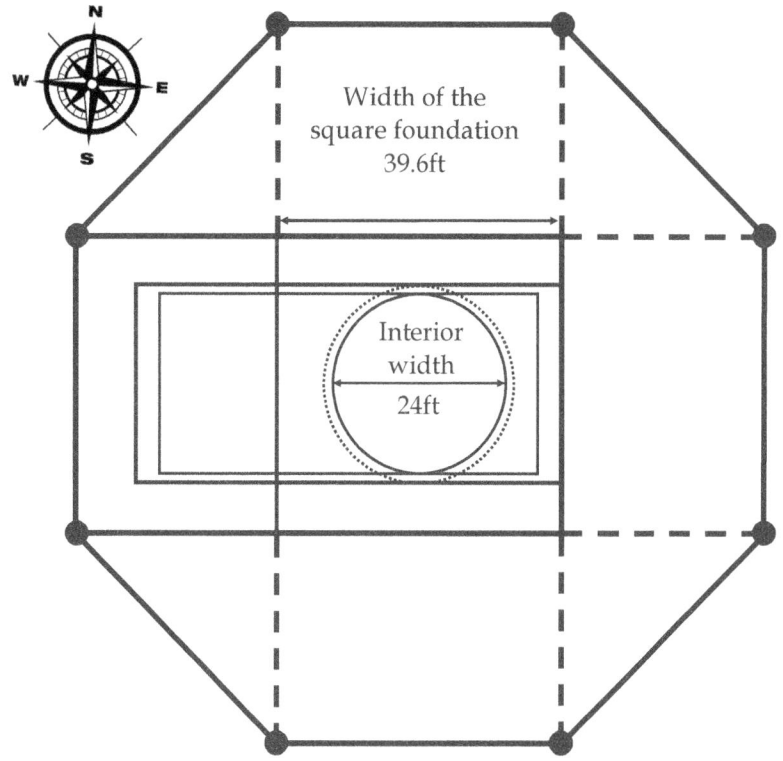

Fig 79. Square foundation.

The diagram above shows the perfect fit of the rectangular chapel within an octagonal scheme. The interior width of the Wattle Church is 24 feet, and its outside width (dashed circle) is 26.4 feet (representing the heavens). The builders constructed the church on a square foundation that measures 39.6 feet wide (representing the earth). The standard gematria value of *Al haarets* ("On the Earth", על הארץ) is 396. It is the same gematria value as *Merukim* ("Anointment," מרוקים) and *Hayshua* ("Salvation", הישועה). The Hebrew root Reish Vav Kuf ("Rock," רוק) gives rise to the term *Merukim*, while the verb *Raqak* ("to smooth, to polish, or to refine," רקק) actively conveys the process of transforming a rough "rock" into a polished "rock," a purification process. Bridging the heavens and the Earth comes naturally with the purification and salvation of the earth and man, which is part of a Master Plan in Elohim's Will.

ST. MARY'S CHAPEL OF GLASTONBURY ABBEY

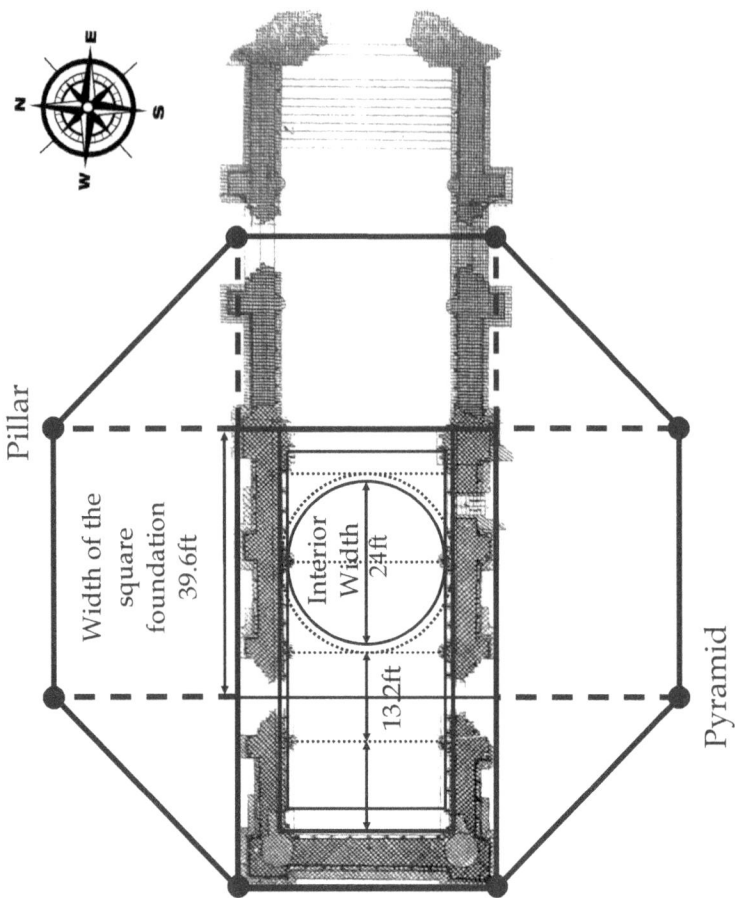

Fig 80. St. Mary's Chapel ground plan
laid over the Old Church diagram.

John Michell discussed this analysis (p 132, New Light on the Ancient Mystery of Glastonbury). This chapter expands on the geometry scheme and the ancient gematria measurements, unlocking lost and forgotten knowledge. The diagram above illustrates amazingly the ground plan of the St. Mary's Chapel laid over the diagram of the Old Church, showing the ingenuity of the 12th-century builders in recording the original proportions of the original geometry scheme in a detailed architecture.

ST. MARY'S CHAPEL OF GLASTONBURY ABBEY

As John Michell mentioned in his analysis:

"The interior walls of the chapel are divided into four bays by pillars at intervals of 13.2 feet (ten times the unit of 1.32 feet). Midway between the first pair of pillars from the east end is the central point of the circular wattle church and of the square on which it stood. The central pair of pillars marks the western limit of the circle. The western side of the original square platform coincides with the central line between the two doorways to the chapel." (p 132, New light on the ancient mystery of Glastonbury).

Here, there is a powerful unit of measurement to highlight in the geometry. This unit is 1.65 feet, the possible original Sumerian cubit. The builders likely used this length in the Temple of Solomon, and Noah's Ark. The diagram shows the measurements of the rectangular chapel (both inner and outer for the wooden building) through sacred geometry (Rose Pattern), allowing us to express these measurements in whole numbers. For example, the width of the *Vesica Piscis* is 13.2 feet, which is eight cubits, and the width of the Wattle Church Circle is 26.4 feet or 16 cubits.

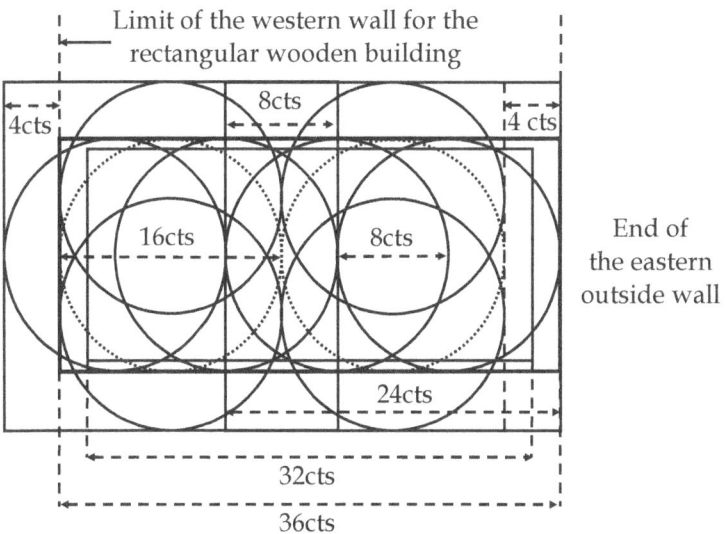

Fig 81. Building in Sumerian Cubit (SC).

ST. MARY'S CHAPEL OF GLASTONBURY ABBEY

The total length of the rectangular chapel with the outside western wall is 67.6 feet, and the theoretical length within the octagonal scheme is nearly 41 cubits. There is only a difference of 0.05 feet between 67.6 feet and 67.65 feet. It is an interesting observation, as it is possible that the builders of the original foundations were working in whole numbers with a cubit of 1.65 feet. The difference of 0.6 inches, approximately three-quarters of a finger width, is not a big deal on the scale of the overall architecture. So, the additional 1.6 feet to the width of 66 feet becomes the cubit itself 1.65 feet for a total length of the rectangular chapel of 67.65 feet. The interval of 8.2 feet becomes 8.25 feet, which is five cubits. We could base the entire geometric layout on this cubit elegantly, expressing all the intervals in whole numbers.

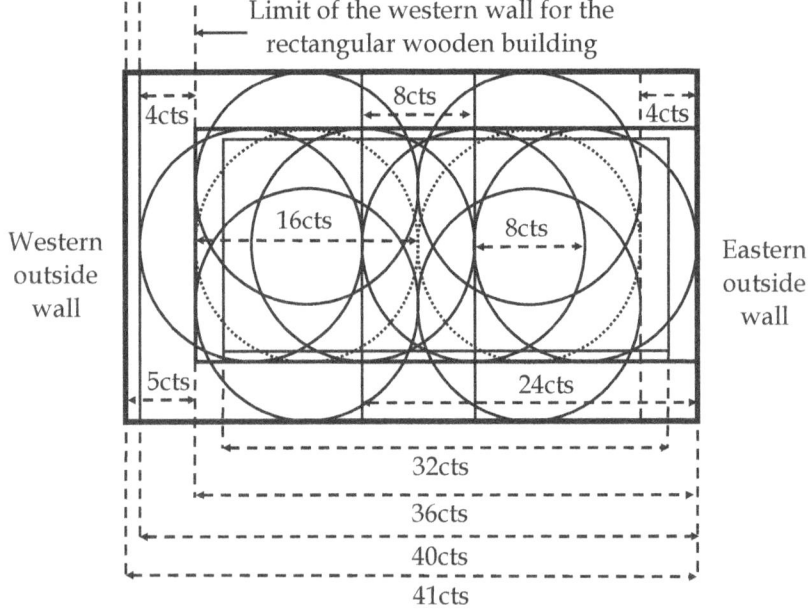

Fig 82. Detailed measures in Sumerian Cubit.

In Hebrew Gematria, 165, a hundred of the original cubit is the standard value of *Nekudah* ("Point," נחודה). Creation began as a "Point" that expanded into a perfect circle, alluding to the squaring circle process.

PI (π) is the irrational number, making this circle wholly and perfectly. The perfect circle represents the heavens, the container of spaces from which everything originates. St. Mary's Chapel's geometric foundation pattern encodes the creation story, with the Wattle Church Circle seen as the center. This pattern expands three times in a threefold manner (26.4 × 3 = 79.2 feet or 48 cubits, the equivalent of twice the width of the square foundation of the Earth (39.6 × 2 = 79.2). Afterward, it becomes a perfect circle, the squaring circle having the same perimeter value as the perimeter of the square containing the circle of diameter 79.2 feet, which is 316.8 feet. 3168 being the Greek gematria value of *Kýrios Iēsoûs Christós* ("Lord Jesus-Christ" Κυριος Ιησους Χριστος) (Fig 79).

All the more, the Hebrew gematria of *Mashiyach Yehushua Eleha* "Lord Jesus-Christ," (משיח יהושוע אלהא) is 792, the same value as the Hebrew word *Hayshua* ("Salvation", הישועה). Gematria gives us significant indications that the sacred geometry of the original proportions was laid out perfectly in alignment with the Designer's Will.

אלהא יהושוע משיח
37   397   358
792

The outside width of the Wattle Church Circle is 26.4 feet. Interestingly, the standard gematria of *Alitheias* ("of truth," αληθειας) is 264. It has the same value as *I parthénia* ("Virginity," η παρθένια) or *Themis* ("Order," Θέμις). *Themis* is Greek mythology's personification and goddess of divine law, will, and justice. 264 is also the standard gematria of *Seder* ("Order," סדר). So, the word "Order" in Hebrew and Greek refers to the number 264, reinforcing that Elohim crafted all creations with order and harmony from the beginning of time.

Let's bring in mind that *ot habrit* ("The sign of the covenant," אות הברית) and *l'vaniym* ("white," לבנים) have a standard gematria value of 132. White, bearing the number 132, identifies *YHVH Elohekhem* (יהוה אלהיכם), "Lord, Elohim of you" (Joshua 4:5)). The number 132 is also the value of the word *Kabal* (קבל) which means "to receive" and is the root of the word *Kabbalah* ("Receiving," קבלה). One-tenth of this value, 13.2 (8 cubits), is the width of the *Vesica Piscis* in the geometric blueprint of the rectangular chapel or the total width of its outside North and South walls in feet. The total width of the outside East and West walls is 14.85 feet (9 cubits). A hundred of this value is 1485, the gematria value of *Christos* ("Christ," Χρειστός). 528 is the triangular number 32, standard gematria of *Leb* ("Heart," לב). The standard gematria value of *Mafteak* ("Key," מפתח) is 528.

$$\begin{array}{cccc} \text{מ} & \text{פ} & \text{ת} & \text{ח} \\ 8 & 400 & 80 & 40 \end{array}$$
$$528$$

The prophet Isaiah mentioned the key. It undoubtedly identifies to "Lord Jesus-Christ" encoded in the story of creation, here presented through sacred geometry and gematria numbers, the original blueprint of the first wattle and daub church and its cells built by Joseph of Arimathea, his followers, and potentially Jesus Himself.

And the key of the house of David will I lay upon his shoulder; and he shall open, and none shall shut; and he shall shut, and none shall open. Isaiah 22:22

ונתתי מפתח בית-דוד, על-שכמו; ופתח ואין סגר, וסגר ואין פתח.

ST. MARY'S CHAPEL OF GLASTONBURY ABBEY

One-tenth of 528 is the interior length of the rectangular chapel, 52. 8 feet (32 cubits), a hundredth part of a mile. The outside length of the rectangle, with the wooden building included, is 59.4 feet (36 cubits). In Hebrew, 594 is the standard gematria value of *Yeshua ben Yosef* ("Yeshua son of Joseph," ישוע בן יוסף). It is the same gematria value of *Avan Israel* ("The Stone of Yisrael," אבן ישראל). These numbers are all part of the same message. The entire length of the rectangular chapel is 67.6 feet (41 cubits). 676 is a very favorite cabalistic number as 676 = 26 × 26, being the square of tetragrammaton *YHVH* or *Yahweh* (יהוה) 26.

In the hexagonal layout of the rectangular chapel discussed by Frederick Bligh Bond (Fig 69), the theoretical value of the length of the rectangle is 68.6 feet. The number 686 is one unit less than 685. 685 is the central spot, the position of the point between the two centers of gravity (center of gravity of the 37th triangle and center of gravity of the 73rd triangle, Fig 44). At position 685, the intersection of the 37th row and 73rd column, the Great Architect encodes the number 3368, the gematria value of Kýriou Iēsoûs Christós ("Lord Jesus-Christ" in Greek, Κύριου Ἰησοῦς Χριστός). Let's recall that the third layer of the first word of Genesis *Bereisheit* ("In the beginning," בראשית), in its full form in Hebrew, has a standard gematria value of 3368.

The sacred numbers involved for the measurements of the rectangular chapel in its possible original proportions, either in the hexagonal or octagonal scheme, hold some essential keys about the story of creation (Genesis, particularly the first verse) and astonishingly seem to refer to the Lord Jesus Christ, as the Great Architect. Gematria ingeniously and elegantly bridges words, numbers, and geometry together, divinely showing that great intelligence, order, and wisdom meticulously crafted all creation. Gematria irrefutably reveals a higher form of Intelligence and Wisdom as the designer of our Universe.

ST. MARY'S CHAPEL OF GLASTONBURY ABBEY

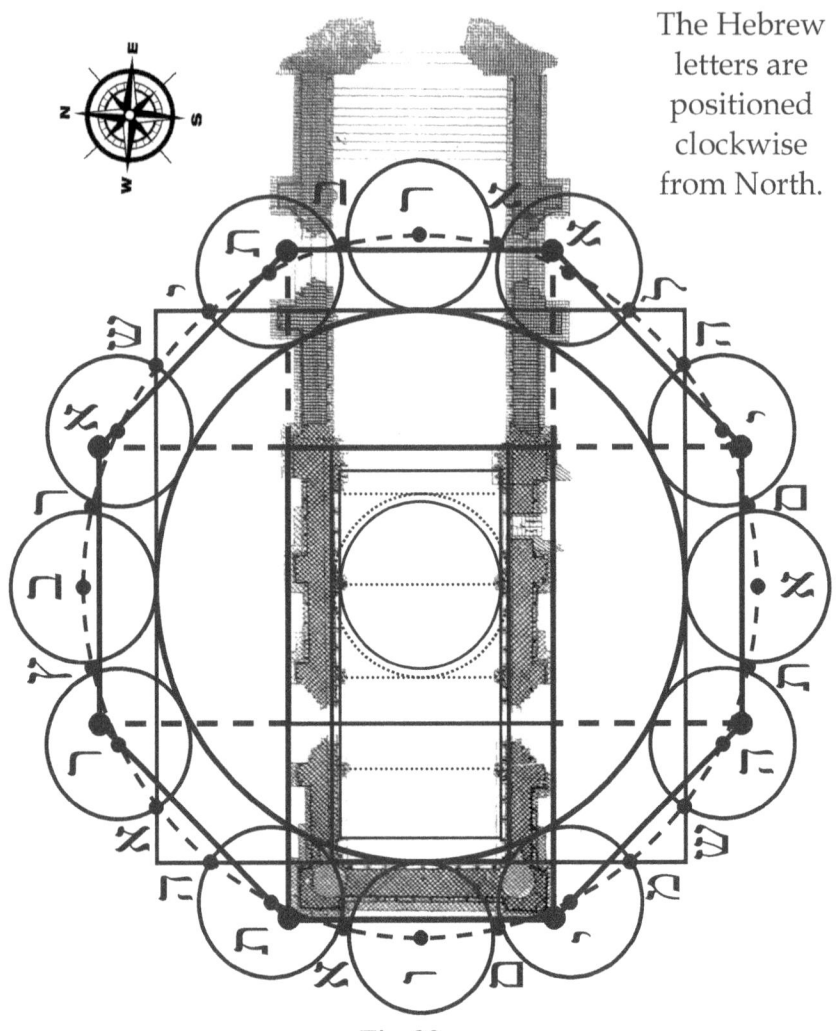

The Hebrew letters are positioned clockwise from North.

**Fig 83.
New Jerusalem Blueprint overlaid on St. Mary's Chapel.**

Above, the diagram shows the New Jerusalem blueprint encoded with the first verse of Genesis, overlaid on the ground plan of St. Mary's chapel. Joseph's followers built the 12 cells along the squaring circle, closely following the edges of the octagon. In this beautiful geometric layout, it became more likely "octagoning the circle." The perimeter of this circle is 316.8 feet (192 Sumerian cubits), the same value as the perimeter of the octagon.

ST. MARY'S CHAPEL OF GLASTONBURY ABBEY

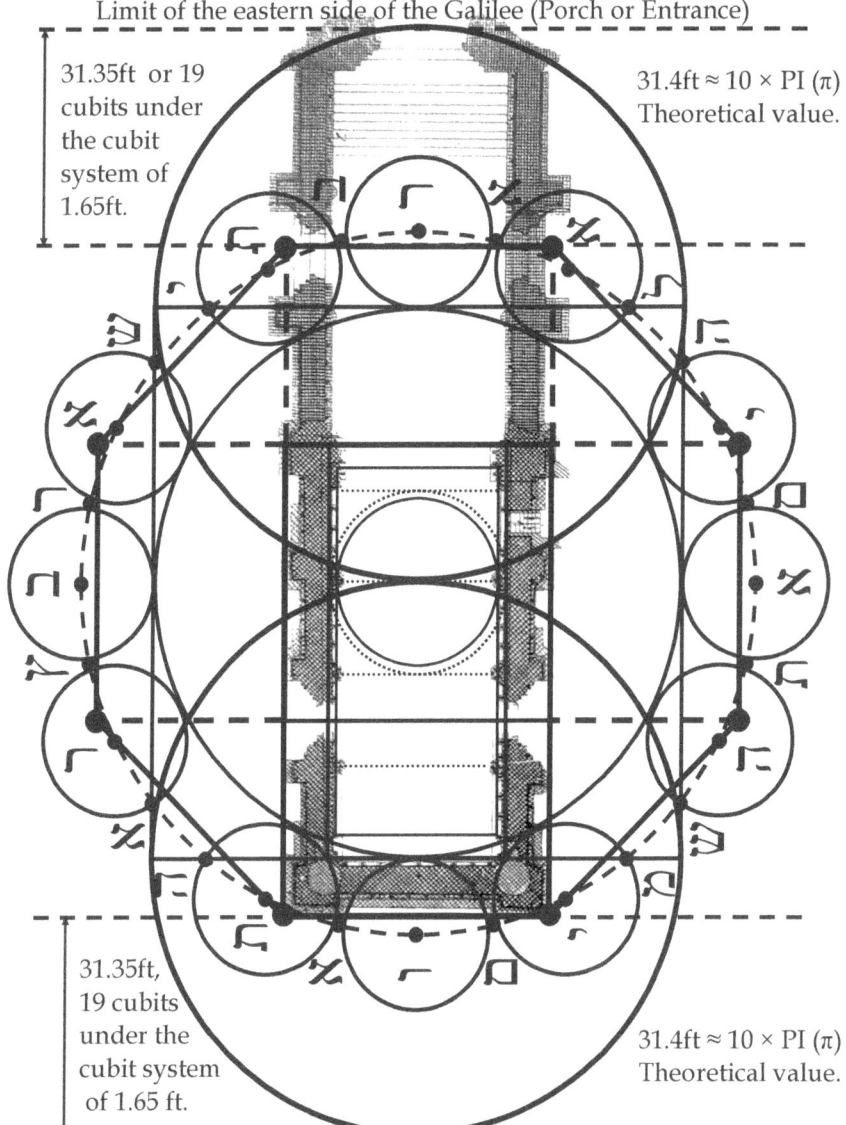

Fig 84. The limit of the eastern side of the Galilee.

Above, the diagram shows the limit of the eastern side of "the Galilee" at the Porch or Entrance by constructing the *Vesica Piscis* with two circles of diameter 79.2 feet. Notice how the geometry fits perfectly the edges of the walls. The length of 31.4 refers to ten times the value of PI (π).

ST. MARY'S CHAPEL OF GLASTONBURY ABBEY

Let's recall that PI (π) is associated with the Holy Name *Sha-dai* (ש-די), the contracted version of *Mi she'Amar Dai L'olamo* ("Whoever said 'enough is enough' for their Universe," מי שאמר די לעולמו). The infinite was constricted into the finite to make it possible for creation to exist. *Sha-dai* (ש-די) has a gematria value of 314, just like PI (π) starts at 3.14. It is interesting to highlight that this measurement related to Their Holy Name *Sha-dai* (ש-די) appears to be the edges of the ground of the Old Church, being the limiter to constrict what is infinite by its divine essence and make room for space and time into a finite vessel. It is, by nature, the story of creation, starting from a singularity "point" at the center of the Wattle Church Circle of diameter 26.4ft, which expanded into a circle of diameter 79.2ft to become a perfect circle of diameter 100.84ft (octagoning the circle). This circle has a perimeter of 316.8ft, 3168 bearing the name of "Lord Jesus Christ" in Greek Gematria.

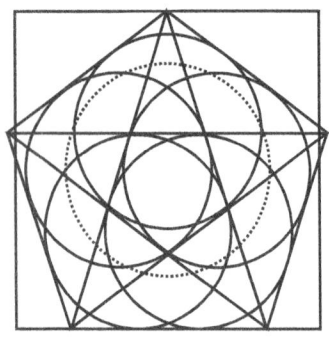

**Fig 85.
The Rose Pattern.**

A square drawn on the height of a pentagon reveals the five-pointed star, truly a Rose Pattern superimposed on the square foundation (platform) upon which the Wattle Church stood. Mathematically, it is possible to prove that the circle's diameter is about 24.5 feet, close to the interior width of the Wattle Church of 24 feet.

The side of the square is 39.6 feet, equal to the height of the pentagon. The circles that make the rose pattern have a diameter close to 24 feet, which is the interior width of the Wattle Church. They are tangent to the lines of the pentagon and the pentagram inside it.

The builders of the Wattle Church constructed its foundations on the pentagram, an essential symbol of Egyptian mysteries in ancient times, including in the school of Pythagoras.

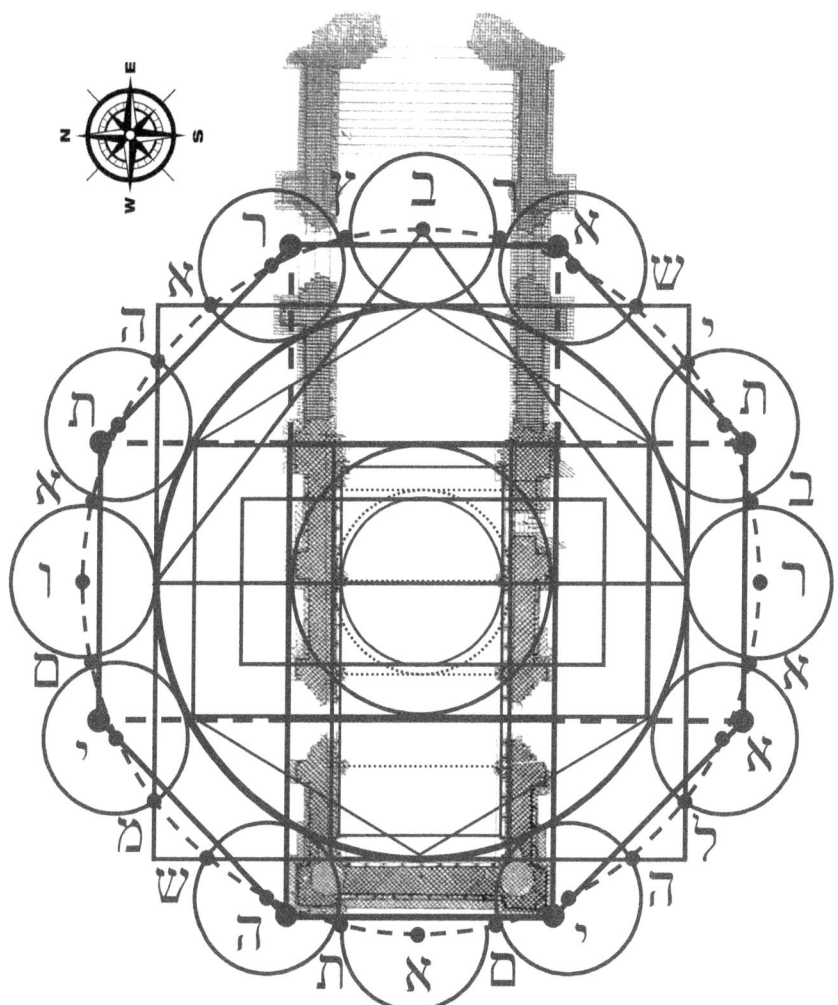

Fig 86. Hexagonal scheme of St. Mary's Chapel in the New Jerusalem Blueprint.

In the diagram above, Bligh Bond discusses the chapel's hexagonal scheme within the New Jerusalem Plan, which fits within Figure 82. The diagram illustrates how geometric construction produces the two geometry schemes: hexagonal and octagonal. The rectangular chapel in the hexagon is abstractly positioned perpendicularly to the vertical ground plan. The top of the Great Pyramid is visible here, pointing eastward toward Stonehenge.

ST. MARY'S CHAPEL OF GLASTONBURY ABBEY

2 Chronicles 3:3 mentions that they measured the Temple (Holy Place and Most Holy Place) according to the original cubit.

"Now these are the foundations which Solomon laid for the building of the house of Elohim. The length by cubits after the ancient measure was threescore cubits, and the breadth twenty cubits."

ואלה הוסד שלמה, לבנות את-בית האלהים: הארך אמות במדה הראשונה, אמות ששים, ורחב, אמות עשרים.

The original cubit measures 19.8 inches in length (1.65 feet). Solomon built the Temple with dimensions of 60 × 20 cubits and designed the perimeter as 160 cubits. We quickly multiply to get the number of inches: 160 × 19.8 = 3168 inches (264 feet), the gematria value of *Kyrios Iēsous Christos* ("Lord Jesus-Christ," Κὺριος Ἰησοῦς Χριστός). It is equivalent to ten times the diameter of the Wattle Church Circle in feet.

The ground plan of Solomon's Temple naturally emerges out of the ground plan of St. Mary's Chapel of Glastonbury Abbey within the New Jerusalem Diagram (Fig 86). For a width equal to 26.4 feet, the diameter of the Wattle Church Circle, three cubits correspond to 79.2 feet, the circle's diameter inscribed a square of perimeter of 316.8 feet. Five-fourths (5/4) of the actual proportions of the ground plan of St. Mary's Chapel gives the proportions of Solomon's Temple. Twenty cubits are equal to 33 feet, and sixty cubits are equal to 99 feet. Thirty-three feet is half of 66 feet, the width of the intersection of two rose patterns (Fig 76). The latter is at the root of the geometric layout of the original Wattle Church within the rectangular chapel without the addition of 1.6ft (or 1.65ft, which is one cubit in the Sumerian cubit system) in the octagonal scheme. It naturally shows the connection between the Middle East and the Western civilization through Joseph of Arimathea and Jesus.

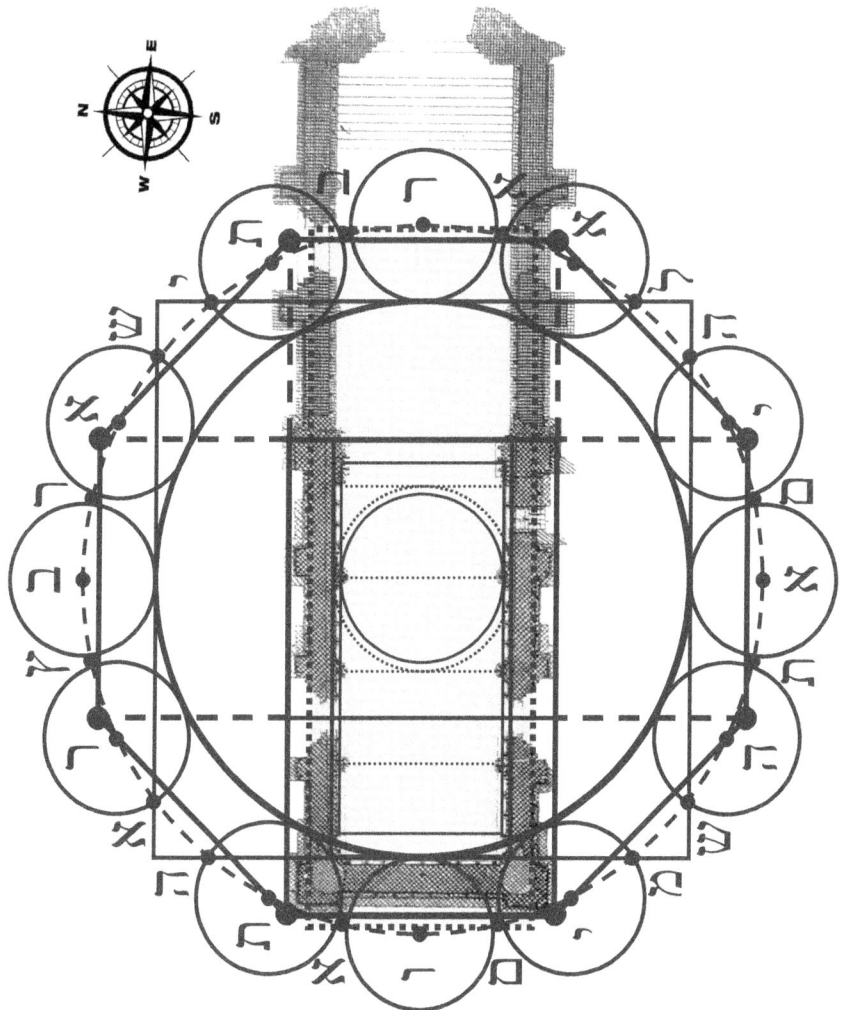

Fig 87. The ground plan of the Temple of Solomon within the New Jerusalem Blueprint.

Above, the diagram shows the ground plan of the Temple of Solomon (grey rectangle and dots for its edges) with the proportions stated in 2 Chronicles 3.3. The rectangular ground plan shares the same center as the Wattle Church Circle and is nearly tangent to the dashed line squaring (or octagonal) circle of diameter 100.84 feet. The difference between the rectangle's length and the circle's diameter is about 1.84 feet (11 inches on each side).

STONEHENGE, A PROTOTYPE OF THE NEW JERUSALEM

STONEHENGE, A PROTOTYPE OF THE NEW JERUSALEM

The diagram below showcases the meticulous plan and reconstruction of Stonehenge. Builders constructed Stonehenge, a potent sacred site and Earth's energy vortex, with remarkable precision at the convergence point of Ley lines. The outer circle, comprised of thirty pillars of Wiltshire sarsen stone, was carefully erected. The builders placed sixty bluestones from the Prescelly Mountains in southwest Wales within this circle. The outer cove, a testament to the builders' skill, consists of five detached trilithons or archways of sarsen stone. The inner cove, originally of nineteen bluestones, was also carefully crafted. The central stone, known as 'the Altar stone,' is a block of greenish, micaceous sandstone from a quarry near Milford, a testament to the builders' attention to detail.

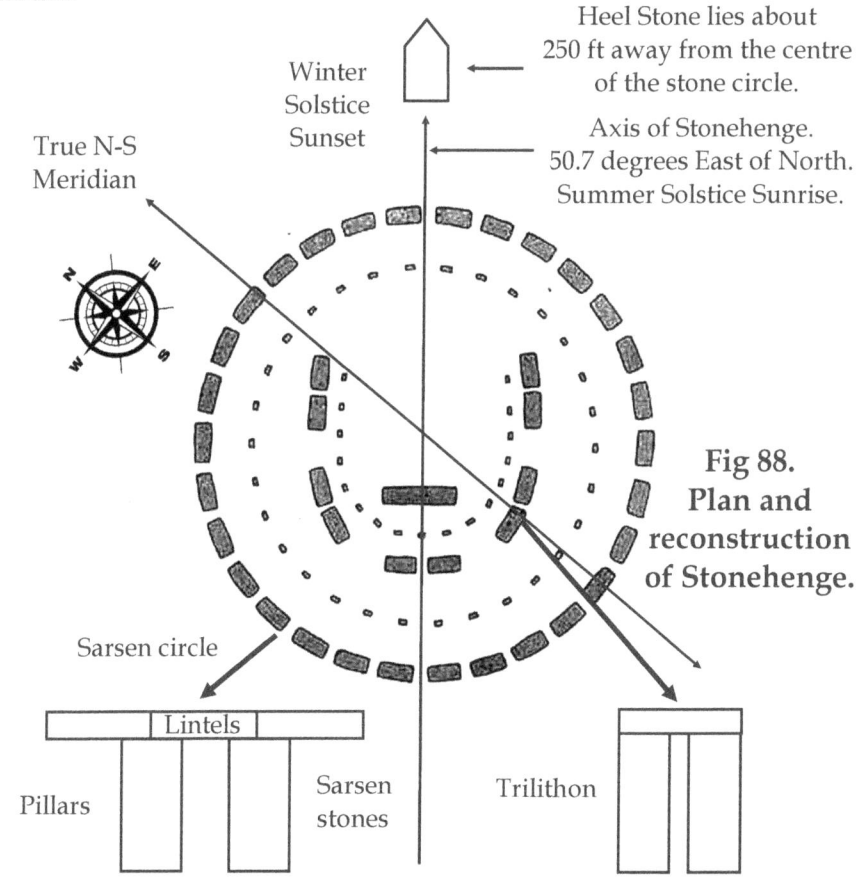

Fig 88. Plan and reconstruction of Stonehenge.

STONEHENGE, A PROTOTYPE OF THE NEW JERUSALEM

The dimensions are as follows:
- Within the inner cove, the remaining stones in the bluestone semi-circle have a diameter of 39.6 feet and stand on the circumference.
- The sixty bluestones stand reasonably on a circle with an outer circumference of 79.2 feet.
- The thirty upright stones (pillars) form the outer sarsen circle, and the builders place the lintels so that the gap between the two pillars spans one-third of three equal sections. The average gap between the pillars is 3.52 feet. 352 is the standard gematria value of *Mishiv* ("He returns," משיב) and *I hodos* ("The Way," η οδοσ). Three lintels atop two pillars give 10.56 feet. The calculation of the circumference of the outer sarsen circle, which has thirty pillars, results in 316.8 feet (a hundredth part of 6 miles) when we multiply 10.56 by 30, and it has a diameter of 100.84 feet. 3168 is the number of *Kýrios Iēsoûs Christós* ("Lord Jesus-Christ," Κύριος Ἰησοῦς Χριστός).

Stonehenge, a cosmic temple, profoundly expresses its essence through the symbol of the squared circle. The square, representing the earth, and the circle, symbolizing the heavens, harmoniously marry these elements in the temple's ground plan and architectural features.

Figure 89 shows the New Jerusalem, a significant spiritual concept superimposed on the Stonehenge Plan, revealing a striking geometric correlation. Numerically, it fits perfectly with the New Jerusalem dimensions superimposed on the Wattle Church Circle's original proportions and cells. The squaring circle is the outer sarsen circle, and the wall of the New Jerusalem is a circle of diameter 79.2 feet inscribed in the square of perimeter 316.8 feet, corresponding to the Stonehenge bluestone circle. The diameter of the inner circle of the New Jerusalem diagram is 39.6 feet, the same as the bluestone semi-circle, further reinforcing the symbolic and geometric correlations between the two.

STONEHENGE, A PROTOTYPE OF THE NEW JERUSALEM

This figure is identical in form and dimensions to the plan of the New Jerusalem in Revelation 21. Each pillar of the Sarsen circle has an average width of 7.04 feet. There are thirty in all, which, when multiplied, gives us 211.2 feet. The Hebrew phrase *ha'almah harah v'yoledet ben v'karat sh'mo Immanu'el* ("a virgin shall conceive and bear a son, and shall call his name Emmanuel," העלמה, הרה וילדת בן, וקראת שמו, עמנו אל) has a gematria value of 2112 in Hebrew (Isaiah 7:14).

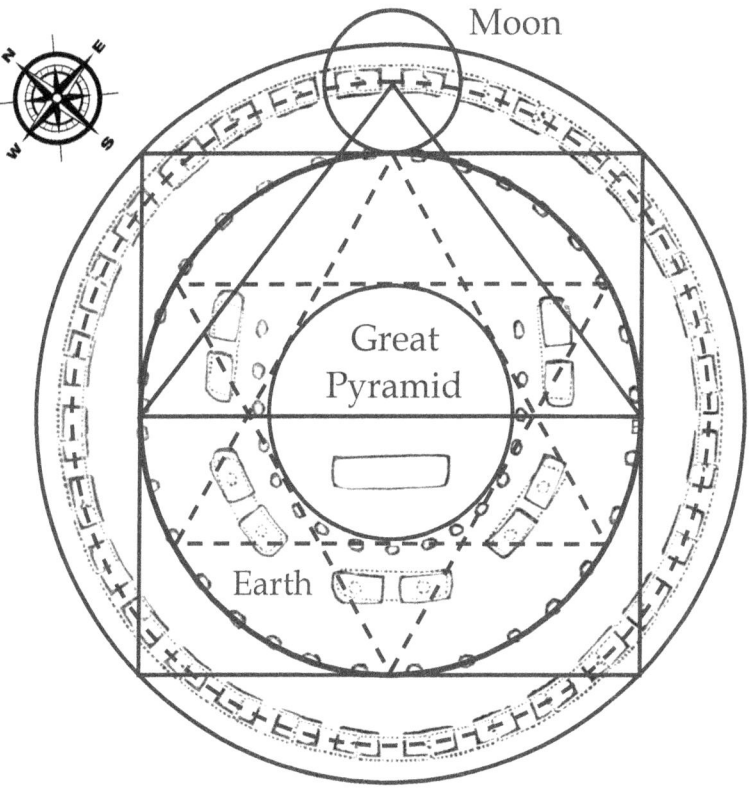

Fig 89. Stonehenge, a prototype of the New Jerusalem.

The Lintels, forming the squaring and perfect circle atop the pillars, have a mean length of 10.56 feet. The standard gematria value of *Sheshon yeshach* ("The joy of Thy salvation," ששון ישעך) is 1056.

STONEHENGE, A PROTOTYPE OF THE NEW JERUSALEM

Below, the diagram shows Stonehenge superimposed on the ground plan of St. Mary's Chapel. The geometric and numeric correlations between the two sacred sites show how accurately the architects built the foundation on a universal blueprint: the New Jerusalem Diagram. The powerful ley line between Stonehenge and Glastonbury Abbey goes through the center of the Wattle Church Circle and the Stone Circle.

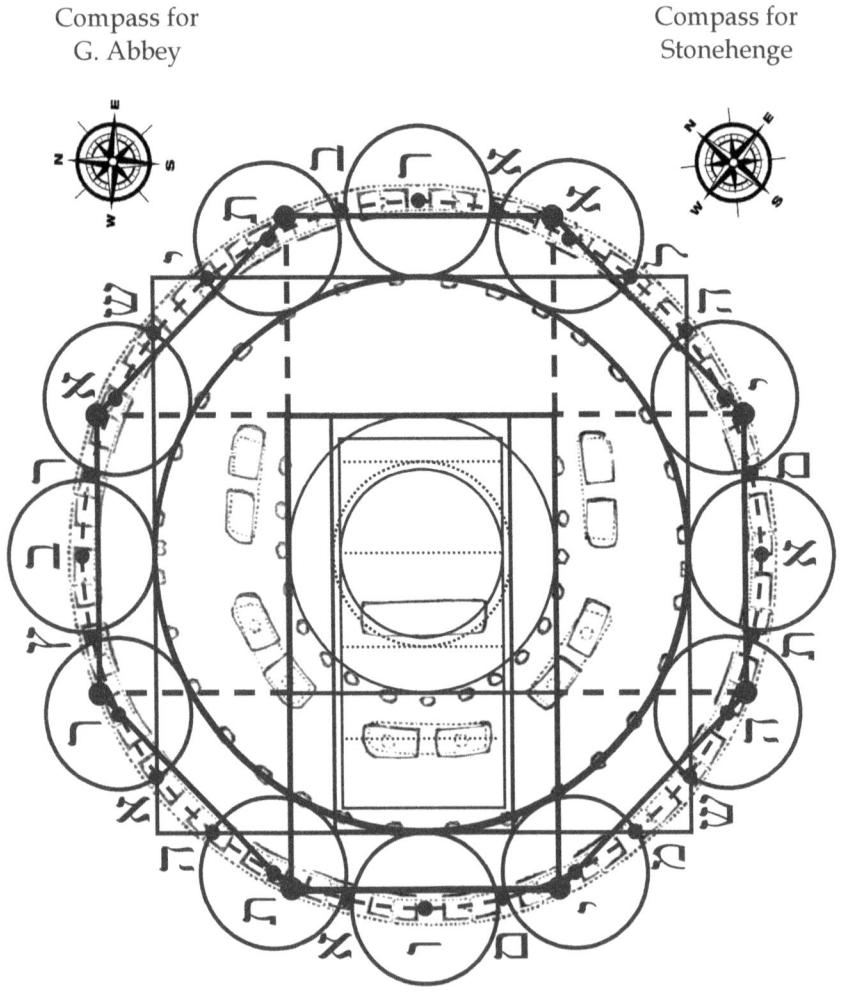

Fig 90. Stonehenge superimposed on the ground plan of the St. Mary's Chapel of Glastonbury Abbey.

THE RECONSTITUTION OF THE LOST PATTERN

THE RECONSTITUTION OF THE LOST PATTERN

Stonehenge is an important sacred site that holds the geometric and numeric blueprint of the New Jerusalem. This blueprint is identical to the original foundation that Joseph of Arimathea, his twelve followers, and potentially Jesus built at Glastonbury Abbey. Stonehenge reveals the story of creation at the beginning of all time, the first pristine emanation of light, emerging from *Ein Sof* ("limitlessness," אֵין סוֹף), the transcendental par excellence.

Bligh Bond's scripts repeatedly emphasized the importance of reconstructing the floor pattern of the Old Church at Glastonbury. One of them said, "You know that in this designing of the Floor lies the future prophecy of Glastonbury, together with the inward secrets of Christianity."

Frederick Bligh Bond asserts that the medieval church builders in Glastonbury employed gematria, an ancient science that encoded mathematical formulae in Biblical texts. They structured the site's original layout based on this knowledge, enabling the use of esoteric principles in constructing the Old Church. Today, it is widely acknowledged that ancient sites such as the Great Pyramid and Stonehenge exhibit signs of the use of Gematria in their design. Bond presented this information at a lecture on the measures of the St. Mary's Chapel in 1916, fully aware that it would challenge the beliefs of many of his contemporaries. The monks of Glastonbury Abbey could have been the ones who introduced him to the subject. In August 1917, the Company of Avalon explicitly references the subject, adding to the mystery and intrigue surrounding the Abbey's construction:

"That which the brethren of old handed down to us, we followed, ever building on their plan. As we have said, our Abbey was a message in ye stones. In ye foundations and ye distances be a mystery — the mystery of our Faith, which ye have forgotten and we also in ye latter days.

THE RECONSTITUTION OF THE LOST PATTERN

"All ye measures were marked plaine on ye slabbes in Mary's Chappel, and ye have destroyed them. So it was recorded, as they who builded and they who came after knew aforehand where they should build....... In ye floor of ye Mary Chappel was ye Zodiac, that all might see and understand the mystery...... Braineton, he didde much, for he was Geomancer to ye Abbey of old tyme."

Bond proposed that the designers of Glastonbury Abbey meticulously laid it out in a geometric pattern of 74ft squares, preserving the symmetry of these squares for centuries until the time of the last Abbot, Whiting. The previous construction, the Edgar Chapel, adheres to this pattern. Eight of these squares have a total length of 592 feet. However, according to John Michell, that length excludes the detached Chapel of St Dunstan at the west end, as his plan shows in Appendix B. If we add an extra square, the whole length becomes 666 feet. The grid which covers the ground plan of the Abbey buildings is four squares deep, with an area of 36 squares (9 × 4). With a square megalithic yard of 7.4 square feet, the total area is 26640, or 666 × 40, square megalithic yards. This meticulous planning and execution of the Abbey's design is a testament to the builders' dedication and skill. The well-known number 666 in gematria refers to the mathematical structure of the first verse of Genesis 1:1. It follows the formula 666 × 3 + 703 = 2701, representing its standard Hebrew gematria. Let's recall that 666 is the canonical number that represents the physical shell (body), while we can view 703 as the spiritual innermost aspect of the being (soul and spirit). The Abbey buildings could represent the body of Christ, while its innermost could be located at the Altar, a representation of the Heart. The builders applied the same principle to place the Wattle Circle church at the center of the New Jerusalem Diagram, along with its 12 cells. Interestingly, counting from the top of Triangle 73, the number 2664 is the counter positioned at the mid-point of its base, as 2701 − 2664 = 37. The last row at the bottom has 73 counters, and 37 is the mid-point.

THE RECONSTITUTION OF THE LOST PATTERN

In August 1917, the Company of Avalon stated: "*In ye floor of ye Mary Chappel was ye Zodiac, that all might see and understand the mystery......*" We can reconstruct the Zodiac on the St. Mary's Chapel floor at Glastonbury Abbey by drawing inspiration from the astounding zodiacal floor of the Lady Chapel in Wells Cathedral, which Thomas Witney probably designed around 1310-19. On some levels, there is a similarity with the geometric layout of St. Mary's Chapel in Glastonbury, as the Wattle Circle church stood on a square platform within an octagonal design. In Well's Cathedral, the builders positioned the central square at the center of an octagon. The central square is a grid of 144 small squares of 6 inches on their side. The total area of the square is 5184 square inches.

On the right, the figure shows the central square of the floorplan of Well's Cathedral. The four zodiac signs are demonstrated within a little circle, each inside a 4 x 4 grid square. At the center is the Lamb of Elohim (אלהים), Yahweh (יהוה).

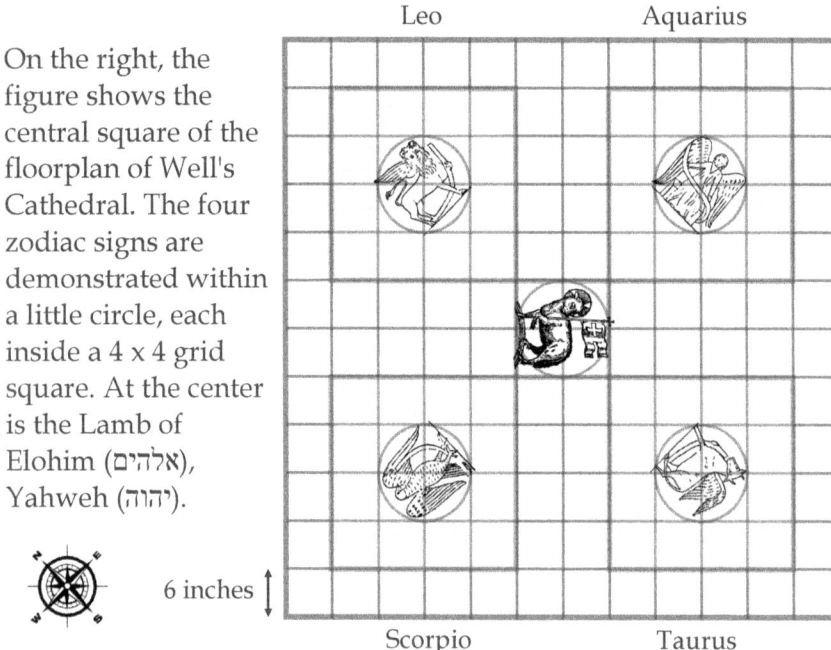

Fig 91. Zodiacal floor of the Lady Chapel of Well's Cathedral.

When we bring the four squares together at the center, they form a grid of 8 x 8, made up of 64 small squares, each measuring 6 inches in total (Fig 92). The ratio between the square foundation upon which the church stood and the central square of Well's Cathedral is 6.6 (39.6 ÷ 6).

THE RECONSTITUTION OF THE LOST PATTERN

The dotted circle inscribed in the square grid 8 x 8 has a diameter of 4 feet and represents the outer wattle church circle, which has a diameter of 26.4 feet.

This figure makes it natural to visualize the Wattle Church Circle as the heavens containing the zodiac signs and the square as the Earth. The circle would represent the movement of Earth's rotational axis, completing a rotation in 25920 years, which is five times 5184 years, a number incorporated in the dimensions of the central square of Well's Cathedral in square inches.

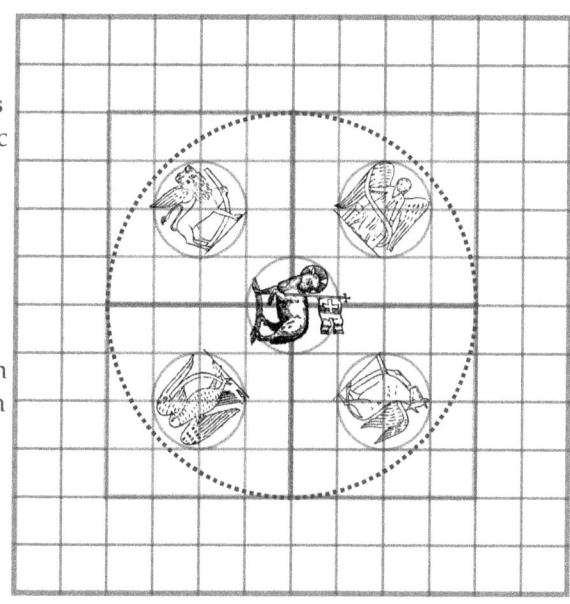

Fig 92. As above, so below.

The number 5184 is among the most important and versatile to ancient navigational and astronomical calculations.

- The intended (coded) slope angle of the Great Pyramid is 51.84 degrees.
- Each side of the Great Pyramid measures 72 Reeds, or 10.56 feet each, which means the base occupies 5184 square Reeds.
- The Precession of the Equinoxes endures for 25920 years (72 × 360) or 5184 years × 5.
- An English league of 16500 feet (10000 Sumerian cubits) converts to a circumference of 51840 feet when multiplied by PI at 3.141818181+ (the form of PI (π) used by the famous Mathematician Fibonacci: 864 ÷ 275).
- The 24883.2-mile circumference of the Earth equates to 518.4 miles × 48.

THE RECONSTITUTION OF THE LOST PATTERN

The original Sumerian cubit is 1.65 feet. A circle with a diameter of 1.65 feet has a circumference of 5.184 feet, with Fibonacci's value of PI at 3.14181818+. Builders likely used this cubit to construct the Temple of Solomon, Noah's Ark, and the original church in Glastonbury Abbey (both inner and outer for the wooden building). By applying the sacred geometry of the Rose Pattern (Fig 85) and combining it with the zodiac figure on the floor of the original church, they created an essential geometric blueprint coded with the numbers 1.65, 5, and 5.184.

Fig 93. The Rose Pattern within the Zodiacal Blueprint.

As well known, the number 5 has a strong relationship with one of the platonic solids, the dodecahedron, and is associated with the fifth element, the ether. The ether is the superfluid element pervading all spaces, including the sphere of the heavens, as shown in the figure above. It is also the divine life force at the origin of all shapes and forms, including the Rose Pattern.

THE RECONSTITUTION OF THE LOST PATTERN

Interestingly, a good approximation of 5 is the product of two fundamental mathematical constants, the golden ratio PHI 1.618033988+ and Fibonacci's PI 3.14181818+. The result is 5.083568604+, close to the value of 5.184, with only a difference of approximately one-tenth (1/10).

$$1.618033988 \times 3.14181818 = 5.083568604$$

We can express Fibonacci's PI using different fractions:

$$PI = 864 \div 275 = 1728 \div 550 = 34.56 \div 11$$

These magnificent canonical numbers 864, 1728, and 3456, those which constantly recur in myths, periods, scriptures, architecture, and so forth, also have an essential connection with the science of gematria. They convey an important message within the creation coding and the New Jerusalem's future prophecy. For example:

- 864 is the gematria of *Ierousalēm* ("Jerusalem," Ἰερουσαλήμ) and ("the sun and the moon," שמש וירח).
- 1728 is the gematria of *Ierousalēm Ierousalēm* ("O Jerusalem Jerusalem," Ἰερουσαλήμ Ἰερουσαλήμ (Mat 23:37)). It is precisely the gematria of *Birushlam ha'ir hakdash ha'amet* ("In Jerusalem the holy city and city of truth," בירושלם העיר הקדש האמת, Isaiah 52:1).
- 3456 is the gematria of *Tís póleos toú theoú mou* ("The City of my God," τῆς πόλεως τοῦ Θεοῦ μου (Rev 3:12)), also of *O gámos toú arníou, kaí i gyní aftoú* ("The wedding of the lamb and his bridge," ὁ γάμος τοῦ ἀρνίου, καὶ ἡ γυνὴ αὐτοῦ (Rev 19:7)). The name of the New Jerusalem is "The City of God" mentioned in Revelations 3:12. The dimensions given for New Jerusalem in Rev 21:16 (12000 furlongs) is 12 × 12 x 12 or 1728 by dropping all the zeros. Our ancestors traced these significant canonical numbers back to common knowledge.

THE RECONSTITUTION OF THE LOST PATTERN

The diameter of the sun is 864000 miles. With a square around the sun, its perimeter would measure 3456000 miles. The standard gematria of *Alithis* ("Truth," αληθης) is 3456000 by multiplication. The root number is 3456, dropping all the zeros.

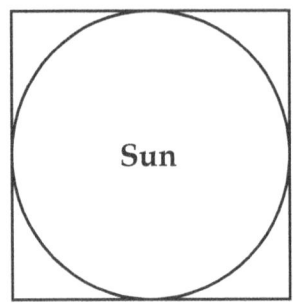

Diameter of the Sun: 864,000 miles.

Perimeter of the square: 3,456,000 miles.

**Fig 94.
Sun's dimensions.**

Fibonacci's PI 3.141818+ (1728 ÷ 550) is as relevant to the calculations of the measurements of the New Jerusalem as expressed in the function of critical canonical numbers referring to the prophecy of the New Jerusalem. A cube of side length 12 units has a volume of 1728. The volume of a cube of 550 would have an approximate side length of 8.2. This number is recurring in the plan of St. Mary's Chapel as the width of its western outside wall in feet (6.6 + 1.6). There are a couple of important points to highlight about 82. First, the 82nd word in the Bible is *Elohim* (איהלם) Genesis 1:8), and the ordinal gematria of the first verse of Genesis is 82. Half of 82 is 41, the number of Sumerian cubits for the total length of the rectangular chapel within the octagon (41 × 1.65 = 67.65), although the theoretical value is 67.6 feet.

בראשית, ברא אלהים, את השמים, ואת הארץ
17 11   17   5   14   5   13
              82

THE POWER OF SPEECH

THE POWER OF SPEECH

The gematria value in the first verse of Genesis 1:1, the value of PI (π), and the gematria value of *Torah* (תורה) are not just coincidental. Still, they form a profound and beautiful symmetry. The standard gematria value of *Torah* (תורה) is 611, and the first 611 digits of PI (π) sum up to 2701 (the standard gematria of Genesis 1:1). The ordinal gematria of *Torah* (תורה) is 17, and the first 17 digits of PI (π) sum up to 82.

3.1 4 1 5 9 2 6 5 3 5 8 9 7 9 3 2 3
1+4+1+5+9+2+6+5+3+5+8+9+7+9+3+2+3 = 82

The number 17 is a hint for the seeker to look at the corresponding position of the Hebrew letter in the Hebrew Alphabet. The 17th Hebrew letter is *Peh* (פ), which means "Mouth." It refers to the power of the spoken word. If Elohim created with Their words, how would it apply to every man and woman made in Their image? Speech has tremendous power. The letter *Beit* (ב) is hidden inside the letter *Peh* (פ) (Fig 95). The sum of the standard gematria of the two letters is 82. It refers back to 10 (8 + 2), *Yod* (י), the center of "the Rings of *Yod*" (Fig 37), the power seat of Elohim, who first spoke "The Word" whose first letter is *Beit* (ב) meaning "House" (first circular ring), and then "The Word" became flesh (second circular ring) to finally be finished as "Adam, the only living creature with a body and a spirit" endowed with the power of speech. The number 82 serves as an essential code of creation that refers to our divine nature in the image of Elohim. The measurements of St. Mary's Chapel encode this, with the outside western wall representing Elohim's Mouth, which first spoke before anything came into existence. The New Jerusalem Diagram is an astounding witness of the story of creation (Genesis) conserved in architecture with sacred and canonical numbers.

Fig 95. Elohim's House; Power of Speech.

Inside Hidden *Beit*

THE POWER OF SPEECH

The sum of gematria values of the first seventeen Hebrew words of Genesis is 5184, with 66 Hebrew letters in total. This divine number is a reflection of the sacredness of the text. Fibonacci's PI is the form of PI used for "11" series numbers. The total length of the rectangular St. Mary's chapel is 66 feet, with an addition of 1.6 feet at the end of the western outside wall (close to the golden ratio 1.618 or 1.65 feet in the Sumerian cubit system). In the "Rings of *Yod*," summing all the numbers in between the rings (601 + 128 + 602), the result is 1331, a perfect cube as 11 × 11 x 11 = 1331, the gematria value of *Mashiyach* ("Messiah," משיח) with the *Mispar Kidmi* method. The phrase *Elohim av natan roch yehad achad chi nifsh Adam* ("Elohim the Father gave a spirit to only one living creature, Adam," אלהים אב נתן רוח יחד אחד חי נפש אדם) has a standard gematria value of 1331.

The 17th word is *Elohim* (אלהים) in Genesis 1:2. The verse mentions the spirit of Elohim when the earth was unformed and void, and darkness was upon the face of the deep. 5184 is a perfect square, as 5184 = 72 × 72. The number 72 is the gematria value of the timeless nature of God's and Goddess' existence ("He/She was, He/She is, He/She will be," יהיה הווה היה). This number is renowned as being the 72-fold name of God and Goddess (Fig 1). The 72 names of God and Goddess is a formula of 72 combinations that Moses used to part the Red Sea.

בראשית, ברא אלהים, את השמים, ואת הארץ
296   407   395   401   86   203   913
2701
והארץ, היתה תהו ובהו, וחשך, על-פני תהום;
451 140 100   334   19   411 420   302
ורוח אלהים
2483   86   220
5184

THE POWER OF SPEECH

Interestingly, the second verse has a total gematria value of 2483, close to 2485 by a difference of 2. The first Hebrew letter of Genesis, *Beit* (ב), has a gematria value of 2, which indicates that the Torah ("The Word") existed before anything came into existence. The second verse states that the earth was unformed and void, and darkness covered the face of the deep. No light was present until the first letter was spoken by Elohim, *Beit* (ב), identifying as the Torah.

Let's recall that the number 2485 is the gematria of the five books of the Torah:

1. Genesis, *Bereisheit* ("Creation," בראשית).
2. Exodus, *Shemot* ("Names," שמות).
3. Leviticus, *Vayikrah* ("And he called," ויקרא).
4. Numbers *Bamidbar* ("In the Wilderness," במדבר).
5. Deuteronomy, *Hadevarim* ("The Second Word," הדברים).

There is a tremendous mathematical formula involving geometry between 2485 and 2701. The number 2701 is the gematria of the first verse of Genesis in Hebrew. Geometrically, it is only separated by the perimeter of the Triangular Number 73, with a total counter of 216 (Fig 23). This number corresponds to the gematria value of *Gevurah* ("Might," "Restraint," גבורה), a sephirah of the Kabbalah, whose function is to hold the inner part, a total count of 2485, considering that 2701 - 216 = 2485.

Thus, the canonical number 5184 has a strong relationship with the Hebrew phrase *Ruach Elohim* ("the Spirit of Elohim," רוח אלהים), the spiritual fire and fiery nature of the Holy Spirit. Its reversed standard gematria is 703, representing the innermost spiritual core, God's and Goddess' breath of divine essence, which vivifies the souls of man and woman and grants wisdom.

THE POWER OF SPEECH

Interestingly, if the number 5184 is divided by 703, it equals 7.37. The standard gematria value of *She'Amar Dai L'olamo* ("Who said 'enough is enough' for their Universe," שאמר די לעולמו) is 737. It is also the "perimeter gematria" of *Gevurah* (גבורה). The contracted version of *She'Amar Dai L'olamo* is the Holy Name *Sha-dai* (ש-די) with a standard gematria of 314. There is a vital link between *Gevurah* (גבורה), its function, and the value of PI (π) in its essence to constrict and enclose the infinite nature of Elohim's Light. The "light" is nothing other than "The Word (Torah)" itself. Remember that the sum of the first 165 digits of PI is 737. The standard gematria value of *Nekudah* ("Point," נקודה) is 165, representing the origin of everything that came into existence. It manifests with the first letter mentioned in the Torah, *Beit* (ב), which contains everything within it. The dot symbolizes the spiritual innermost aspect of Elohim's House, situated within *Beit* (ב), which we can visualize as the *Nekudah* ("Point," נקודה). Number 737 also expresses the Absolute Truth of Their Being from "The Heart" with "Wisdom" = 700 + 37 = 737; That of a "Primary Being," *Metzuy Roshon* (מצוי ראשון), *Bekar lekal nivra* ("The firstborn of every creature," בכר לכל נברא), *Mashiyach* ("Messiah," משיח), all expressing a threefold nature in the creation. First, through the three primary colors: Red, 284; the standard gematria value of *Theos* ("God," θεος). Yellow, 228; the standard gematria value of *Ohr Yah* ("Light of Yah," אוריהו). *Yah* (יהו) is the first three letters of *Yahweh* (יהוה); Blue 188; the standard gematria value of *B'tzelem Yahweh* ("In the Image of Yahweh," בצים יהוה). Then, through the three aspects of the Spiritual Flame *Shalhevet* (שלהבת): *Eish* ("Fire," אש) 301, *Nogah* ("Brillance," נגה) 58, *Chashmal* ("Electrum," חשמל) 378 (Ezekiel 1:4). The Hebrew word *Shalhevet* (שלהבת) meaning "Flame," has a gematria value of 737.

Fig 96. Power of Speech through the Point *Nekudah* (נקודה) **(spiritual innermost).**

Inside hidden 'Beit'

THE PROPHECY OF MELKIN

THE PROPHECY OF MELKIN

Our exploration begins with a thorough discussion of the intricate connections between the canonical numbers in the measurements of St. Mary's Chapel and the story of creation (Genesis). We will then delve into the meticulous process of determining the potential location of Joseph of Arimathea's grave, employing the sciences of gematria, sacred geometry, and the first verse of Genesis. The medieval text 'The Prophecy of Melkin' predicts Glastonbury's future and describes the alleged hidden grave of Joseph of Arimathea as follows:

"The Isle of Avalon, with greed for the death of pagans, before all others in the world, for the entombment of them all. Decorated beyond all others by the chanting spheres of prophecy and for all time to come, adorned shall it be by them that praise the Most High. Abbadare mighty in saphat, noblest of pagans, has fallen on sleep with 144,000 saints, among these, Joseph of Arimathea has found perpetual sleep in a marble tomb and he lies on two forked line next to the southern angle of an oratory, where the wattle is prepared above the mighty maiden and where the aforesaid 13 spheres rest. For Joseph has with him in his sarcophagus two vessels white and silver, filled with the blood and sweat of the prophet Jesus. When his sarcophagus is discovered, it will be seen whole and undefiled, and will be open to the entire world. From that Time those who dwell in that noble Isle will lack neither water nor the dew of heaven. For a long time before the day of judgment (ludioailem) in Josaphat, open shall these things be and declared to the living".

Prophecy of Melkin

The text states Joseph's grave "lies on a two-forked line next to the southern angle of an oratory." Two ley lines could cross near the southern angle of St. Mary's Chapel, which is highly possible because an existing fork for the springs lies at the east-southern angle. Saint Joseph's Well stands there.

THE PROPHECY OF MELKIN

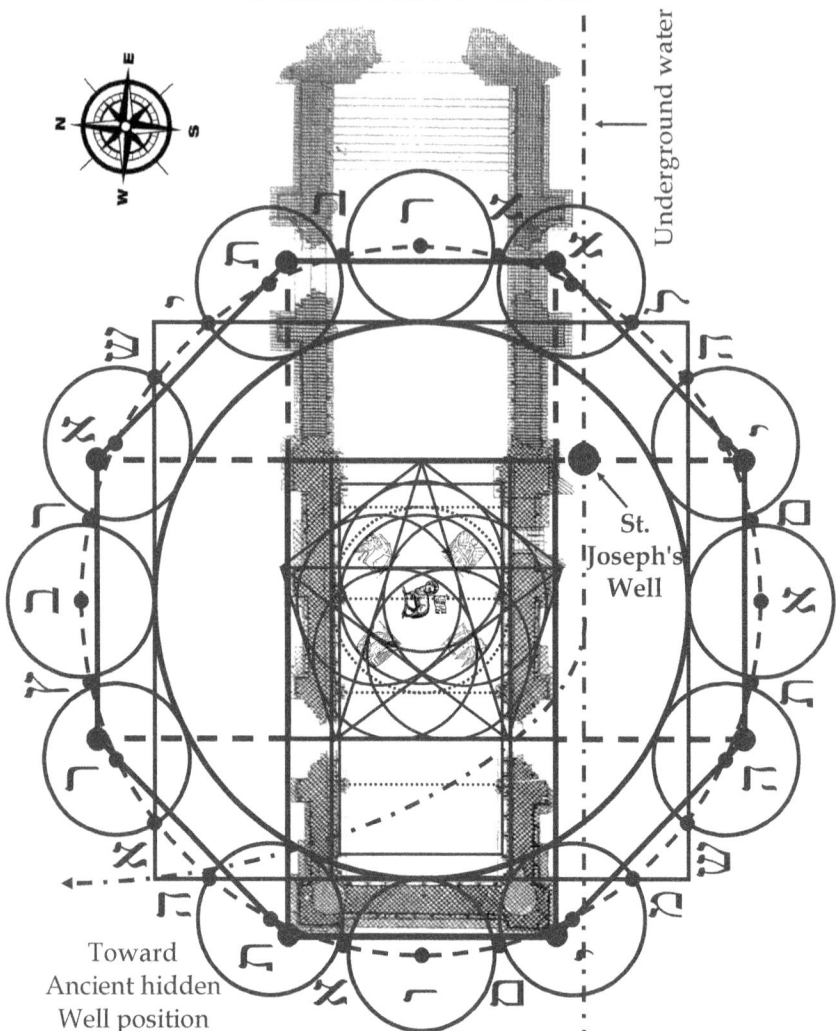

Fig 97. Reconstitution of the lost pattern (Rose Pattern & Zodiacal Blueprint) on the floor plan of St. Mary's Chapel.

The above figure shows the Rose Pattern, a zodiacal blueprint of the floorplan of the Wattle Church Circle. The lion is oriented toward the True North of Stonehenge when superimposed on St. Mary's Chapel. The underground water spring lines are two forked lines near the southern-east angle of the chapel, near St. Joseph's Well. There are 12 spheres corresponding to the 12 cells of Joseph's followers positioned along the octagon or dashed squaring circle.

THE PROPHECY OF MELKIN

Melkin describes the 13th sphere as Joseph's cell. The significance of the number 13 often connects it to Joseph and his disciples. It is natural to think that Joseph's grave lies close to his cell, serving as an indicator. To find his grave, one must consider the overall ground plan of St. Mary's Chapel and the Galilee as part of a bigger picture. For this, the universal blueprint of the spiral observed in nature, known as Fibonacci's spiral, will potentially lead the way in our search for Joseph's grave. This spiral, constructed using Fibonacci's numbers (1,1,2,3,5,8,13), is significant as the number 13 emerges after the number 8, which is associated with the octagon, a key element in the design of St. Mary's Chapel. The architects of St. Mary's Chapel identified the number 5 as the root of the original foundations through the Pentagon or the Rose Pattern. They associated the number 8 with the octagon, which serves as the source of the New Jerusalem Diagram. The design team will delimit the spiral with a square, positioning its opposite sides in alignment with the outside western wall of St. Mary's Chapel and the eastern limit of Galilee at the Porch (from West to East). In this geometric construction, a fascinating discovery awaits. If we take the square's side length as five times the diameter of the outside Wattle Church Circle, we find an excellent numerical correlation: 5 x 26.4 = 132 feet. A golden rectangle with a long side of 132 will contain a golden spiral of 316.8 feet, with 3168 being the standard gematria of *Kýrios Iēsoûs Christós* ("Lord Jesus Christ," Κύριος Ἰησοῦς Χριστός). This discovery is significant, as the spiral bears the number of Lord Jesus Christ. Identifying the singularity of the spiral as the location of Joseph's grave seems highly relevant. Here, we present an excellent design witnessed throughout millennia, from the beginning of time, encoded in a pearl of wisdom through the science of gematria, sacred geometry, and the story of creation (Genesis). As the mysteries unravel, the significance of these discoveries comes to light. The New Jerusalem will finally reveal itself, the bride of the lamb, as Joseph's grave reveals itself to the World.

THE PROPHECY OF MELKIN

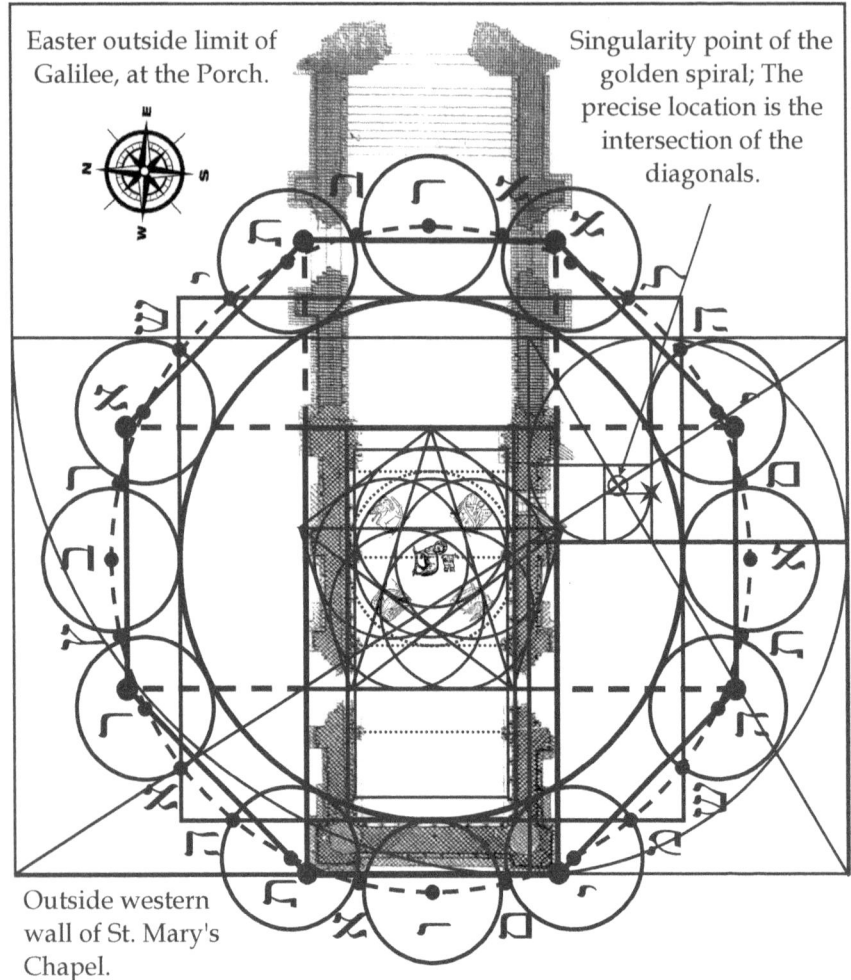

Fig 98. The Fibonacci Spiral points to the precise location of Joseph of Arimathea's grave.

Above, the diagram shows the golden spiral, which is 316.8 feet long and ends on a marker, which could well be the location of Joseph's grave at the southern angle of St. Mary's Chapel. We can locate the singularity of the spiral using the two diagonal lines of the golden rectangles: one line crosses the golden rectangle with sides measuring 132 and 81.58 feet, and the other line crosses the golden rectangle with sides measuring 81.58 and 50.42 feet.

THE PROPHECY OF MELKIN

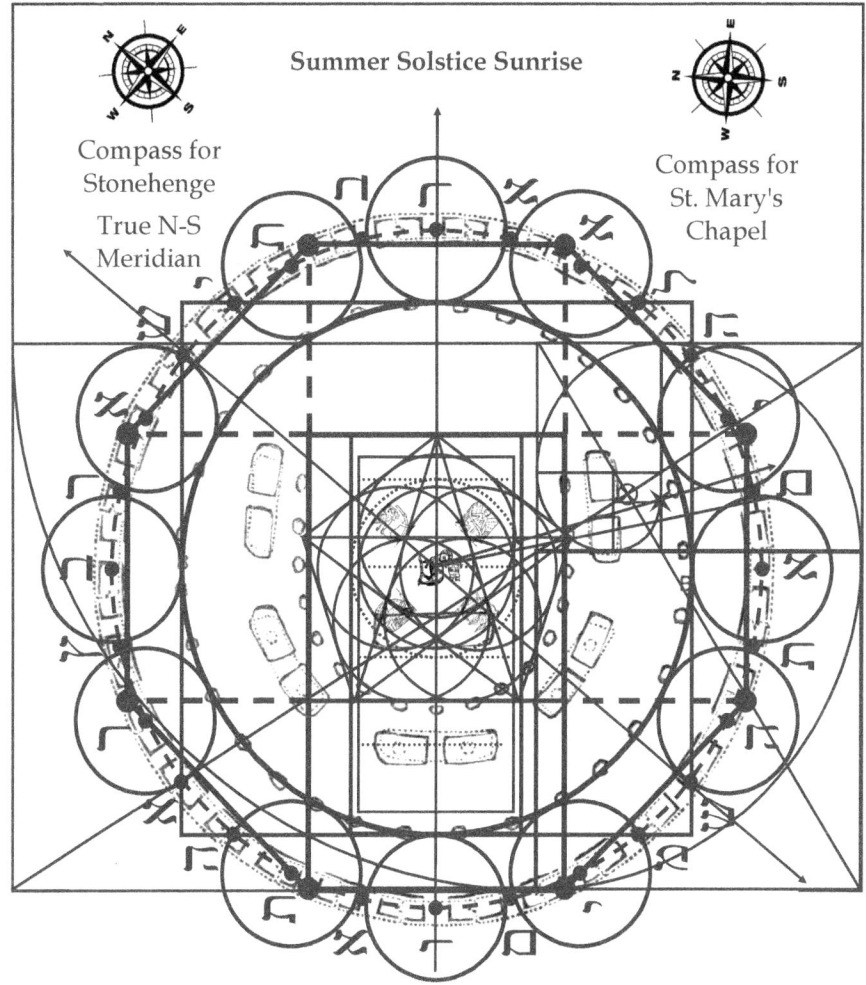

Fig 99. Stonehenge, a prototype guide of the New Jerusalem Blueprint and the possible location of Joseph's grave.

Above, the diagram shows Stonehenge superimposed on Fig 98. The actual North-South Meridian for Stonehenge passes through the two Hebrew letters *Shin* (ש) of the first verse of Genesis. *Shin* (ש) expresses the threefold nature of all things and corresponds to life itself, the breath of life, the fifth element, the ether. It "gives light" and "shines" as *Eish* ("Fire," אש), and it came after the first letter *Aleph* (א) in the emergence of the building blocks of creation

THE PROPHECY OF MELKIN

The arrow starting from the center of the Wattle Church Circle, at the lamb, and passing through the 5th Hebrew letter *Mem* (מ) of the 3rd word of Genesis 1:1, *Elohim* (אלהים), points to the Winter Solstice Sunrise. The 13th Hebrew letter, *Mem* (מ), possibly indicates the location of the 13th sphere, Joseph's cell. Melkin mentioned 13 spheres, stating, "where the wattle is prepared above the mighty maiden and where the aforesaid 13 spheres rest." In the New Jerusalem design (Fig 99), we positioned each Hebrew letter apart by dividing the circle into 28 sections, which resulted in an angle of $360 \div 28 = 12.85$ degrees. The angle between the Summer Solstice Sunrise pointing to the 8th Hebrew letter *Reish* (ר), of the second word *Bara* ("created," ברא) and the letter *Mem* (מ) of *Elohim* (אלהים), is 77.14 degrees, as there are six sections apart from each other. We can calculate the angle between the winter/summer solstice sunrise and the East; it is 39.3 degrees with a tilt angle of Earth of 23.4 degrees (Appendix C). The total angle between the Summer and Winter Solstice Sunrises is 78.6 degrees, only 1.46 degrees from *Mem* (מ) of *Elohim* (אלהים). On another note, the distance between the center of the Wattle Church Circle and the possible location of Joseph of Arimathea's grave is about 36 feet Northeast, about 15.7 degrees facing the current altar of Mary's chapel (Appendix D).

We can mathematically calculate the exact angle between the vertical line passing through the center of the square foundation (lamb) (toward the Summer Solstice Sunrise for Stonehenge) and the potential location of Joseph's grave. The result is about 74 degrees (Appendix D). Interestingly, 74 corresponds to the English ordinal gematria of *Jesus* and the Hebrew standard gematria of *Yasad* ("Founded," יסד). It means "to set; to be found; to set down; to appoint; to assign; foundation, beginning" - also a variant spelling of the name of the ninth Sephirah, *Yesod* ("Foundation," יסוד). The 74th prime number is 373, which matches the gematria value of *Logos* ("Word," λογος) from John 1:1. The term *Logos* ("Word," λογος) identifies Jesus. The number 86 first appears in PI (π) at position 74, and 86 corresponds to the gematria value of *Elohim* (אלהים). So Elohim also identifies Jesus in the threefold (trinity) divine nature with the Father and the Holy Spirit (Mother). Gematria presents us with many essential keys reinforcing the veracity of Melkin's prophecy, including the reconstitution of the Rose Pattern with the Zodiacal Blueprint.

THE CELTIC CROSS CONNECTION

In early times, before Christianity was born, cross-slabs presented powerful Celtic and Pictish symbolism. Sacred geometry intimately connected sacred numbers encoded in the Holy Scriptures. The designers show that they gained some ancient knowledge and wisdom from the dawn of humanity. An interesting standing stone is an example of a particular cross in Dunblane's Cathedral of Scotland, potentially dating back to the early 9th century. The next page shows the front side of the slab cross depicting the Celtic Cross with four little circles at the corners of the two main lines that make up the cross. Those little circles seem encircled by a bigger circle, which is unimportant in the first approach. However, the Celts and Picts were carving their symbolism with a deeper meaning through mathematics and geometry. Combining these aspects with the numbers previously discussed and developed in the New Jerusalem Diagram scheme opens a new dimension in understanding the energy flow within the earth and cosmic realms. We will discuss this section further. Each line along the side crosses through two little circles with a snake at the bottom and a spiral at the top. Each line could represent the conduct of earth and cosmic energies. The snakes represent the earth's energies circulating into the ground while the spirals represent the etheric energies pervading throughout space; in other words, cosmic energies. These four circles, the main characteristics of the Celtic and Pictish cross-slabs, could be a geometric representation of the manifestation of the ether, the fifth element, from which four vortices conduct earth and cosmic energies in equilibrium.

On the reverse of this cross-slab, a designer arranged five circles geometrically (Fig 100), similar to the geometric layout of the zodiacal floor of Mary's Chapel shown in Fig 91. This intriguing similarity raises a thought-provoking question: Did the Celts and Picts possess some knowledge about this design? The possibility of their understanding of such complex geometric patterns adds another layer of fascination to the study of these ancient artifacts.

THE CELTIC CROSS CONNECTION

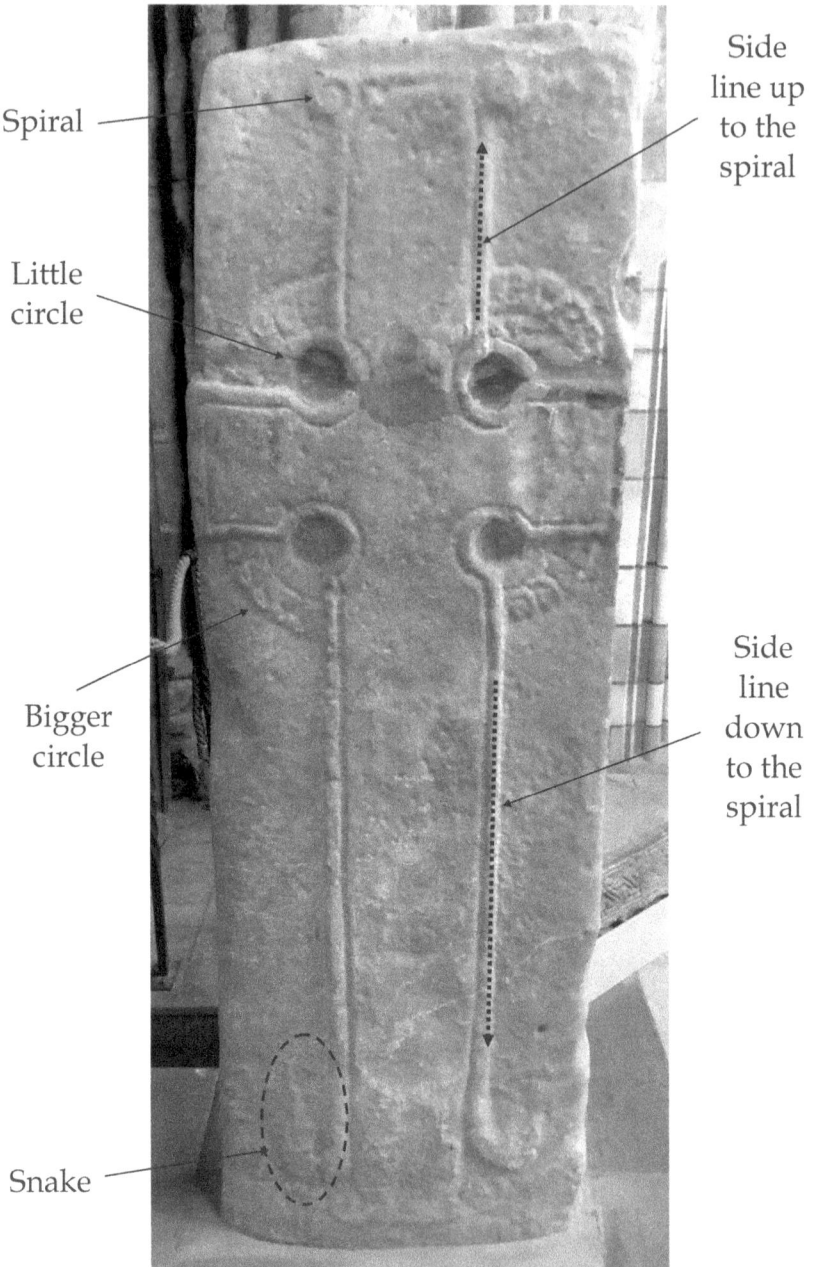

Fig 100.
Standing Stone of Dunblane's Cathedral of Scotland.

THE CELTIC CROSS CONNECTION

Fig 101. Reverse of the cross-slab (Fig 100) compared with the zodiacal floor pattern of St. Mary's Church (Fig 92).

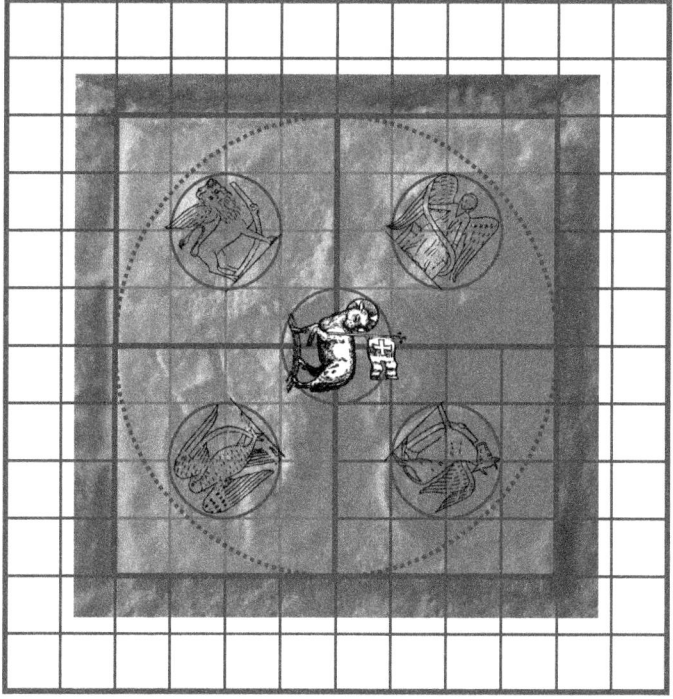

THE CELTIC CROSS CONNECTION

Stoneworkers meticulously formed this design on cross slabs, such as the reverse of Rosemarkie Stone, shown below, showcasing their exceptional skill and precision.

Fig 102. Reverse of Rosemarkie Stone.

The designer places small circles containing interesting geometric patterns at each square's corners. As depicted below, a circle inscribed within each square corresponds to each zodiac sign. The bigger circle on the front side of Dunblane Cathedral's cross slab in Fig 99 would correspond to the circle scaled down to the ratio 1:√2.

An outer Wattle Church Circle of St. Mary's Chapel with a diameter of 26.4 ft scales down to a circle of diameter 18.667ft. 186 is a harmonic number referring to the nature of the light and a numerical signature of Elohim and Yahweh.

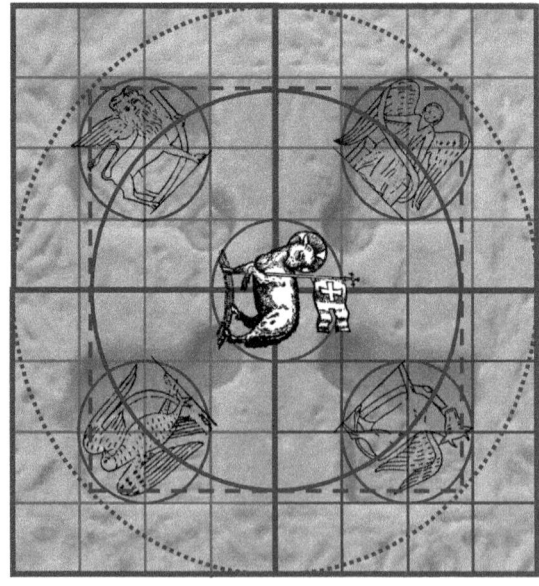

Fig 103. Zodiacal Blueprint of St. Mary's Chapel overlaid on the reverse of Rosemarkie Stone.

THE CELTIC CROSS CONNECTION

If correctly matched, the center of the slab cross coincides with the lamb of Elohim/Yahweh. It also naturally coincides with the Rose Pattern, as previously discussed. Below is shown the bigger circle potentially corresponding to the scaled-down circle of the outer Wattle Church Circle of Mary's Chapel at Glastonbury Abbey by a ratio of 1:√2. This could be called "The Light Circle," similar representation of a halo of light, strengthened by the number 186 as a reference to the nature of the light.

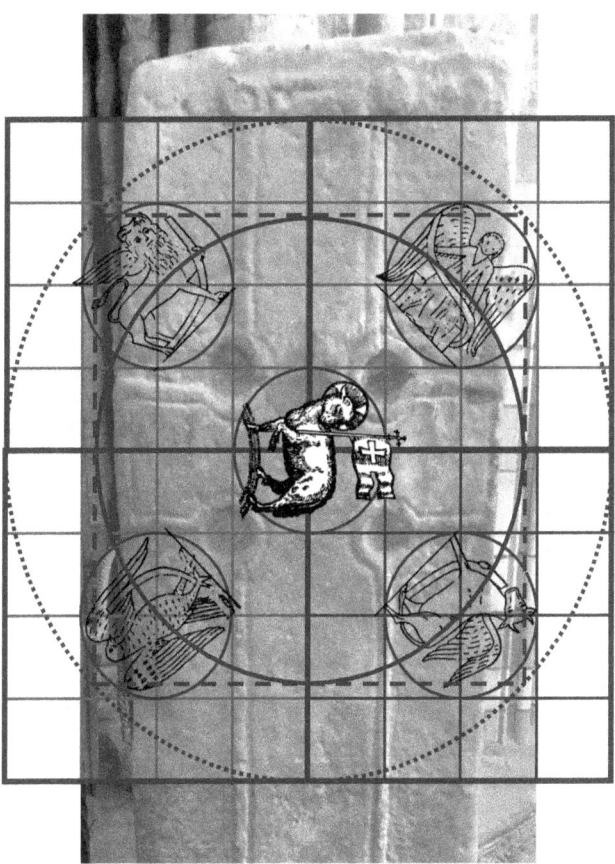

Fig 104. The "Light Circle" (halo) and the zodiacal blueprint of the cross-slab of Dunblane's Cathedral.

The number 186 is the Hebrew standard gematria of *Makom* ("Place," מקום), implying "The Place of Light".

THE CELTIC CROSS CONNECTION

The design involves duplicating a square in eight directions (above, below, to the sides, and diagonally) to create a 3x3 grid using compasses and straight edges through the eight-pointed star and tangential circles. To the original square, vertical and horizontal central axes plus an enclosing circle are used to facilitate the addition of a same-sized square concentrically but diagonally. The lines forming these two squares are then extended to their first intersections with each other, creating an eight-pointed star.

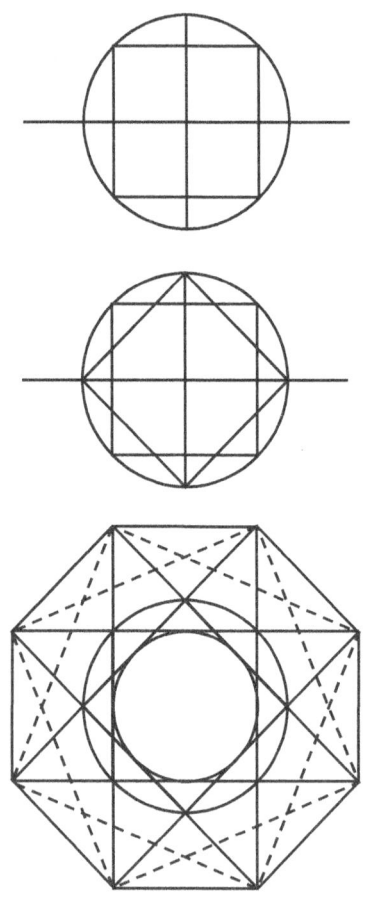

Fig 105.
The progressive construction of the eight-pointed star.

This geometric principle is the first stage of producing the Celtic Cross. The four little tangential circles characteristic of the standard Celtic Cross are added on the corners of the original square and tangential to the circle inscribed in that square. Then, tangential to these, four circles with the same radius as the central circle are added with centers on the diagonal axes (or vertical axes/horizontal axes). The artist encloses these four new circles with a square, creating a regular 3 x 3 grid, which results in the Celtic Cross, as seen on the reverse of the Rosemarkie Stone or the front side of the Standing Stone in Dunblane's Cathedral.

Fig 106. The geometric construction of the Celtic Cross.

Interesting ratios naturally appear between the circles:
- There is a ratio of 1:√2 between the circle inscribed in the eight-pointed star (central circle) and the circle passing through the center of the four little circles, which is the same ratio as the forearm to the deltoid tuberosity of the humerus, if measured from the fingertips. This particular ratio defines the Egyptian Royal Cubit as a sacred proportion within the human body (Figs. 53-55). A little circle would be of diameter √2-1 with a central circle of diameter 1.

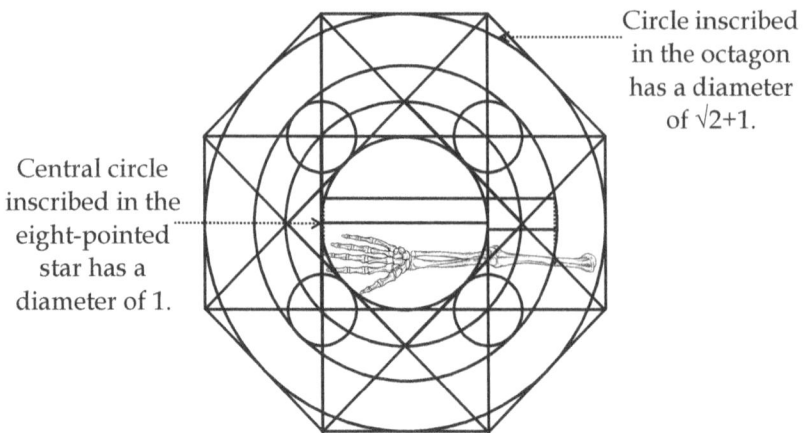

Fig 107. The geometric construction's ratios are 1:(√2+1) and 1:√2.

- The ratio between the circle inscribed in the eight-pointed star and the circle inscribed in the octagon is 1:(√2+1).

A beautiful geometric and mathematical relationship exists between the circles involved in the previous ratios, a testament to the elegance of these ancient designs. Incrementing or decrementing by one the diameter of the circle (square root of 2) enclosing the four little circles, respectively, results in the circle inscribed the octagon and the little circle. The circle's diameter enclosing the four little circles is 2√2-1.

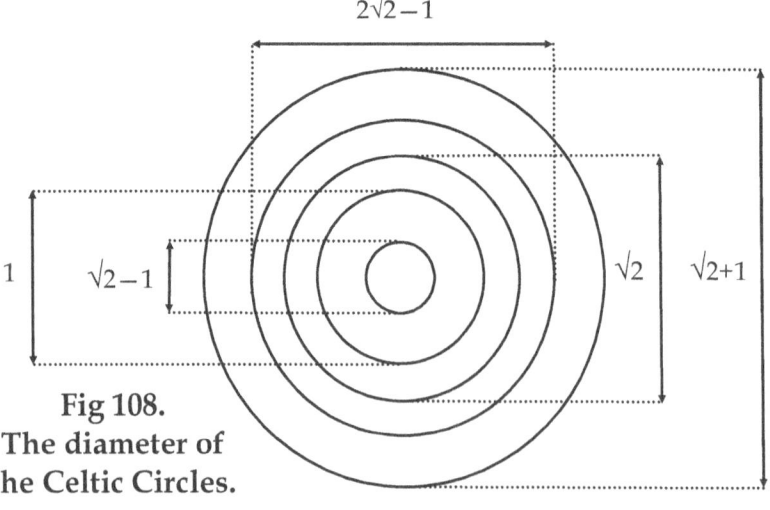

Fig 108. The diameter of the Celtic Circles.

THE CELTIC CROSS CONNECTION

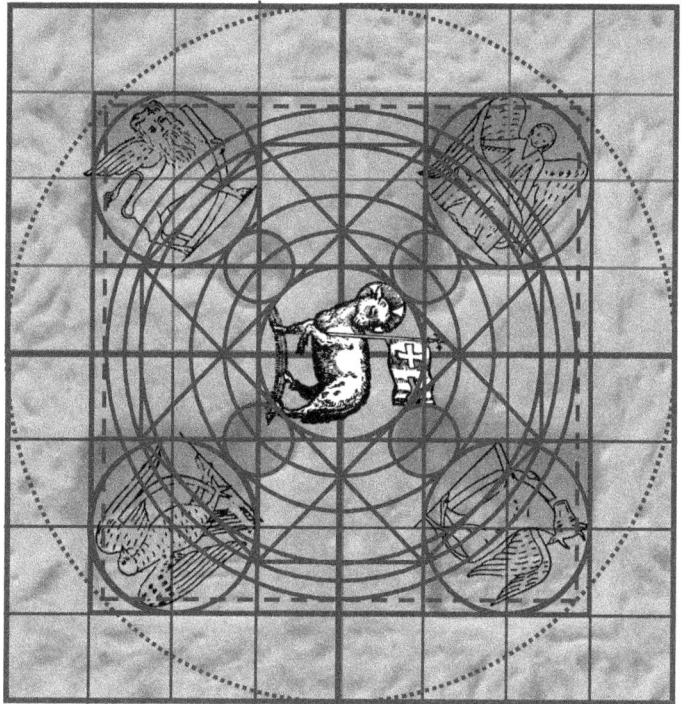

Fig 109.
Construction geometric of the Celtic Cross overlain on the reverse of the Rosemarkie Stone with the Zodiacal Blueprint of St. Mary's Chapel.

The "Solar Wheel" is formed simply from an outer circle enclosing the original eight-pointed star and an inner circle enclosing the four small tangential circles. The double diameter of the circle enclosing the four tangential small circles is $4\sqrt{2}-2$, which is 3.65685, close to one-hundredth of a solar cycle in days (365.2423).

It is interesting to highlight that a circle with a diameter of 2.613 inscribes the octagon, which is one-hundredth of a natural C in Hz (261). The circle passing through the center of the four circles enclosing the four zodiacal signs, each placed at the corner of the Celtic design, has a diameter of $2\sqrt{2}$. Half of that circle is the circle passing through the four tangential small circles with a diameter of $\sqrt{2}$.

It follows that the dashed circle representing the outer Wattle Church Circle has a diameter of 4 on this particular scale. Using the feet as the measure of the length, the diameter of the outer church circle being 26.4ft, in its actual proportions, the ratio between these two different scales is 6.6. As discussed in the seventeenth chapter, *The Reconstitution of the Lost Pattern*, the ratio between the square foundation upon which the Wattle Church Circle stood and the central square of Mary's Chapel floor in Wells' Cathedral is 6.6. The square foundation is drawn on the height of a pentagon, revealing the five-pointed star, truly enclosing the Rose Pattern.

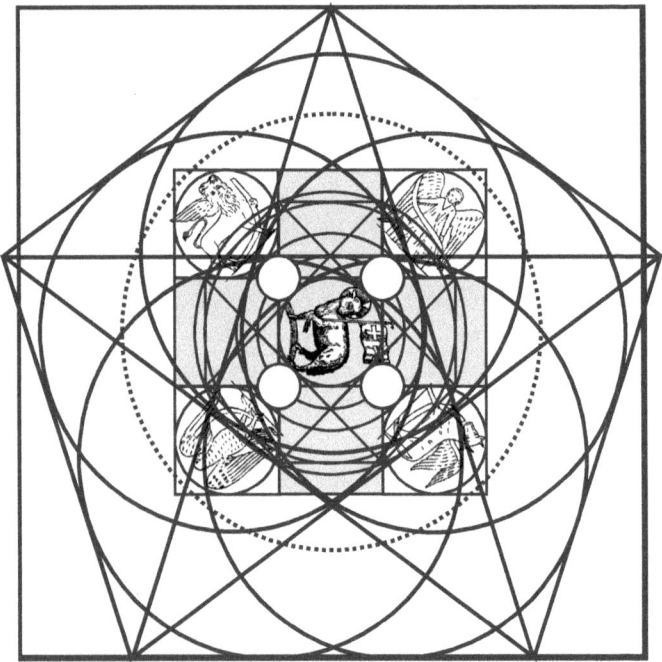

Fig 110.
The unification of the Celtic Cross with the Rose Pattern and the Zodiacal Blueprint of St. Mary's Chapel.

The Celtic Cross is enclosed within the Rose Pattern, bringing the origin of Early Christianity back to ancient times among the Celts and Picts. Natural ratios based on √2 carry a wealth of information for the seekers of truth.

THE CELTIC CROSS CONNECTION

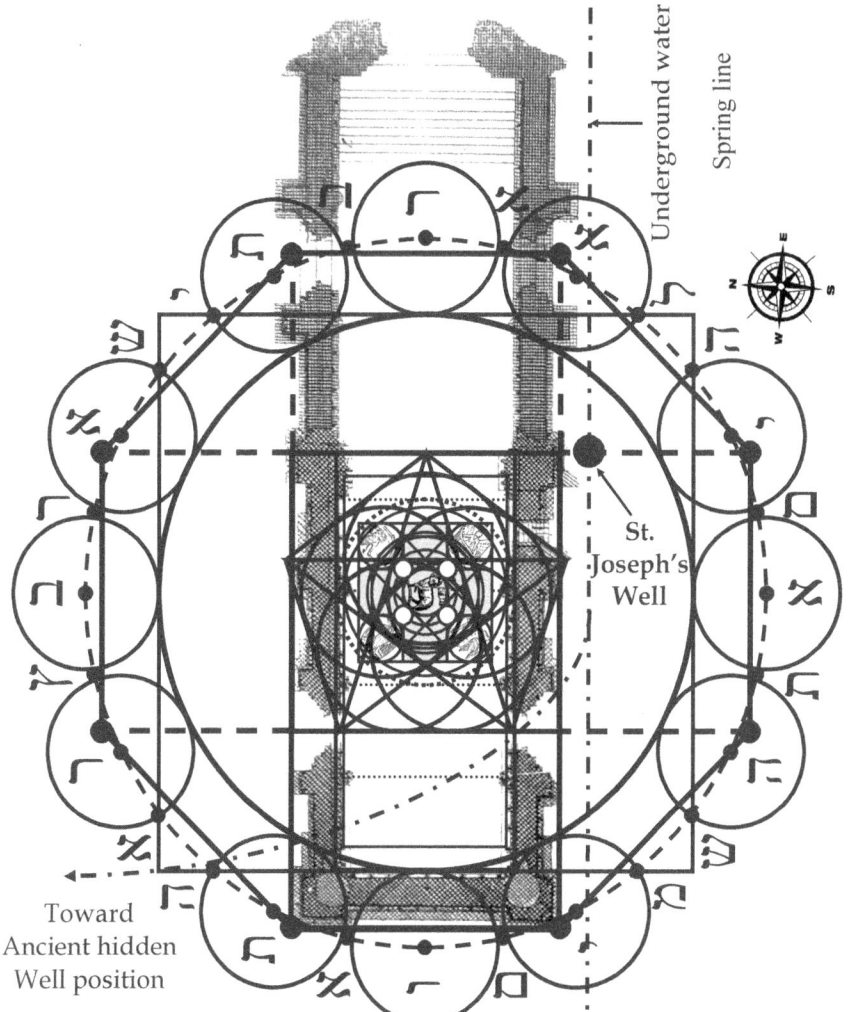

Fig 111. Unified Design of the New Jerusalem Diagram: a bridge between early Christianity and ancient Celtic Cultures.

Above the figure, we can position the Celtic Cross at the center of the original Wattle Church Circle within the Rose Pattern. This correlation reveals how early the Ancient Celtic culture still influenced Christianity. We can now clearly see a geometric fractal between the octagon that originates from the construction of the Celtic Cross within the foundation square of side length 39.6 ft and the octagon constructed from the rectangular Mary's Chapel.

THE CELTIC CROSS CONNECTION

The scale ratio between the octagon of a side-length one and the octagon within the square foundation is 6.6. It is the same scale ratio between the geometric layout on the floor of Mary's Chapel in Wells' Cathedral and the ground plan of St. Mary's Chapel in Glastonbury Abbey. So, the perimeter of the octagon within the foundation square is 52.8ft or 32 Sumerian cubits with a side length of 6.6ft or 4 Sumerian cubits. As previously discussed, 52.8ft is the interior length of the rectangular chapel, a hundredth part of a mile (Fig 77). The octagon design in the New Jerusalem Diagram, which builders constructed from the rectangular Mary's Chapel, features the 28 Hebrew letters of the first verse of Genesis spaced out along its line. This octagon has a perimeter of 316.8 feet or 192 Sumerian cubits, and each side measures 39.6 feet, or 24 Sumerian cubits. The scale ratio between these two octagons is 6 (a side length of 39.6 divided by a side length of 6.6).

Further, the geometric design of the octagon is a geometric fractal with a scale ratio of 6.6 from the construction of the Celtic Cross. The fractal leads to a third octagon with a perimeter of 348.48ft (8 × 6.6 × 6.6). This particular number holds the information of the previous measurement of 316.8ft of the octagon of the New Jerusalem Diagram, as 348.48 = 316.8 + 31.68, another interesting fractal within a fractal bearing the number of Lord Jesus Christ. We can interpret the octagon with a perimeter of 316.8 ft as the inner body. In comparison, the octagon of perimeter 348.48ft can be construed as the envelopes of the body, like the skin is for the flesh. The circle's diameter with the same perimeter of 348.48ft has a value of 110.9166+ft (111 - 1 ÷ 12) with the Fibonacci's value of PI at 3.14181818+. Number 111 is the full standard value of *Aleph* (אלף), "One" 1, where everything begins. Figure 112 shows the fractal nature of the octagons within the New Jerusalem Diagram, an essential blueprint of Genesis 1.1, incorporating the Rose Pattern and the Zodiacal Wheel of the floor plan of St. Mary's Chapel. It unifies important symbolism, further bridging early Christianity and ancient Celtic cultures.

THE CELTIC CROSS CONNECTION

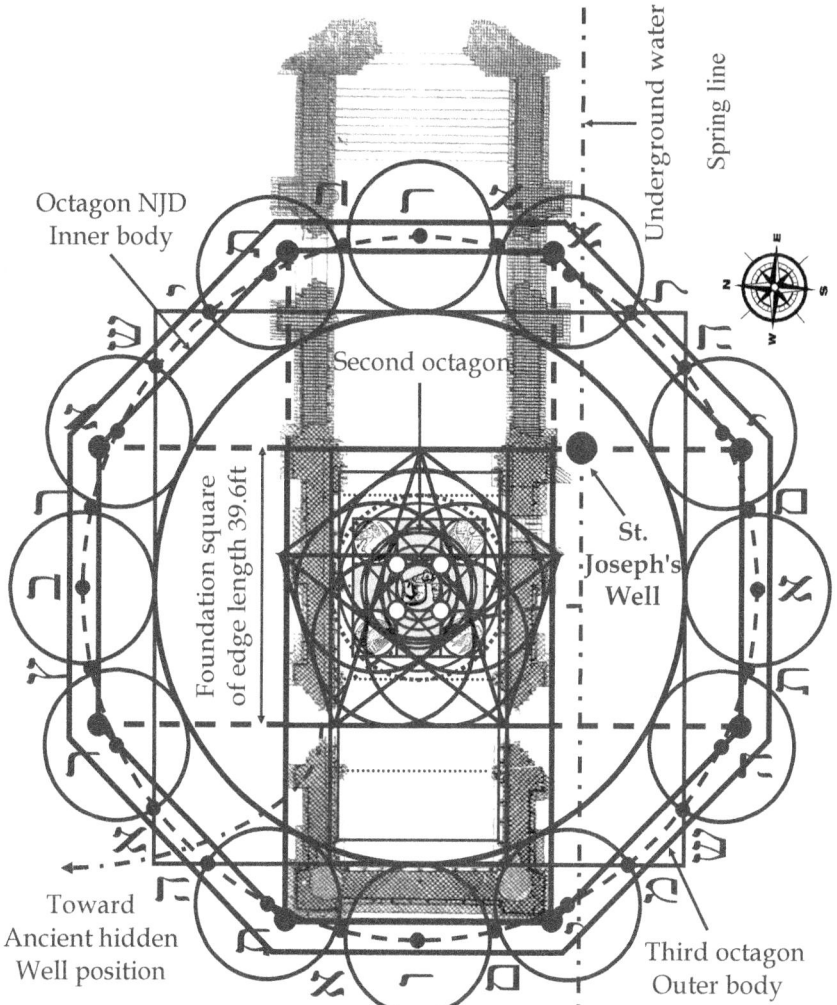

Fig 112. A bridge between the fractal nature of the Celtic Cross and the New Jerusalem Diagram.

The third octagon emerges from the geometric fractal out of the construction of the Celtic Cross with a progressive scale ratio of 6.6, seen as the outer body (envelop). The first octagon has a side length of 1, so a perimeter of 8. The foundation square, which has a side length of 39.6 ft, encloses a perimeter of 52.8 ft for the second octagon with a side length of 6.6 ft. The third octagon has a side length of 43.56ft, so a perimeter of 348.48ft. The side length of the second octagon, 6.6 multiplied by 6, is 39.6ft. The New Jerusalem Diagram octagon has a side length representing the inner body. The next foundation square has a side length of 261.36ft, about 33 times the perimeter of the first octagon.

ROSSLYN CHAPEL

ROSSLYN CHAPEL

As previously discussed, and illustrated in Fig 86, the Temple of Solomon's proportions are meticulously encoded in Mary's Chapel's ground plan with a well-known Sumerian Cubit measurement system (1.65 ft). The rectangular ground plan shares the same center as the Wattle Church Circle. With remarkable precision, William Sinclair scaled the proportions of the Temple of Solomon to Rosslyn's ground plan when he built the 15th-century Chapel.

We can divide the geometric layout of Rosslyn Chapel into 28 cells of 9.9 ft or 6 Sumerian cubits. The number 28, a perfect number, holds significant symbolism as there are 28 Hebrew letters in the first verse of Genesis. Rosslyn Chapel, often called the Bible in stone, encodes numerous facets of the Bible through symbolism or numbers (Gematria). The approach of its construction seems to be very similar to the method used by the builders of St. Mary's Chapel of Glastonbury Abbey and, previous to this, built upon the Wattle Church Circle laid out by Joseph Arimathea.

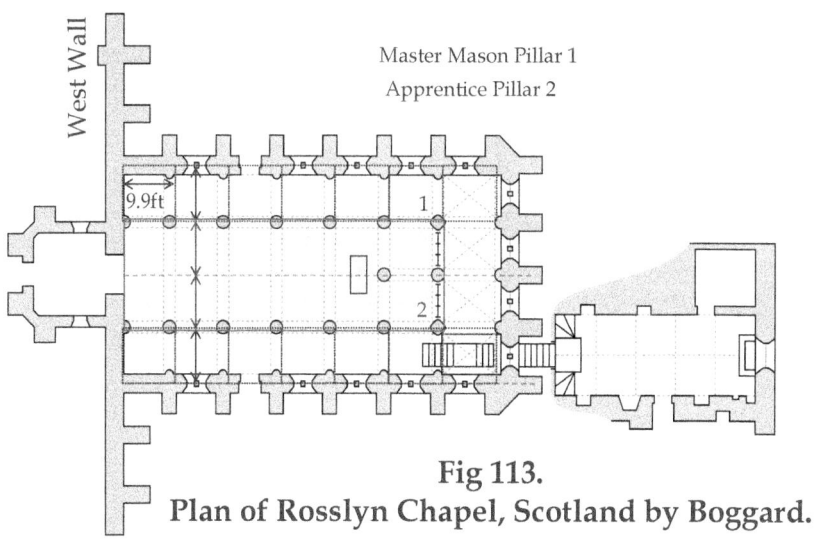

Fig 113.
Plan of Rosslyn Chapel, Scotland by Boggard.

Above, the diagram shows Solomon's Temple proportions scaled to Rosslyn's ground plan (seen as the grey rectangle), scaled down to a ratio of 1.666+:1, a major sixth's ratio of 3:5. The width is 19.8ft, and the length is 59.4ft.

Keep in mind that the length of the rectangular St. Mary's Chapel of Glastonbury Abbey is 59.4 feet, with an interior length of 52.8 feet, a hundredth part of a mile (Fig 77). The measurement of 59.4 feet defines the limit of the western wall for the rectangular wooden building. The proportions of Solomon's Temple, as stated in 2 Chronicles 3.3, the height is 30 cubits or 49.5 ft for the Sumerian Cubit of 1.65ft. The new height of the Temple of Solomon's proportions scaled to Rosslyn's ground plan is thereby 29.7ft, which is about double the height of the Lady Chapel. Standing fifteen feet high, seven and a half feet deep, and extending thirty-five feet of the Chapel, the Lady Chapel plays a crucial role in the overall design. Half of the height is 14.85ft (9 Sumerian Cubits), considered to be the total width of the outside East (8.25ft) and West (6.6ft) walls of the rectangular St. Mary's Chapel of Glastonbury Abbey. A hundred of this value is 1485, the gematria value of *Christos* ("Christ," Χρειστός). The ancient measurements in Glastonbury Abbey are potentially the same values used to build Rosslyn Chapel.

The pendant keystone of the high ceiling directly aligns with the center of the Wattle Church Circle on the ground. The carved projection at the center of the roof sits on the second rib from the east and displays the St Clair (or Sinclair) shield and cross, which two hands hold. To understand the function of the Rosslyn Chapel, one must consider the correlations between the Rose Pattern, the Celtic Cross, and the Temple of Solomon, with the keystone serving as an essential piece of the puzzle laid out on an ancient geometric scheme of the New Jerusalem Diagram.

Fig 114. The Keystone of Rosslyn Chapel.

ROSSLYN CHAPEL

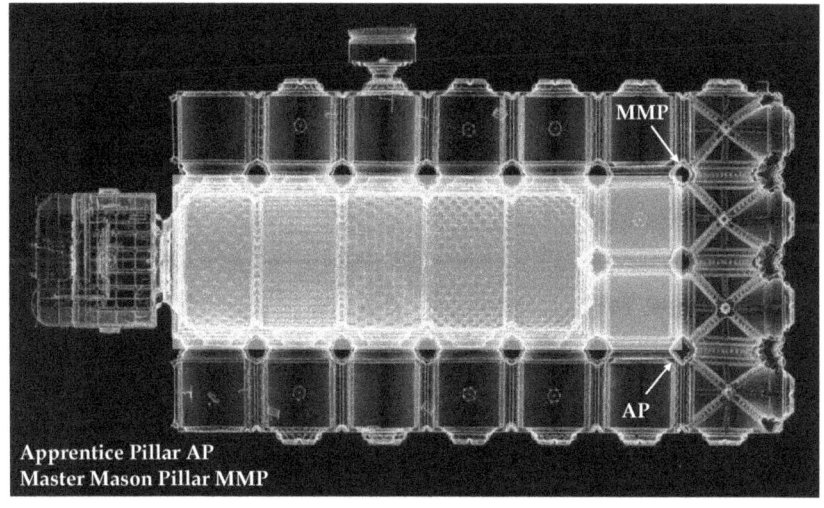

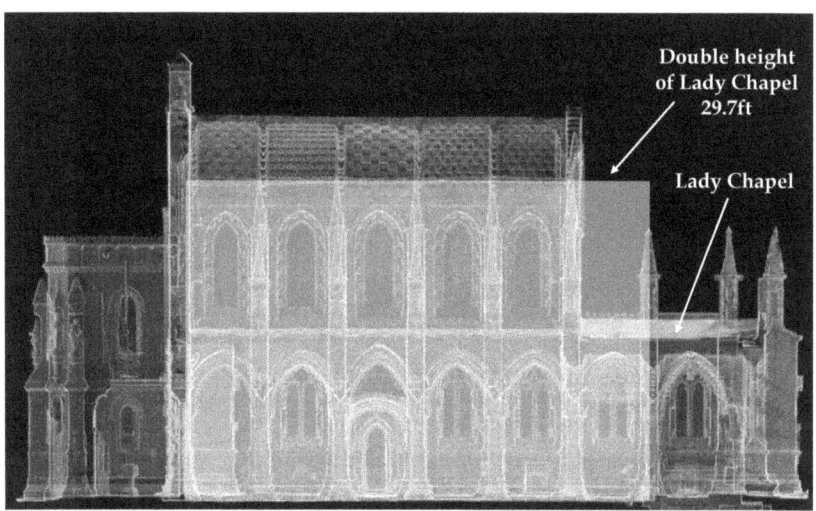

Fig 115. Background Laser Scans by CyArk.

The proportions of Solomon's Temple, when scaled down to Rosslyn's Chapel's ground plan and height, are shown above. Laser scans are instrumental in observing the Lady Chapel's double-height elevation. On the arches of the Lady Chapel, carved rectangular cubes/prisms protrude outwards, revealing intriguing geometric patterns.

There are 216 rectangular prisms, three of which are missing, revealing 13 distinct geometric patterns. These configurations are the focus of ongoing research.

Fig 116. Rectangular Prisms of Rosslyn Chapel.

The perimeter of the Triangular Number 73 is 216, totaling up to 2701, the gematria value of Genesis 1.1. So, 216 is relevant. The Triangular Number 73 holds everything into place in the creation, with 216 the gematria value of *Gevurah* ("Might," "Restraint," גבורה), a Sephirah of the Kabbalah, the function is to have the inner part, a total count of 2485, considering that 2701 - 216 = 2485 (gematria of the five books of the Torah). *Gevurah* (גבורה) constricts and encloses the infinite divine light in finite "vessels" and holds the inner part to make the creation possible. Although we interpret these rectangular prisms as musical notes with a specific frequency related to a geometric pattern (cymatics), we can also construe them as containers that constrict the infinite light in our physical reality. So, the function of these rectangular prisms could be transcribing an abstract infinite light from the highest Sephirah *Kether* ("Crown," כתר) to an entirely clear, comprehensible, and perceptible light in our physical reality. That is a combined work of the Father representative of the Sephirah *Chokmah* ("Wisdom," חכמה) and the mother for *Binah* ("Understanding," בינה) that the infinite light is finite and perceptible to our naked eye.

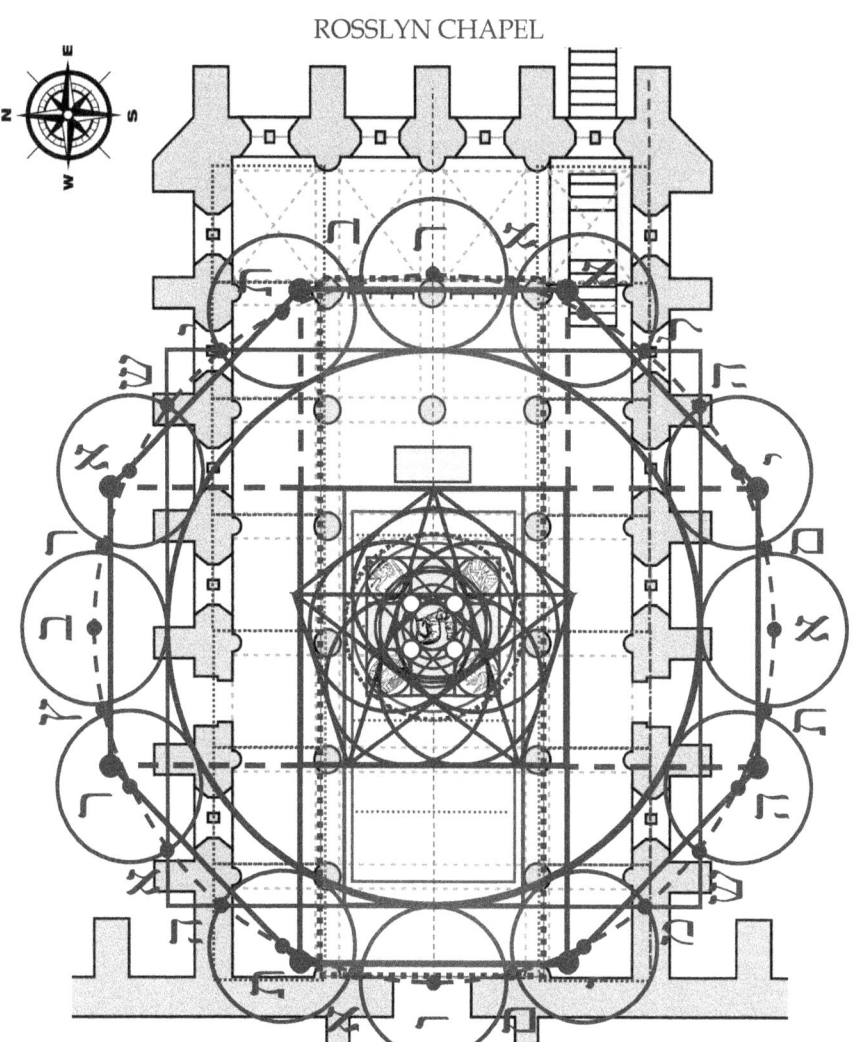

Fig 117. Rosslyn Chapel floorplan within the Unified Design of the New Jerusalem Diagram.

Above is a figure showing Rosslyn Chapel's ground plan scaled up to the original foundations of St. Mary Chapel of Glastonbury Abbey to a ratio of 1.666+:1, a major sixth' ratio. The center of the Rose Pattern shares the same center as the rectangular ground plan of Solomon's Temple (light grey area). From this exact location, higher up to the ceiling, is the pendant keystone.

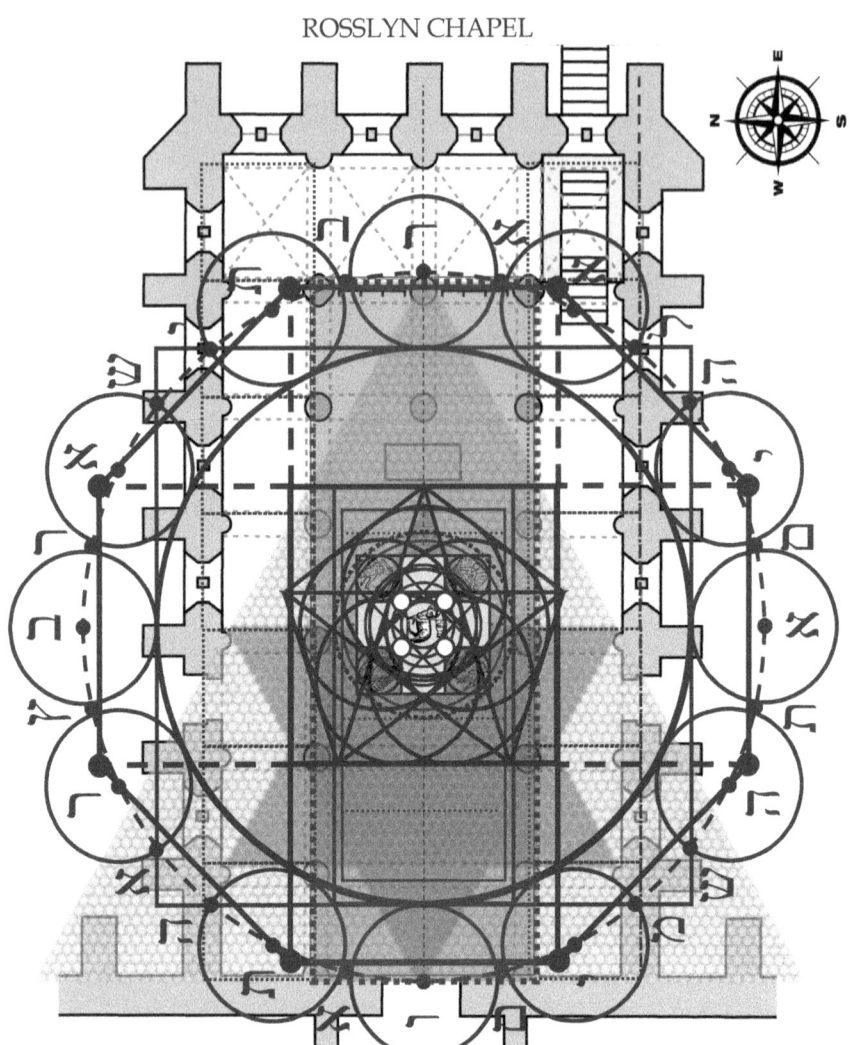

Fig 118. Triangular Number 73: Its Height Equals the Temple of Solomon's Length – Aligned with the Unified New Jerusalem and Rosslyn Chapel Floorplans.

The above figure shows the overlapping between the Triangular Number 73, the geometric blueprint of Genesis 1.1, and the combined floorplans of Rosslyn and St. Mary's Chapel of Glastonbury Abbey. The first reverse star prime number is a highlighted star with 937 counters. The Lamb is precisely located at the central spot 685, encoding the full signature of Jesus, "Lord Jesus Christ.

ROSSLYN CHAPEL

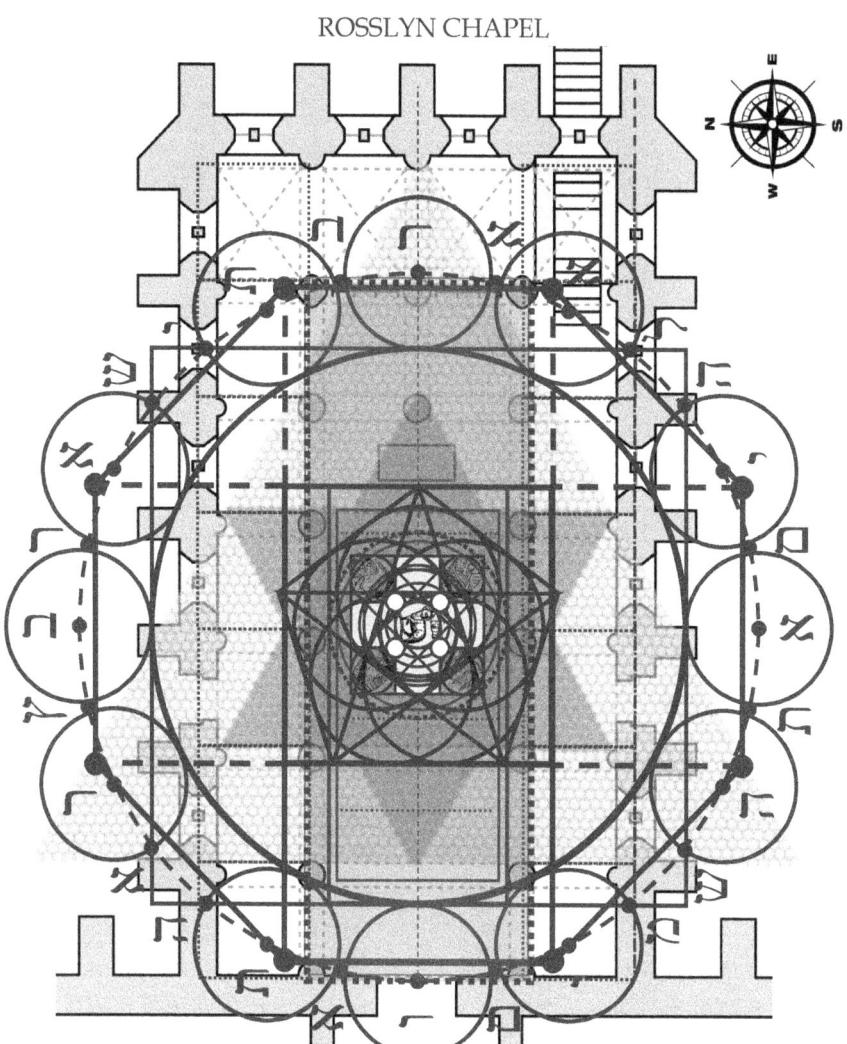

Fig 119. Triangular Number 73 Elevated:
Apex Aligns with the Eastern Wall and Central Axis of the Zodiac Rose and Lamb.

The above figure is the same as Fig. 118. Still, the triangular number 73 has been elevated by 9.9 feet, causing its apex to align precisely with the inner edge of the eastern wall along the central axis. This axis passes directly through the center of the zodiac floor, marked by the rose pattern and associated with the Lamb, revealing a deeper harmonic correspondence between number, geometry, and sacred architecture.

The 13th star number, a reverse star number, carries the frequency/vibration of 117Hz, as 117 multiplied by 8 equals 936. This number, 117, is significant in the Bible Code, as it is the 117th word in the Bible that is *Elohim* (אלהים) in Genesis 1.11. The decimal 11.7 squared results in 137, the standard gematria of *Kabbalah* (קבלה). The number 137 refers to the fine structure constant, a crucial constant in physics considering the inverse ratio of 137, *Alpha* (α), is 1/137.

The center of the star number 937 is indexed at position 1201 in Genesis 1.1, counting the first counter as one from the top and going down across each row. The 49th row is the row in which the middle counter is the centroid or center of gravity of 2701, the total counter of the Triangular Number 73. The number 1201 is the 197th prime, and 197 is the 45th prime. *Adam* ((אדמ) has a standard gematria of 45. The centroid located at 1201 refers to Adam and Eve (197th prime number and 197 is the 45th prime number) at the center of gravity of a *Metzuy Roshon* ("Primary Being," מצוי ראשון) who spoke with Wisdom. The Primary Being created Adam in Their image to serve as the intermediary between Them and the entire creation. In Figure 117, the last Adam, *Immanuel* (עמנואל), serves as a "sign" and "seal" of Elohim's Covenant, presented with the different layers. He represents the center of the Zodiacal Wheel and the Rose Pattern, the embodiment of the Divine Feminine, the innocent and pure lamb. A profound truth encoded in ancient architecture and brought to the surface with the language of numbers based on gematria, geometry, philosophical and esoteric insights.

Fig 120.
The distillation of heavenly dew, a stage in the alchemical work pictured by Walter Crane in his frontispiece for 'The High History of the Holy Grail.'

APPENDIX

A. The mathematical correlation between the Royal Cubit, the hyper dodecahedron and the Sun.

This appendix provides a comprehensive understanding of the calculations supporting this statement. Let's delve into the details: considering the diameter of the Sun as 864000 miles and the transitional layer between the top of the chromosphere and the lower corona as 2387.308 miles (= 3842 km) from the Sun's surface (bottom of the photosphere). The number 3842 corresponds to the total sum of the standard gematria of the first 42 Hebrew letters of the Torah from Genesis 1.1.

The total diameter D of the circle is then:

$$D = 864000 + 2387.308 \times 2$$
$$= 864000 + 4774.616$$
$$= 868774.616 \text{ miles}$$

The circumference C is:

$$C = 868774.616 \times \pi$$
$$= 2729335.952 \text{ miles}$$
$$= 4392400.438 \text{ kms}$$
$$\approx 4.4 \times 10^6 \text{ kms}$$

The circle's circumference is the same as the perimeter of the square (squaring the circle). We can calculate the side of the square b.

$$C = 4 \times b$$
$$b = 1098110.109 \text{ kms}$$

APPENDIX

Nesting this geometric shape 42 times is the same as dividing each square side by $\sqrt{2}$ 42 times.

$$s = b \div (\sqrt{2})^{42} = 0.5237 \text{ kms}$$

This value is one-thousandth of the Royal Cubit RC:

$$s = 1000 \times RC = w = h \div \sqrt{3}$$

s could be the width of the *Vesica Piscis* for a height h equal to the side of the dodecahedron cell of a 120-cell (hyper dodecahedron).

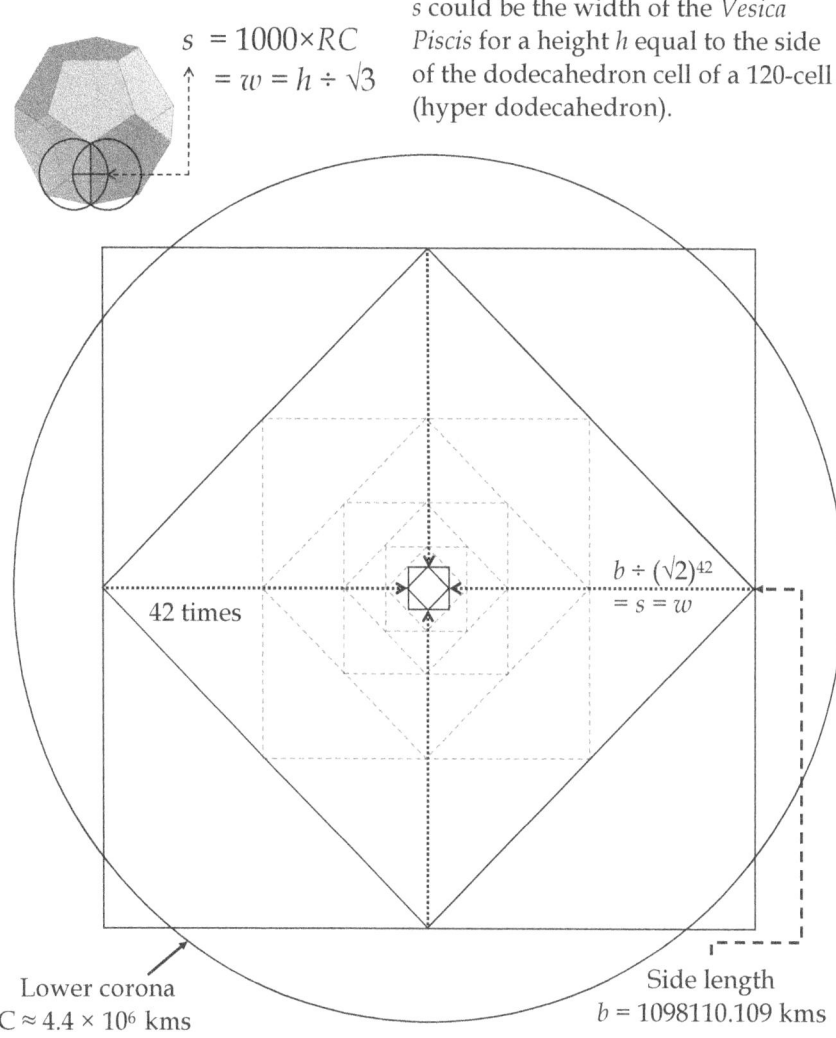

42 times

$b \div (\sqrt{2})^{42} = s = w$

Lower corona
$C \approx 4.4 \times 10^6$ kms

Side length
$b = 1098110.109$ kms

Fig 121. A bridge between the Sun's dimensions and the Royal Cubit.

APPENDIX

B. A plan of Glastonbury Abbey by Frederick Bligh Bond.

In the early part of the twentieth century, archaeologist Frederick Bligh Bond made a significant discovery about the construction of Glastonbury Abbey. He found that builders constructed it over a regular grid of squares measuring 74 ft or 888 inches, which corresponds to the Greek gematria value of Iesous ("Jesus," Ιησους). As shown in the plan below, this discovery provides a fascinating insight into the state of knowledge in 1912.

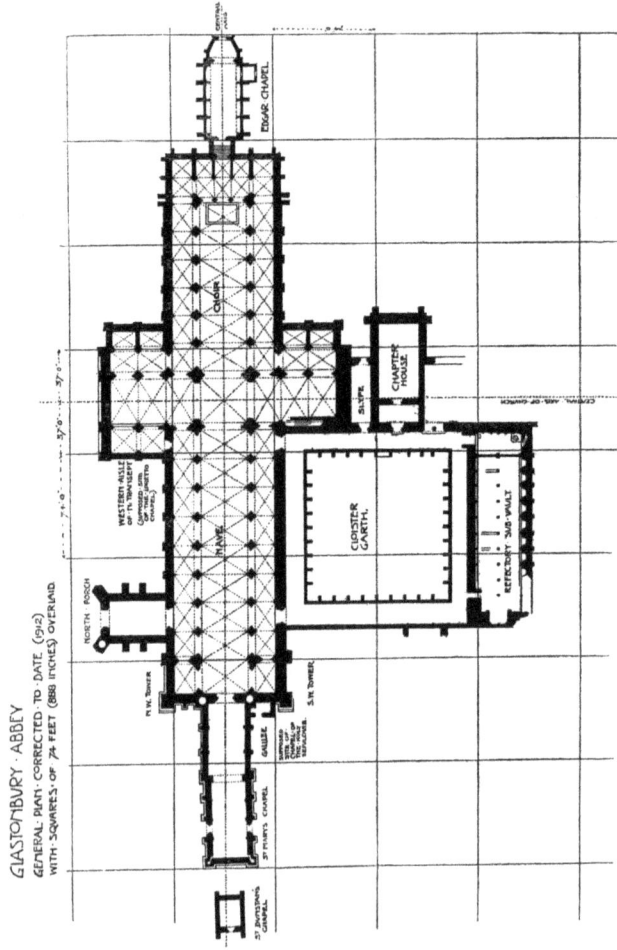

Fig 122.
A Plan of Glastonbury Abbey by Frederick Bligh Bond.

APPENDIX

C. Formula to calculate the angle between the east-west line and solstice sunrise or sunset at latitude L.

To calculate the angle, D, between the east-west line and solstice sunrise or sunset at latitude L, use the following equation:

$$\sin(D) = \sin(T)/\cos(L) \text{ with } \sin(T) = \sin(23.4) = 0.397$$

The angle T is the title angle of Earth. Use a calculator expressing all the numbers in degrees. For example, the latitude of St. Mary's Chapel of Glastonbury Abbey is L = 51.1467. Type" arcsin (sin (23.4) ÷cos (51.1467))" in degrees. Sin (D) = 0.633, so D = 39.3 degrees. Note that 0.633 is close to 0.6336. The number 6336 is relevant in measuring the Ark of Noah, as its full length is 6336 inches, a significant measurement in the context of the Ark's construction. Divide this number by 2, and 3168 is the Greek standard gematria value of *Kyrios Iēsoûs Christos* ("Lord Jesus Christ," Κύριος Ἰησοῦς Χριστός).

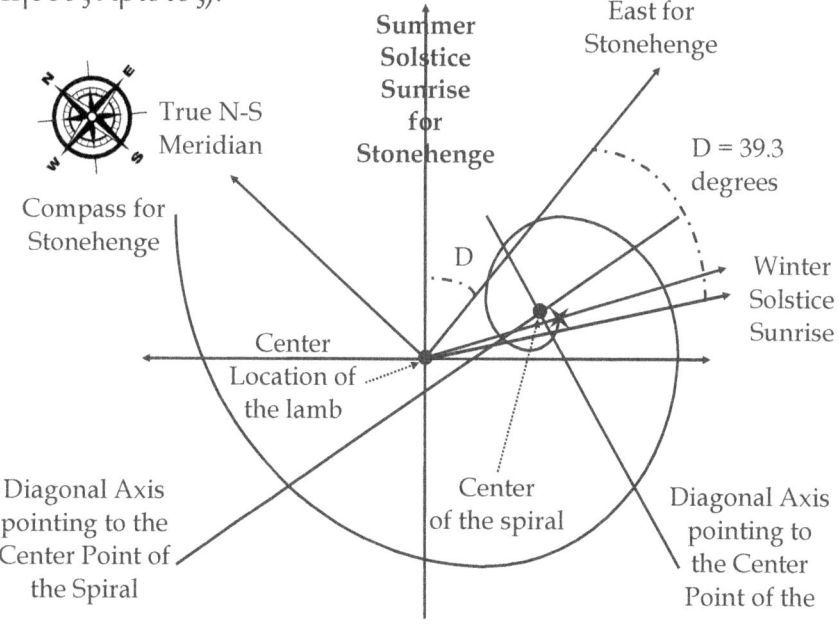

Fig 123. The geometric layout of the Fibonacci Spiral.

APPENDIX

D. Detailed calculations of the exact angle between the vertical line passing through the center of the square foundation (lamb) (toward the Summer Solstice Sunrise for Stonehenge) and the potential location of Joseph's grave.

Consider the triangle OBC in Figure 123 below (a section of Fig 99). O is the center of St. Mary's Chapel (the lamb). C is the star position, the possible location of Joseph's grave, and B is the orthogonal projection of C on the segment OB. The exact angle sought is the same as OCB.

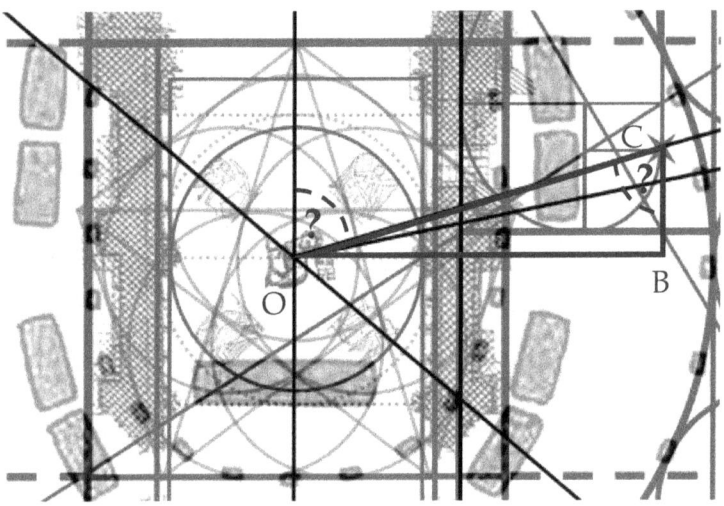

Fig 124. The right-angled triangle OBC.

To calculate OB, we need to consider some other segments. First, we note that the side length of the Golden Rectangle, a rectangle whose side lengths are in the golden ratio, across the width of St. Mary's Chapel measures 132 ft, while the square's side length is 31.2 ft, corresponding to 13 in the Fibonacci sequence (Fig 124). After making a few geometric considerations, we calculate the segment OB as follows:

$$OB = 132 \div 2 - 31.2 = 34.8 \text{ft}$$

APPENDIX

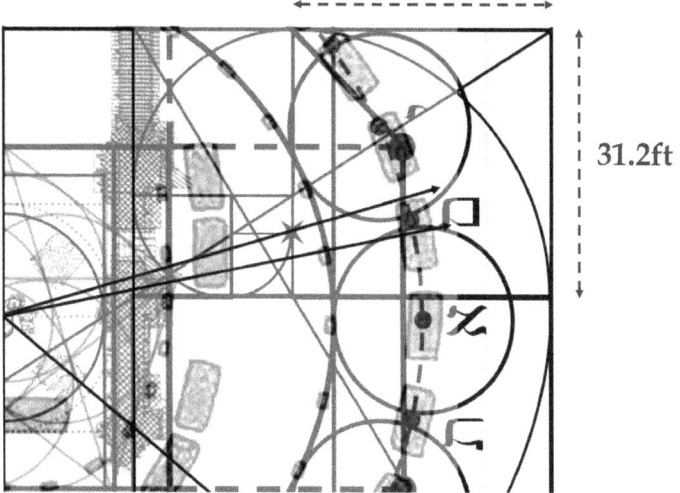

Fig 125. Consideration geometric to calculate OB.

To calculate BC, we need to consider some other segments. The medium diagonal of the octagon measures 95.6ft, so we take half of that, which is 47.8ft. We also look at the other segments involved in constructing the spiral with the golden rectangles. The relevant segments are the squares with 2, 8, and 34 side lengths from the Fibonacci Sequence, a sequence of numbers where each number is the sum of the two preceding ones.

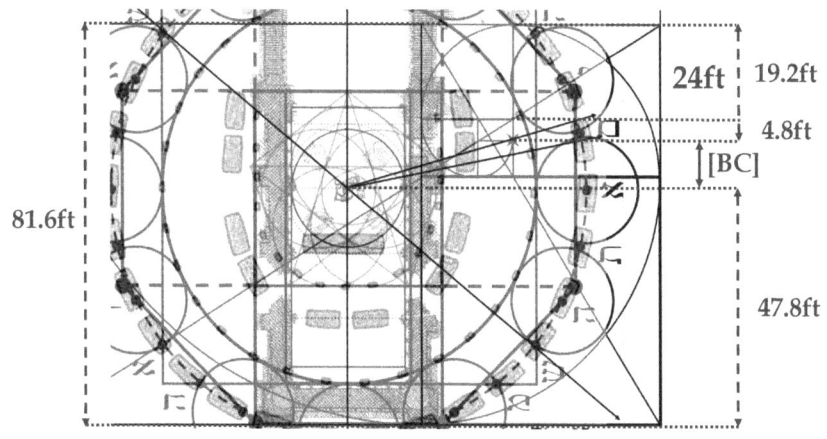

Fig 126. Considerations geometric to calculate BC.

APPENDIX

After a few geometric considerations, we calculate the segment BC as follows:

$$BC = 81.6 - 47.8 - 24 = 9.8 \text{ft}$$

To calculate the exact angle OCB between the vertical line passing through the center of the square foundation (lamb) (toward the Summer Solstice Sunrise for Stonehenge) and the potential location of Joseph's grave, you need to know the segments OB and BC:

$$\text{Tan(BOC)} = [BC] \div [OC] = 9.8 \div 34.8 = 0.2816$$

$$BOC = 15.727 \text{ degrees}$$

$$OCB = 90 - BOC = 74.273 \text{ degrees}$$

E. Detailed calculations of the distance between the center of the square foundation (lamb) and the potential location of Joseph's grave.

We can consider the right triangle OBC in B from Figure 123 to calculate the distance between the center of the square foundation (lamb) and the potential location of Joseph's grave.

Applying the Pythagorean Theorem, we have:

$$OB^2 + BC^2 = OC^2$$

$$OC = \sqrt{(OB^2 + BC^2)}$$

Given that OB = 132 ÷ 2-31.2 = 34.8ft and BC = 81.6 - 47.8 - 24 = 9.8ft (obtained from Appendix D), it results in:

$$OC = \sqrt{1307.08} = 36.16 \text{ft}$$

APPENDIX

F. Gematria Systems (Hebrew, Greek and English)

Hebrew letters	Name	Standard value	Reduced value	Ordinal value	Reverse value
א	Aleph	1	1	1	400
ב	Beit	2	2	2	300
ג	Gimel	3	3	3	200
ד	Dalet	4	4	4	100
ה	Heh	5	5	5	90
ו	Vav	6	6	6	80
ז	Zayin	7	7	7	70
ח	Chet	8	8	8	60
ט	Tet	9	9	9	50
י	Yod	10	1	10	40
כ	Kaf	20	2	11	30
ל	Lamed	30	3	12	20
מ	Mem	40	4	13	10
נ	Nun	50	5	14	9
ס	Samekh	60	6	15	8
ע	Ayin	70	7	16	7
פ	Peh	80	8	17	6
צ	Tsade	90	9	18	5
ק	Kuf	100	1	19	4
ר	Reish	200	2	20	3
ש	Shin	300	3	21	2
ת	Tav	400	4	22	1

Fig 127. Hebrew Standard, Reduced, Ordinal, and Reverse Gematria.

APPENDIX

Hebrew letters	Full form	Full Standard value	Full Reduced value	Full Ordinal value
א	אלף	111	12	30
ב	בית	412	7	34
ג	גימל	83	11	38
ד	דלת	434	11	38
ה	הא	6	6	6
ו	וו	12	12	12
ז	זין	67	13	31
ח	חית	418	13	40
ט	טית	419	14	41
י	יוד	20	11	20
כ	כף	100	10	28
ל	למד	74	11	29
מ	מם	80	8	26
נ	נון	106	16	34
ס	סמך	120	12	39
ע	עין	130	13	40
פ	פה	85	13	22
צ	צדי	104	14	32
ק	קוף	186	15	42
ר	ריש	510	6	51
ש	שין	360	9	45
ת	תו	406	10	28

Fig 128. Hebrew Full Standard, Reduced and Ordinal Gematria.

APPENDIX

Greek letters	Name	Standard value	Reduced value	Ordinal value	Reverse value
α	Alpha	1	1	1	800
β	Beta	2	2	2	700
γ	Gamma	3	3	3	600
δ	Delta	4	4	4	500
ε	Epsilon	5	5	5	400
ζ	Zeta	7	7	6	300
η	Eta	8	8	7	200
θ	Theta	9	9	8	100
ι	Iota	10	1	9	80
κ	Kappa	20	2	10	70
λ	Lambda	30	3	11	60
μ	Mu	40	4	12	50
ν	Nu	50	5	13	40
ξ	Xi	60	6	14	30
ο	Omicron	70	7	15	20
π	Pi	80	8	16	10
ρ	Rho	100	1	17	9
σ	Sigma	200	2	18	8
τ	Tau	300	3	19	7
υ	Upsilon	400	4	20	5
φ	Phi	500	5	21	4
χ	Chi	600	6	22	3
ψ	Psi	700	7	23	2
ω	Omega	800	8	24	1

Fig 129. Greek Standard, Reduced, Ordinal and Reverse Gematria.

APPENDIX

Letters	Standard value	Reduced value	Ordinal value	Reverse value
A	1	1	1	800
B	2	2	2	700
C	3	3	3	600
D	4	4	4	500
E	5	5	5	400
F	6	6	6	300
G	7	7	7	200
H	8	8	8	100
I	9	9	9	90
J	10	1	10	80
K	20	2	11	70
L	30	3	12	60
M	40	4	13	50
N	50	5	14	40
O	60	6	15	30
P	70	7	16	20
Q	80	8	17	10
R	90	9	18	9
S	100	1	19	8
T	200	2	20	7
U	300	3	21	6
V	400	4	22	5
W	500	5	23	4
X	600	6	24	3
Y	700	7	25	2
Z	800	8	26	1

Fig 130. English Standard, Reduced and Ordinal Gematria.

LIST OF FIGURES

LIST OF FIGURES

1. Table of the 72 names of God and Goddess.
2. The Holy Grail.
3. The Ideal Circle.
4. The Tetragrammaton — Man in Yahweh's Image.
5. The Phoenix and Pyramidion.
6. Joints of the Hand.
7. The Fibonacci Spiral / Golden Ratio.
8. A quarter of a circle.
9. The Tetragrammaton - Humankind in the Image of Elohim.
10. A 2D projection of the E8 root system.
11. Matter and Time encapsulate the Spoken Word.
12. The inner structure of the Hebrew letter *Aleph* (א).
13. The Hebrew letter *Shin* (ש).
14. The Pentagrammaton - The Integration of *Shin* (ש).
15. Fire in the Middle.
16. Hexagonal Ring 6.
17. Hexagon 7.
18. Hexagonal Ring 42.
19. Snowflake 55.
20. Signature of 6.
21. The Kabbalah Blueprint.
22. The Emergence of Life.
23. Triangular Number 7.
24. Genesis Triangles.
25. Star Number 73 and Hexagon 37.
26. Centroid of Triangular Number 73.
27. Centered hexagonal numbers.
28. Triangular relationship between Elohim, Yahweh, and Genesis 1.1.
29. Triangular Numbers T73 and T70.
30. Sign of the Covenant.
31. Light and Colours.
32. The Cube of Light.
33. Hexagon/Star pairs.
34. The three aspects of a flame.
35. Elohim's Triangle.

LIST OF FIGURES

36. Threefold of Elohim's *Ch'i* (י'צ).
37. The Great Image.
38. The Triangle and Rings of *Yod* (י).
39. The Rings of *Yod* (Reduced values).
40. The First Word (18 Hexagram 37 and 13 Hexagon 19).
41. Square root of 153 within the Triangle.
42. Triangular Number 17. 5 - 12 - 13.
43. The Macroscopic and Microscopic connection.
44. Jesus' name decoded in Genesis 1.1.
45. Interpretation of Triangular Number 73.
46. Jesus' Code.
47. Light connection with 666.
48. The regular dodecahedron.
49. Hyper dodecahedron in four dimensions.
50. 120 dodecahedral cells.
51. The Cube of Light.
52. The geometric origin of the Royal Cubit.
53. *Vesica Piscis* and Royal Cubit.
54. Hieroglyph of the Royal Cubit.
55. Deltoid tuberosity.
56. The 1:$\sqrt{2}$ ratio in the arm.
57. The 1:$\sqrt{2}$ ratio in the square.
58. The Royal Cubit and the Sun.
59. The visible Corona in a Solar Eclipse.
60. Sun's Lower Corona.
61. *Vesica Piscis* expanded in a fractal manner.
62. Next Iteration.
63. Numerical Values of the *Vesica Piscis*.
64. The Diagram of the New Jerusalem with Key 117.
65. The Celestial City described by John Michell.
66. A Universal Design.
67. Numerical and Geometrical Blueprint of Genesis 1.1.
68. The God's & Goddess' Particle.
69. The hexagonal/octagonal layout of the rectangular Mary's Chapel of Glastonbury Abbey.
70. Geometric discussion by Bligh Bond.
71. Wattle Church Circle in Elohim's Particle.

LIST OF FIGURES

72. Love 16 (וי).
73. Spelman's illustration of the plaque from Glastonbury Abbey describes the Old Church's history.
74. Bligh Bond's discoveries.
75. The outer enclosure.
76. The Vesicae Piscium.
77. Detailed measurements of the original building.
78. Octagonal fit of the building with detailed measurements.
79. Square foundation.
80. St. Mary's Chapel's ground plan laid over the Old Church diagram.
81. Building in Sumerian Cubit (SC).
82. Detailed measures in Sumerian Cubit.
83. New Jerusalem Blueprint overlaid on St. Mary's Chapel.
84. The limit of the eastern side of the Galilee.
85. The Rose Pattern.
86. Hexagonal scheme of St. Mary's Chapel in the New Jerusalem Blueprint.
87. The ground plan of the Temple of Solomon within the New Jerusalem Blueprint.
88. Plan and reconstruction of Stonehenge.
89. Stonehenge, a prototype of the New Jerusalem.
90. Stonehenge superimposed on the ground plan of the St. Mary's Chapel of Glastonbury Abbey.
91. Zodiacal floor of the Lady Chapel of Well's Cathedral.
92. As above, so below.
93. The Rose Pattern within the Zodiacal Blueprint.
94. Sun's dimensions.
95. Elohim's House; Power of Speech.
96. Power of Speech through the Point *Nekudah* (נקודה) (spiritual innermost).
97. Reconstitution of the lost pattern (Rose Pattern & Zodiacal Blueprint) on the floor plan of St. Mary's

LIST OF FIGURES

Chapel.
98. The Fibonacci Spiral points to the precise location of Joseph of Arimathea's grave.
99. Stonehenge, a prototype guide of the New Jerusalem Blueprint and the possible location of Joseph's grave.
100. Standing Stone of Dunblane's Cathedral of Scotland.
101. Reverse of the cross-slab (Fig 100) compared with the zodiacal floor pattern of St. Mary's Church (Fig 92).
102. Reverse of Rosemarkie Stone.
103. Zodiacal Blueprint of St. Mary's Chapel overlaid on the reverse of Rosemarkie Stone.
104. The "Light Circle" (halo) and the zodiacal blueprint of the cross-slab of Dunblane's Cathedral.
105. The progressive construction of the eight-pointed star.
106. The geometric construction of the Celtic Cross.
107. The geometric construction's ratios are $1:(\sqrt{2}+1)$ and $1:\sqrt{2}$.
108. The diameter of the Celtic Circles.
109. Construction geometric of the Celtic Cross overlain on the reverse of the Rosemarkie Stone with the Zodiacal Blueprint of St. Mary's Chapel.
110. The unification of the Celtic Cross with the Rose Pattern and the Zodiacal Blueprint of St. Mary's Chapel.
111. Unified Design of the New Jerusalem Diagram: a bridge between early Christianity and ancient Celtic Cultures.
112. A bridge between the fractal nature of the Celtic Cross and the New Jerusalem Diagram.
113. Plan of Rosslyn Chapel, Scotland by Boggard.
114. Fig 114. The keystone of Rosslyn Chapel.
115. Background Laser Scans by CyArk.
116. Rectangular Prisms of Rosslyn Chapel.
117. Rosslyn Chapel floorplan within the Unified Design of the New Jerusalem Diagram.
118. Triangular Number 73: Its Height Equals the Temple of Solomon's Length — Aligned with the Unified New Jerusalem and Rosslyn Chapel Floorplans.

LIST OF FIGURES

119. Triangular Number 73 Elevated: Apex Aligns with the Eastern Wall and Central Axis of the Zodiac Rose and Lamb.
120. *The distillation of heavenly dew, a stage in the alchemical work* pictured by Walter Crane in his frontispiece for 'The High History of the Holy Grail.'
121. A bridge between the Sun's dimensions and the Royal Cubit.
122. A Plan of Glastonbury Abbey by Frederick Bligh Bond.
123. The geometric layout of the Fibonacci Spiral.
124. The right-angled triangle OBC.
125. Consideration geometric to calculate OB.
126. Considerations geometric to calculate BC.
127. Hebrew Standard, Reduced, Ordinal, and Reverse Gematria.
128. Hebrew Full Standard, Reduced, and Ordinal Gematria.
129. Greek Standard, Reduced, Ordinal, and Reverse Gematria.
130. English Standard, Reduced, and Ordinal Gematria.

ACKNOWLEDGMENT

Writing The Quantum Blueprint has been a meaningful journey of exploration and growth. For the past two years, I have poured my heart into this work, and I am very thankful for everyone who has helped me along the way.

To the unseen forces of the universe—Elohim, Great Spirit, the One Source—your guidance and inspiration have influenced every page of this book. I am profoundly grateful for your guidance.

To my readers—your curiosity and desire to learn keep this work alive.

To my friends, family, and guides—thank you for your support, patience, and strong belief in this vision.

This book helps you gain a deeper understanding and encourages your transformation.

With deep gratitude,
Salah-Eddin Gherbi

ABOUT THE AUTHOR

Salah-Eddin Gherbi is a dedicated researcher with a unique approach to uncovering the mysteries of the universe. He combines ancient wisdom and modern science, drawing from his background in theological studies and fundamental Physics, including Astrophysics. Gherbi's years of study have focused on the intricate connections between sacred texts, numerical codes, and geometric patterns. His ability to translate complex concepts into engaging and comprehensible narratives is a testament to his unique qualifications. His first book, "The Fifth Element: The Rainbow Bridge Between the Dimensions," 2nd edition, was published in September 2023.

Salah-Eddin Gherbi's work extends beyond research and writing. He has co-authored books on Soul Alchemy, designed to support individuals in their personal and spiritual development. His collaboration with Sue Cawthorne led to the creation of an online accredited course, "Law of Attraction and Manifestation Training," aimed at self-help and global transformation. Gherbi's dedication to promoting healing and well-being on all levels, including using his innate knowledge of gematria through Intuitive Numerology, is a testament to his altruistic motives.